THE DO'S AND TABOOS OF HOSTING INTERNATIONAL VISITORS

Other books by Roger E. Axtell

Do's and Taboos Around the World: A Guide to International Behavior, second edition, John Wiley & Sons, 1990.

The Do's and Taboos of International Trade: A Small Business Primer. John Wiley & Sons, 1989.

THE DO'S AND TABOOS
OF HOSTING
INTERNATIONAL VISITORS

Roger E. Axtell

WILEY

John Wiley & Sons
New York • Chichester • Brisbane • Toronto • Singapore

This publication is designed to provide accurate and authoritative information in regard to the subject matter covered. It is sold with the understanding that the publisher is not engaged in rendering legal, accounting, or other professional service. If legal advice or other expert assistance is required, the services of a competent professional person should be sought. FROM A DECLARATION OF PRINCIPLES JOINTLY ADOPTED BY A COMMITTEE OF THE AMERICAN BAR ASSOCIATION AND A COMMITTEE OF PUBLISHERS.

Copyright © 1990 by Roger E. Axtell
Published by John Wiley & Sons, Inc.
All rights reserved. Published simultaneously in Canada.

Reproduction or translation of any part of this work beyond that permitted by section 107 or 108 of the 1976 United States Copyright Act without the permission of the copyright owner is unlawful. Requests for permission or further information should be addressed to the Permission Department, John Wiley & Sons, Inc.

Library of Congress Cataloging-in-Publication Data

Axtell, Roger.
    The do's and taboos of hosting international visitors / Roger
Axtell.
        p.   cm.
    Includes bibliographical references.
    ISBN 0-471-51572-8. — ISBN 0-471-51570-1 (pbk.)
    1. Business etiquette—United States.   2. Business entertaining—
United States.   3. Visitors, Foreign—United States.   I. Title.
HF5389.A98   1990
395'.52—dc20   89-48995
                                                              CIP

Printed in the United States of America

    10 9 8 7 6

To, who else, but "the hostess with
the mostest," my wife, Mitzi.

PREFACE

Pick up any Sunday newspaper and it will probably contain a hefty section devoted to travel. Week in and week out, headlines on travel stories announce a familiar refrain: "Shoppers Love Dublin," or "Relax in Antigua," or "Prime Minister Invites Tourists to Jamaica."

Then wander into any bookstore, and the shelves labeled "Travel" will be bursting with guides to every geographic destination from Alaska to Zambia. Swelling that assortment to the second power are more travel books on specific slices of travel: biking, bed and breakfasts, hideaways (which, after buying that particular book are hideaways no longer), traveling safely, traveling healthfully, and traveling with pets both safely and healthfully.

Now turn to the bookcases on business-oriented subjects. There you'll find an increasing number of books on how to do business in other countries: how to negotiate with the Japanese, how to license your technology in Europe, how to travel inexpensively to world capitals, how to find Third World customers, how to get involved in barter and countertrade, and of course the old standby, how to speak the language once you and your attaché case arrive there.

With any or all of these books, you are taught to travel to any far-reaching spot in the world, vacation or do business there, and return happy and successful.

But what about the flip-side? What happens when the stream of transnational travelers flows in *this* direction? What happens when those hordes come *here* to do business on our home ground? Where are all those "how to" books when those international visitors arrive in the United States? In a single word, what about *hosting?*

Every day, an increasing number of frantic phone calls are received in offices of chambers of commerce, universities, embassies, and trade groups. They all have the same theme: "I have guests coming next week from Argentina (or Austria, or Angola, or

Australia, or wherever). What should I do about hosting them? What protocol should I know? Will they have any special religious or dietary needs? Will they speak English? Where do I get an interpreter? Am I expected to give them gifts?" The most common plea, of course, is "Do you have any suggestions on how I should *entertain* them?"

All good questions. In those college courses we took on international business, we may have learned all about the rewards of managing positive cash flow in hyperinflationary international markets. But no one uttered one word of advice about the rewards of managing a positive *visit* by international customers to satisfy a hypernervous management. This book should help fill that gap.

In fact, this book is actually the third leg of a trilogy on international business and behavior. The first book, *Do's and Taboos Around the World*, was published by John Wiley & Sons in 1986 and provided a guide to international behavior on protocol, lingo, gestures, and gift-giving. In four years, over 100,000 copies have been sold and it has been printed in Japanese, two versions of French (one for Canada, one for France), Finnish, Portugese (for Brazil), German, and Hungarian, with more language versions to come.

The second book, *The Do's and Taboos of International Trade: A Small Business Primer*, (Wiley) was issued in the spring of 1989. It is a "how-to" book for medium and small-sized businesses on breaking into international trade. It is a step-by-step guidebook on exporting, licensing, joint ventures, or whatever form your business may take overseas. In addition, it instructs on the laws, on pricing, on payments, on financing, on shipping, and on managing and motivating overseas distributors.

This third book, the one you are holding, is intended to complete a triangle: the first book formed the base, dealing with behavior when traveling abroad; the second side of the pyramid explained how to break into international trade; and now this side instructs how to host your international visitors when they come to the United States.

Note that the operational phrase in all three books is "Do's and Taboos." The emphasis is, quite simply, on what to do and what *not* to do. All three books are laced with anecdotes. That is because, whenever advising someone, it seems more effective and entertaining to inform through true stories than through vague concepts.

For many of these anecdotes and case studies, and indeed for much of the information in this book, I am indebted to scores of audiences around the country who participated in seminars and workshops I have conducted on the subject of international business and behavior. I have yet to give an after-dinner program—and I do 30 or 40 each year—and not have someone from the audience approach me afterward with a wonderful true experience from their own world of international business and behavior. I always warn them good-naturedly: "Be careful. This is one way I conduct my research. Maybe you should consider writing your own book." Invariably, though, they laugh and eagerly share their knowledge in a wonderful spirit of camaraderie that seems to reside among people who travel and work in the global marketplace.

Therefore, as you will see, the stories and lessons assembled in this book come from governors and shipping agents, from students and professional diplomats, and especially from those well-traveled colleagues in international manufacturing, law, marketing, accounting, tourism, and service industries who ply the world of commerce.

WHAT WILL YOU LEARN IN THIS BOOK?

First, you will discover that the word *hosting* in the title of this book has a broad meaning—hosting involves not only the act of entertaining but also "relating" to other people. In academic circles, this is part of what is called "cross-cultural communication" or "intercultural relations."

You will learn about protocol, courtesies, comportment, and behavior. You will learn how to become more worldly, more cosmopolitan, more statesmanlike. You will also learn that the French seem to have a corner on terminology in this field, just as with good dinner menus. The key word *etiquette* is of French origin, but you will also learn the mysterious, deeper meaning of that peculiar and almost undefinable French phrase *savoir faire*, which in our parlance signifies "knowing," "being cool and composed." For the French, *savoir faire* means much more than that, and you will learn in this book, graphically and in story form, exactly how that term is interpreted by the French. Other French words appropriate for this book are: *élan*, meaning "enthusiasm," "style," "flair"; and *panache*, meaning "with verve and dash." The objective is not only to acquire *savoir faire* and *élan* but, in good Old English, to be *couth* as well (i.e., refined, suave, knowledgeable).

If, about now, you're thinking "What I'll be learning is which wine to serve French guests or how to make small talk with an Arab," you will be pleased to know there is more, much more, than just that. You will also find solid business information designed to make you a world-wise executive and business negotiator. Here are a few examples. You will learn:

- □ How to work effectively through foreign language interpreters

- □ How to defuse loaded and antagonistic questions about American foreign policy

- □ How to be especially adroit at conducting business with the Japanese, or the British, or the Canadians

- □ How to avoid social *faux pas* that could ruin a perfectly good business deal

- □ How to use certain business negotiating tactics depending on which culture is sitting across the bargaining table

- □ Most of all, you will read how to be a considerate and understanding human being with people from other cultures. And that, after all, should be the cornerstone of any business relationship.

A WORD ABOUT WORDS

Just a moment ago, we said "hosting" was too limiting a word. This book will also aid you in becoming more cosmopolitan, more statesmanlike, more worldly. Maybe the best phrase of all is "internationally genteel." The *American Heritage Dictionary* defines *genteel* as "refined in manner; well-bred, polite; free from vulgarity or rudeness; fashionable; elegant; striving to convey a manner of appearance of refinement and respectability." Is there any among us who would not want to be so described?

Another key word used in the title of this book is "taboo." For your next cocktail party conversation, you might like to know that "taboo" is really *tabu* which means "forbidden" and originated as *tapu,* a Tongan word for "sacred" or "exceedingly marked."

You will also find in this book frequent use of the phrase "the American way" of protocol or customs. I also refer to "we Americans" in describing some trait or common action. I realize this is tricky territory. Whenever we deal with generalizations or stereotypes about a culture—even our own culture—we are tiptoing through minefields. There is only one thing worse than stereotypes, it is said, and that is ignorance, so we all use them. But, if you read here about a so-called "American custom" or stereotype and you disagree, I hope you will be generous and forgiving. When describing the behavior of any given culture, please remember that there is no single definitive source book that documents every act of behavior of every member or group or culture.

WHAT THIS BOOK CONTAINS

A friend impishly suggested that the title of this book might be "People with Foreign Accents Are Not Hard of Hearing." We Americans do tend to believe, mistakenly, that volume will breed comprehension. This book is about that fault and many more.

One premise in this book is that knowing appropriate protocol in business can be as important as business discussions themselves. Chapter 1 presents evidence to support that claim and, in fact, proposes that proper hosting is a valuable business skill. In Chapter 2, we examine how others view Americans and learn what questions they typically ask about us and our society. Then, in Chapter 3 we touch on the core of hosting and examine "How To Entertain." Following that are two chapters, one on "Dining" and one on "Social Drinking," important twin adjuncts of hosting. In Chapter 6, we step into the typical American business office to learn exactly what our guests find peculiar about American business protocol. Chapter 7 is a case study, and Chapter 8 offers insights and tips for using language translators and interpreters. Succeeding chapters deal with specialized subjects: gift-giving, the Japanese, the British, the Canadians, hotels, young people, and a variety of other aspects of hosting. Chapter 12 contains a country-by-country quick reference list with specific tips to remember and use (carefully) with guests of specific nationalities. When you are entertaining someone from, say, Singapore you can quickly flip to the section in that list titled "Singaporeans" and be armed with potentially useful tidbits about the behavior and habits of the people there.

Finally, in the Appendix, you will find a series of lists to make your hosting job easier, plus a case study that illustrates how to collect more hosting information on your own.

The hope, then, is that this book will add new knowledge to your personal storehouse about stereotypes, about expectations, about idiosyncrasies, and about customs in America and elsewhere.

Above all, we should be aware that in the universe of behavior, the Earth does not necessarily revolve around an axis centered in North America. While it might understandably seem that way, we should remember the wry observation of lecturer/trainer James Bostain who cautions his audiences by saying "I know it seems startling, but we must bear in mind that fully 95 percent of the world is un-American."

ROGER E. AXTELL

ACKNOWLEDGMENTS

For the reader, acknowledgment pages can be pretty boring stuff. However, each name represents an important contributor to this book whom it would be totally unfair to overlook. Note the wide range of backgrounds and specialties. Without these names, the book would be far less informative.

V. Lynn Tyler at the David M. Kennedy Center for International Studies at Brigham Young University, Provo, Utah, provided excerpts, advice, and much encouragement.

Sara Malin contributed research for several of the lists in the Appendix. She is a recent graduate of the University of Wisconsin (Oshkosh) in international business and will surely be a leader in the new wave of trade ahead.

My thanks also go to **Richard J. Deasy** and **Maureen Gavigahn** at the National Council for International Visitors (NCIV) for their encouragement, support, and assistance.

Robert F. Froehlke, Chairman of IDS Mutual Fund Group, Minneapolis; **William A. Guenther**, S.C. Johnson Wax Co., Racine, WI; and **Fran S. Meyers** of the Wisconsin World Trade Center, Milwaukee, each considered the material in this book and provided both encouragement and endorsements.

My brother, **Dean R. Axtell**, is a world-wise and well-traveled business executive who supplied helpful information for case studies and other examples.

I also am deeply indebted to the people at the **Metrolina World Trade Association**, Charlotte, NC, for staging a series of seminars, workshops, and after-dinner programs in 1988 and 1989 that provided momentum for this book. To the wonderful **Ingeborg Hegenbart** (Southern National Bank), **Samuel P. Troy** (U.S. Department of Commerce), **Don Haack** (Donald Haack Diamonds), **Wayne Cooper** (Arcon Manufacturing, Inc.), and others—all international business professionals—I offer my sincere thanks.

Good friends **Dr. Paul Odland** and his wife **Barbara**, and **John** and **Freda Gibb**, provided helpful anecdotes and research that brighten the text.

Four California friends devoted much of a week's summer vacation in northern Wisconsin to reviewing the manuscript and offering helpful suggestions. They are **Dale** and **Marion Levander** and **Carol** and **Sterling Blakeman**.

Larry Greb, retired senior marketing officer with S.C. Johnson Wax Co., is constantly alert to humorous anecdotes in international business and, as always, provided several for this work.

In Lima, Peru, **Jack** and **Marie Ottiker** seem to have a special sense for observation and good humor. Jack is a former executive with W. R. Grace, Braniff Airlines, Parker Pen Co., and currently heads the American Chamber of Commerce in Lima. Over the years, Jack and Marie have provided me with much information on international behavior and customs.

My thanks go, too, to **Katherine Schowalter**, Editor at John Wiley & Sons, New York, for her support and confidence, and also to her assistant, **Laura Lewin**. My literary agent, **Sally Wecksler**, not only negotiated the contract for this book but offered useful comments and contributions for the text.

Dr. Robert Shuter at Marquette University, Milwaukee, WI, is an authority on cross-cultural communication, and he allowed me to use examples and information from his vast experience.

Professional translators/interpreters **Dr. Jo Ann Church** and **Dr. Marvyn Bacigalupo** in Nashville, TN, reviewed Chapter 8 on "Using Interpreters." They helped ensure accuracy and contributed very useful tips and anecdotes.

Tax expert **P. Donald Carson** of Manpower Inc., Milwaukee, WI, made certain my comments on entertainment as a business expense for tax purposes were correct.

Dr. Rolf Wegenke, international trade expert for Wisconsin, kindly provided observations and statements from his extensive experience.

For Chapter 10, "Doing Business With Special Groups—Canadians, Japanese, British," I owe thanks to the following: Canadian Consul in Chicago, **Randolph C. Stansfield**; Vice Consul **Caroline Cracraft** of the British Consulate General (Chicago); and, finally, to the staff of the **Japanese External Trade Organization** (JETRO) in Chicago.

If you *still* consider all this as "just a list of names," I challenge you to try writing a book without friends, associates, and experts like them. It can't be done.

CONTENTS

=1

HOSTING AS A
BUSINESS SKILL

"If it be appropriate to kiss the
Pope's slipper, by all means do so."

*—Lord Chesterfield, founder of
modern etiquette, in 1750.*

———— □ ————

When a delegation of buyers from the People's Republic of China came to Nashville in 1988, export executive Ken Kirkpatrick arranged for top drawer treatment. At the welcoming dinner, he carefully preordered the best cuts of prized American prime ribs of beef. As is the custom in most fine American restaurants, the beef was served rare. The Chinese took one look at the meat, blanched, and refused to touch it. Kirkpatrick quickly discovered they were totally unaccustomed to rare red meat. In fact, they were repulsed by what they considered raw meat sitting in a pool of reddish brown blood.

———— □ ————

In Grand Rapids, Larry Bratschie, marketing executive for a large manufacturer of office furniture, once hosted a key group of Japanese customers. Knowing that the Japanese were great gift-givers, Bratschie purchased sterling silver pocket knives for each guest. He had them carefully wrapped Japanese-style (pastel colored paper, no bows) and positioned at each place at the dining table. As the Japanese opened their gifts, each guest suddenly went mute. Each carefully set the knife back in the gift box and stared stiffly into the distance. As the guests left the dinner table, the gifts remained behind, untouched. Later, Bratschie learned that in the

1

Japanese culture the act of presenting a knife as a gift can be a symbol of suicide.

———— □ ————

C. Edward Boggs of Bluefield, West Virginia, hosted his West German distributor, a husband and wife duo, and, wanting to make a good first impression, he ordered a dozen long-stemmed red roses placed in their hotel room. Unknown to Boggs, sending a bouquet of even-numbered flowers is considered bad luck among West Germans. Even worse, sending red roses to a German woman can have strong romantic overtones (the rose is a symbol of secrecy, as in the Latin phrase *sub rosa*). What Boggs had inadvertently done was make a pass at his distributor's wife.

———— □ ————

These three anecdotes illustrate that in the world of international etiquette there exists a tangled thicket of customs, habits, protocol and behavior that can confuse and trap the most accomplished business professional.

Old Lord Chesterfield's advice wears well even today, especially among aspiring business types. Without some up-to-date knowledge of international behavior, the modern business career climber could easily have a few rungs missing from his or her ladder of success.

The Business Executive in A.D. 2000

Last year, the prestigious *Wall Street Journal* documented the need for future CEO's to develop a true cosmopolitan nature. In a series of articles aimed at the year 2000, the *Journal* headlined one segment with these words: "Going Global: The Chief Executives in Year 2000 Are Likely to Have Had Much Foreign Experience."

This is how the *Journal* profiled the typical CEO of that coming era:

His (or her) undergraduate degree is in French literature, but he also has a joint M.B.A./engineering degree. He started in research and was quickly picked out as a potential CEO. He zigzagged from research to marketing to finance. He proved himself in Brazil by turning around a failing joint venture. He speaks Portuguese and French and is on a first-name basis with commerce ministers in half a dozen countries.

Then various sources went on to say "The world is going to be so significantly different it will require a completely different kind of CEO. He must be multienvironment, multicountry, multifunctional . . . ." A Westinghouse executive exhorted aspiring executives to "Travel overseas. Meet with the prime minister, the ministers of trade and commerce. Meet with the king of Spain and the chancellor of West Germany."* All of this is blue chip business advice.

What the *Journal* was saying in so many words was this: When that new circle of princes and potentates of business comes to America, will the aspiring CEO be able to demonstrate one important skill—the skill of hosting? Stated succinctly: Thou shalt be comfortable, both here and abroad, with thy global colleagues. The CEO in the year 2000 must be worldly, learn how to make guests feel at home, know and respect their protocol, cater to their customs, and generally win their hearts through his or her acts and their stomachs.

Successful international business executives agree that one of the first revelations learned by a true global manager is that "other nationalities value the personal relationship" more than many Americans do in business. True, Americans are widely known for openness and friendliness. True, many are known for informality and gregariousness. But among many other cultures, Americans are considered negatively ethnocentric. American-style friendship is often considered shallow and short-lived. In many non-Western business cultures, strong *personal* relationships are sought and coveted. That leads us to the operational word *hosting* used throughout this book. In fact, that specific word is examined in fine detail in Chapter 3.

At this point you couldn't be blamed for protesting, "Hosting? What's so important about hosting? Everyone knows that, in business, signing the contract is what's important."

* Reprinted by permission of *The Wall Street Journal,* © Dow Jones & Company, Inc. 1989. All rights reserved worldwide.

And you might continue, "But as long as you've brought it up, what's so difficult about hosting? I'm a good host. I know something about manners. Frankly, though, on the business priority list, hosting is low on the agenda. Here in the United States we're all business." And that just may be the answer to why hosting is so important. Because, "Here in the United States, we're all business."

In other parts of the world, there is more—much more—to business than just business: Socializing, friendships, etiquette, grace, patience, protocol, and a whole list of other such cultural traits are, indeed, integral parts of business. And that is precisely what this book is all about.

Here is a classic example of the premise that "business is more than just business" involving hundreds of millions of investment dollars involving thousands of new jobs:

———— □ ————

In the late 1970s, when a dozen states in the United States eagerly huffed and panted over landing the much-coveted Nissan automobile factory, the winner turned out to be the state of Tennessee. Later, it was learned that while there were many reasons for choosing that state—location, labor force, incentives—one strong factor was the sincerity and sensitivity and style of the Tennessee contacts and negotiating team. The easy manner of the Tennesseans, the slower pace and the personal touch, made a marked impression on the Japanese for whom style is almost as important as substance.

Lamar Alexander, Tennessee's Governor at that time, personally courted the Japanese with charm and patience. The Japanese liked that. They especially liked the fact that someone of his position and stature would personally visit them over and over again. The Nissan victory and investment in Tennessee was followed by others: Toshiba, Sharp, and Japanese-owned Bridgestone soon built there. Today, Tennessee boasts of having fully 10 percent of all Japanese investment in the United States. Why? One key reason was because the Japanese decisionmakers were comfortable with the people they dealt with and were impressed with the *personal* side in the Tennesseans' business comportment.

———— □ ————

How do we become acquainted and then comfortable with other people? We will be examining many of the ways to do this. For example, one traditionally proven method is to invite them into our homes; invite them into a part of our lives. Let them see the pieces of antique furniture we're so proud of; let them see the time-line photos of our kids from tykes, to trikes, to teens, to matriculation. And, yes, let them also see the paint peeling in the bathroom. On a more intangible level, it also takes a special set of business skills and abilities like empathy, respect, and objective judgment. Later in this chapter, seven specific intangible business skills are explained in detail.

One important aspect of this whole sociological process is what we call *hosting* or, to use a contemporary therapy session favorite, *relating* to others. This is not to say that Americans are lousy hosts or have difficulty relating to other cultures. As I have repeatedly emphasized in my other books, I do not believe in the 30-year-old stereotype of the so-called "Ugly American." That's a false rap. That perception, born via a 1950s novel with that title followed by a movie starring Marlon Brando, suggested that all Americans were inconsiderate, loud, brash, bold, and brutish. Not true. We are, in fact, generally known as an exceedingly friendly people. As well as being friendly, we are also considered informal; but many of our international visitors consider our informality and friendliness as only skin deep. Americans usually do not reveal their inner selves easily. We do not make deep friendships easily, preferring instead to have a loose "circle" of friends. But "Ugly Americans"? No. Distinguished British public relations expert Ian Kerr suggests instead that "Maybe 'Uninformed Americans' would be more apt than 'Ugly Americans.'"

Perhaps Americans are "uninformed" because we must travel thousands of miles before bumping into other significantly different cultures. In Europe, one can drive for only a few hours and cross several different cultural enclaves. We Americans just don't have that kind of opportunity to learn about new customs for socializing, entertaining, or doing business with distinctly different cultures.

The hints in this book are intended to make that experience easier and more successful. In international business, proper hosting and proper attention to all the cultural graces can be just as important to your business success as the quality or price or timely delivery of your product or service.

The S. C. Johnson Wax Co. in Racine, Wisconsin, is a privately held company, but its sales are estimated in the billions of dollars with half, at least, coming from outside the United States. As a result, Johnson has constructed an impressive, tasteful guest facility called "The Council House" which each year hosts hundreds of international business executives. The manager of that facility, William A. Guenther, says "Knowing the appropriate protocol, customs and etiquette when hosting business guests from overseas can often be more significant than the business discussion itself."

AVOIDING BLUNDERS AND FOOLISH NOTIONS

This book examines our society from the outside looking in. It is like the magical mirror in "Snow White and the Seven Dwarfs" except this one responds to the question:

> Mirror, mirror on the wall,
> How do others view Americans all?

To be good hosts it is important to hold that penetrating mirror before us and confront the images that others hold of Americans. The Bible teaches that it is necessary to know oneself in order to understand others. Knowing your true self will help you understand others and thus more easily resolve a host of other challenges.

Scottish poet Robert Burns put it even more memorably with this familiar refrain:

> O wad some Pow'r the giftie gie us
> To see oursels as others see us!
> It wad frae mony a blunder free us,
> And foolish notion.

This book will help us do just as Burns wished, to see ourselves as others see us. And, this may also ". . . from many a blunder free us, and foolish notion."

What are some examples of those *blunders* and foolish *notions*? In the blunder category, here are just a few:

□ Jumping to a first-name basis with an Englishman or Frenchman (or woman)

- □ Ignoring the strict dietary rules practiced by a devout Buddhist, Hindu, Jew, or Muslim visitor

- □ Flashing the "O.K." gesture to a Brazilian

- □ Giving a clock to a visitor from China

- □ Clapping a Japanese or Taiwanese businessman on the back

- □ Jumping right into business discussions with a Latin

- □ Asking someone from Great Britain "What do you do for a living?"

Dr. Rolf Wegenke, international business expert for the state of Wisconsin, says "We're surrounded by innocent, inadvertent potential blunders. In the space of just a few weeks, I found that the Mayor of Milwaukee had wrapped gifts in white paper for a Korean buying delegation, that the Governor's mansion was planning to serve pork to a group of Muslims, and that a Johannesburg Riesling wine was on the menu for some visiting black Africans."

And what about those foolish *notions* Burns wrote about? This refers to assumptions or general impressions we all collect and carry around in our mental and emotional baggage. Here are just a few:

- □ Every culture enjoys some form of a "cocktail hour."

- □ All Latin cultures take *siestas.*

- □ The very best place to entertain is an ethnic restaurant featuring food from your guest's home.

- □ Interpreters accurately convey your every word.

- □ The Japanese tend to avoid eye contact because they're shy.

- □ Shaking hands is always done with a firm grasp and direct eye contact, just as our fathers taught us.

- □ We communicate effectively with signs and hand gestures.

- □ Germans are hyperefficient, the French are romantics, Italians are demonstrative, and Orientals are inscrutable.

These are common stereotypes, popular generalizations; but they can also be misleading. It's like saying all Americans are hard working, friendly, monolingual, sometimes loud, and often a bit brash. Before setting right these possible blunders and notions, let us first examine why all these foreigners come to the United States. What draws them here? And what implications does this have for the U.S. business community?

WHY VISITORS COME

Visitors from other countries are streaming into the United States in unprecedented numbers. In 1987, some 30 million international visitors poured into America. In 1988, stimulated by a cheaper dollar, that figure increased 13 percent to about 33.5 million.

In 1989, 38.5 million visitors came, and in 1990 the 41 million figure could be topped. That's like having the combined populations of the states of Alabama, Arizona, Arkansas, Colorado, Iowa, Kansas, Kentucky, Minnesota, Nebraska, Oregon, South Carolina, and Wisconsin arrive and depart over 12 months.

It is estimated that these international visitors to the United States in 1990 will have spent $49.8 billion and in 1990 expenditures will hit $50 billion. The U.S. Travel and Tourism Government Affairs Council has published an impressive list of intriguing ways of measuring this spending: They spend $3 billion on lodging alone, but they also consume an amount of beef equivalent to all the cattle in Utah; they eat enough potatoes to fill over 4700 boxcars; and they use enough toilet tissue to wrap around the world more than 100 times.

Most of these visitors come purely as tourists feeding a $260 billion industry (combining U.S. earnings from foreign and domestic tourism). They also come as students, to visit family members, and for cultural exchange missions. But the largest growing proportion comes for pure business reasons: as buyers, sellers, negotiators, investors, and expatriate workers. Japan and Great Britain rank as numbers one and two in the tourist department, but in the business investment category the positions are reversed. By 1988, the British had accumulated $32 billion in investments in the United States compared to Japan's $12 billion. One reason for this is that the Japanese have been investing here for only 25 years whereas the British have had investments in this country for over three centuries. After these two, the Canadians and West Germans are the most active investors, and thus, guests in the United States.

Much of this foreign investment in the United States is in the form of real estate and government securities. But, according to the U.S. General Accounting Office, foreign acquisition of American corporations is rising dramatically. These foreign acquisitions, as a share of all takeovers in the United States, has increased from 6 percent in 1984 to 9 percent in 1987 and to 13 percent in the first half of 1988.

Is this a friendly invasion or not? Interestingly, according to the U.S. General Accounting Office, of the 1281 foreign takeovers during that 4 1/2 year period, only 17 were hostile or were resisted by the target company's board of directors.

CROSS-CULTURAL TRAINING FOR BUSINESS

Much of this book deals with the short-term, business or tourist visitor from other lands, but there are many who come to America for more than just short visits. What about those who come for longer visits or even move here permanently?

Asians are the fastest growing nonwhite minority in the United States. Between 1970 and 1980, the number of Asians in the United States grew by 141 percent. Between 1980 and 1985, the number of Asian Americans grew another 50 percent, to reach a total of about 5.1 million.

This class of visitor—the one that takes up residence and becomes employed here—is having such an impact on American business that a whole new profession is growing within college and corporate walls. It is called variously "cross-cultural training," "intercultural communication," or, the newest buzz word, "creative diversity." This training helps Americans work more effectively with people from other cultures, whether here temporarily or permanently.

Motorola Inc. of Chicago and Intel Corp. in Santa Clara, California, have created special departments to concentrate solely on training employes from different ethnic, economic, and social backgrounds to work with one another. Among other things, that means teaching Americans to work smoothly and efficiently with the growing number of new citizens or temporary workers who are Hispanics, Asians, and—just as important—work with that other important generic group, gender. They learn about social and cultural styles and customs of each group. They also learn to respect the others' background and viewpoint. The objective is obvious: It is to mold a more harmonious and productive workforce. In diversity there is an opportunity for more creativity, and every business sees a profit in that.

Going International Inc., a San Francisco consulting firm, started business five years ago with what has become a standard orientation textbook guide to cross-cultural management. That book is titled, appropriately, *Going International* (Random House, 1985) and was soon followed by a series of well-accepted instructional videos dealing with behavior overseas and how managers should be trained for overseas assignments. One of those videos even deals with the problem of "re-entry," referring to the time when American managers and their families return to the United States and encounter difficulty re-adjusting to American ways and change. More recently, Lennie Copeland and Lewis Griggs, the authors and producers, founders, and leaders of Going International, have embarked on new films and training programs for corporations that turn this matter of cultural diversity into generating a positive force rather than causing divisive turmoil. Thus we now have the term *creative diversity* or *valuing diversity,* as Copeland and Griggs have labeled it.

At more and more colleges and universities, it is now possible to obtain advanced degrees in fields of intercultural development. Additional information and training is also offered by groups such as the following:

- ☐ Intercultural Communication Institute, (8835 SW Canyon Lane, Portland, Oregon 97225).

- ☐ Society for Intercultural Education, Training and Research, (SIETAR) 1505 22nd St., NW, Washington, DC 20037.

- ☐ The Key Man Course at the American Graduate School of International Management (also known as "Thunderbird"), (Glendale, Arizona 85306).

- ☐ The Intercultural Press, Inc., (P.O. Box 768, Yarmouth, Maine 04096). Write for the free directory of publications.

☐ Sage Publications, Inc., (2111 West Hillcrest Drive, Newbury Park, California 91320) is another publisher specializing in texts on cross-cultural communication.

☐ The Business Council for International Understanding Institute (BCIU) in Washington, DC (202-686-2771) issues various publications and has for several decades helped train people for overseas assignments.

☐ The Monterey Institute of International Studies (425 Van Buren St., Monterey, California 93940).

☐ The National Council for International Visitors (NCIV) is a national network of private voluntary and community-based organizations that create professional and hospitality opportunities for international visitors and students. There are 103 NCIV community organizations and university centers across the country. The address of the headquarters for NCIV is 1623 Belmont St. N.W., Washington, DC 20009 (1-800-523-8101).

☐ Finally, specialists at the David M. Kennedy Center for International Studies at Brigham Young University (Provo, Utah 84602) have an extensive collection of resource information on this subject. This Center publishes a vast amount of intercultural material, among them a series of excellent leaflets called *CULTURGRAMS*. These are leaflets, one for each of about 100 countries, containing concise information on greetings, visiting, eating, gestures, personal appearance, demographics, lifestyle, and government.

☐ For American businesses interested in training their employes for postings abroad, an excellent resource book is *The New Expatriates* by Rosalie L. Tung, Ballinger Publishing Co., 1988, Cambridge, MA. This book compares the selection and training procedures of expatriate assignments using a sample of U.S., European, and Japanese multinational companies. Dr. Tung lists the criteria used in selecting candidates for overseas assignments, reviews the kinds of training those companies provide, gives failure and recall rates of expatriates, and provides the factors that contribute to an expatriate's ability to perform successfully.

We blithely talk about choosing a career in "the world of business" not realizing the complete accuracy of that phrase. Whether it is a delegation of buyers from Taiwan, or a transferred employee from your European subsidiary, or—perhaps the most traumatic of all— the arrival of your new corporate owners from Japan, the Middle East, or West Germany, the cold truth is that American businesspersons must learn to cope and communicate well with people from other cultures.

WHY A MANAGERIAL SKILL?

Fully 10 years before *The Wall Street Journal* articles described the globally minded CEO of the year 2000, authors and educators Philip R. Harris and Robert T. Moran described the manager of the future:*

> The manager who knows only his or her own country is doomed to become obsolete. Most organizations can no longer afford to employ culturally myopic managers.
>
> The cosmopolitan manager is required—one who is an intercultural communicator and transmitter.
>
> The terms *international* and *cross-cultural* are frequently used interchangeably and therefore incorrectly. Almost any international experience must be cross-cultural, but it is also possible to have a cross-cultural experience without leaving one's own country.

Harris and Moran define cosmopolitan as "belonging to the world; not limited to just one part of the political, social, commercial, or intellectual sphere; free from local, provincial, or national ideas, prejudices, or attachments."

Another writer quoted in the Moran-Harris text, Brent R. Ruben, lists seven skills, or abilities, that mark an effective multicultural manager. Here they are, with explanations paraphrased:

1. *Respect.* This means the capability of demonstrating respect in whichever way a specific culture requires: respect for age,

---

* Excerpted, with appreciation, from *Managing Cultural Differences,* by Philip R. Harris and Robert T. Moran, copyright 1979 by Gulf Publishing Co., Houston, Texas. Used with permission. All rights reserved.

respect in manner of speech, respect with eye contact, respect with hand or body gestures, respect for personal privacy, and so on. Among the Japanese, for instance, the mere exchanging of business cards borders on ceremony, and it is important to respect and respond to this fact.

2. *Tolerating Ambiguity.* This refers to the skill of reacting positively to new, different, and at times, unpredictable situations. For instance, how do you react when a Latin hugs you, or a Middle Easterner walks arm-in-arm with you in public? By American standards, these are not only mixed but often uncomfortable signals. A cosmopolitan businessperson quickly tolerates them.

3. *Relating to People.* This means placing the management of people on an equal level with "getting the job done." Too often, American managers are totally result-oriented without sensitivity to the "people" ingredient.

4. *Being Nonjudgmental.* This is the ability to withhold judgment until all information is accumulated, while also taking into account cultural idiosyncrasies that could color judgment. Why do the Japanese seem to move at glacier-like speed when making decisions? Don't rush to judgment; there is an explanation. (See Chapter 10 on hosting the Japanese.)

5. *Personalizing One's Observations.* This is the skill of recognizing that each person sees the world from his or her own platform of observations—like the allegory of the group of blind people examining an elephant for the first time: each person had a clear, but completely different perception of what an elephant was depending on which part of the elephant they were touching.

6. *Empathy.* This skill, the ability to place yourself in another person's shoes, is one of the higher level skills in intercultural relationships. As one counselor explains, "If your colleague has a stone in his shoe, it is helpful to know what type of discomfort is involved—just don't go to such an extent that *your* foot starts hurting."

7. *Persistence.* This is the companion word to "patience." Both are firm requirements in dealing with people from other societies

around the world. But usually it should be the George Bush "kinder and gentler" kind of patience and persistence. In rare cases, it may even be acceptable to be persistant to the point of downright firmness. One of my mentors, a highly successful British international executive, explained it this way: "It's O.K. to pound on the table once in a while. Just make certain, first, you are absolutely right and, second, you do it very sparingly."

Is it possible to wrap all these abilities into a single word? I think so. One word is "statesmanlike." Another two-word phrase suggested by Dr. Charles T. Vetter, Jr. is "citizen ambassador." In global business, being a statesman who cares about people encompasses the seven skills above plus three more: dignity, professionalism, and propriety. As we said, in the business world it is also sometimes necessary to be firm. That still doesn't rule out statesmanlike conduct. As one writer says, a statesman is ". . . a person who can tell you to go to hell in such a way that you actually look forward to the trip." These qualities are then all contained in a mein of grace and respect and goodwill.

This matter of being cosmopolitan, of managerial mobility between cultures, is becoming more and more vital in business. Human resource specialists are spending more time assisting and training employes who come from and go to different lands. As a result, as with many professions, a new vocabulary has emerged. *Expatriate* has been used for decades to describe an American employee who is posted to an overseas work assignment. But with more overseas nationals coming to the United States, a new term *inpatriate* has been adopted. And then, of course, each of those can become a *repatriate*, or someone who is returned to their home country after an assignment in a different nation.

A CASE STUDY

Moving from country to country can be a true test of personality, of business skills, and especially of one's family. Here is a typical case study, reported last year by the Associated Press news service,* that illustrates just how foreign the United States can be:

* Reprinted, with permission, from the Associated Press Inc.

In 1988, Chrysler Motors Corp. and Mitsubishi Motors Corp. built a joint-venture factory, Diamond-Star Motors Corp., in the ironically named location of Normal, Illinois, a college town of 38,000 in the heart of corn country.

Mitsubishi transferred some 50 Japanese employees to Normal for postings of from three to five years. In addition, 200 Japanese technicians journeyed to Normal for six-month assignments to train their American colleagues to operate 470 robot assembly machines designed by Mitsubishi. About 100 Americans also went to Japan to study, first-hand, operations there.

Diamond-Star's chairman, G. Glenn Gardner, reported that "There has not been any prejudice or anything like that. But the language barrier has been an absolute nightmare. It's been 10 times worse than I ever imagined. And things like body language are so much different. For three years now, I've been working with Japanese executives and I'm just now catching on to Japanese body language."

Quite wisely, the company trained newly hired American employees to speak basic English and to use appropriate hand gestures with their Japanese counterparts. They also taught the Americans to respect important Japanese history and culture.

On the Japanese side, the visitors were complimentary of their American hosts. Complaints centered on entertainment and food, especially a lack of fresh fish and other staples of their diet.

The wife of one Japanese worker said "I like America. I never get homesick, but I'm not satisfied with the shopping. In Tokyo, I can get anything I want. Here, I can't get everything, especially Japanese food and fashionable clothes."

"The U.S. is super, other than its fast food," said a Japanese manager. "When I brought my daughter home from three weeks at summer camp with no Japanese food, I promised her a trip to the best sushi restaurant in Chicago. She said, 'No, Daddy, I want a hamburger and a Coke.'"

On the plus side there is also golf, according to another Japanese manager. It is so much cheaper in the United States than in Japan. But on the negative side, the American education system is less demanding and Japanese children attend special classes each Saturday emphasizing Japanese language, culture, mathematics, and social studies.

THE ROLE OF BUSINESS ETIQUETTE

Etiquette, according to national platform speaker Herbert V. Prochnow, ". . . is learning to yawn with your mouth closed." At a different level is Charlotte Ford's definition in her *Book of Modern Manners*, (Simon and Schuster, New York, 1980): "This is what etiquette is all about—it's the graciousness to coexist peacefully and productively in the lives that we, as individuals have set up for ourselves. And as we travel farther and faster between different worlds with their differing cultural demands, we must become ever more flexible and adaptable."

Ford then offers this especially provocative insight: "In China, the ideograph for 'tradition' is the same one for 'good manners.' The two are inevitably linked."

As further evidence for the importance of intercultural etiquette, read this definition of the closely linked word "protocol" from a book titled *Protocol, the Complete Handbook of Diplomatic, Official and Social Usage*, by Mary Jane McCaffree and Pauline Innis (Prentice-Hall, 1977):

> The term protocol comes from Greek words meaning "the first glue," and indeed it may be said that protocol is the glue which holds official life in our society together. Whether on the local, state, national or international level, proper protocol is vital in assuring that relations between the officials of organizations and government are conducted with minimum friction and maximum efficiency.

If protocol is the glue that holds part of our lives together, it seems worthwhile to avoid becoming *un*glued.

Even in beginning classes on etiquette for young children, two basic rules are taught that seem to make good sense for anyone living in our shrinking global village. Those two rules are: Don't ever comment or call attention to someone else's bad manners, and don't ever do anything that will cause someone else to be embarrassed.

At a seminar I once conducted in North Carolina, a member of the audience rose and issued this challenge: "I understand clearly what etiquette and protocol are, but can you give me examples of how business is risked or even lost by insufficient attention to them?"

My answer was this. How would you react if a salesperson came into your office, gave you a limp handshake, and would not make direct eye contact. And what if he or she spoke with a toothpick sticking out of their mouth, picking their teeth throughout the conversation? Then how would you feel if he or she spit on the floor, or actually blew their nose without benefit of a handkerchief and flipped the result on the ground?

My guess is you would not only be turned off, but you would turn them out as fast as possible. Regardless of what product or service that person was selling, you would look for quick excuses to kick them out the door.

These examples of behavior are not fanciful exaggerations. As you will learn in the pages of this book, and perhaps from personal experience, in several important cultures a limp handshake is actually the preferred custom. The same applies to avoiding first names, direct eye contact, and touching. And, yes, even toothpicks, burping, and avoidance of handkerchiefs are accepted public behavior in a few places around the world.

If you're still unconvinced, how would you feel about a conversation with a person who suddenly asks you "How much do you earn each year?" Or, "How much is your house worth?" Again, in certain other cultures, these are common and perfectly acceptable questions.

Without an awareness and capability to deal with such examples, what might be at first blush a promising business situation could develop into a short and certainly not sweet relationship. The point here is that, quite literally, business in international circles can succeed or fail with the very first greeting. Etiquette or protocol or comportment or whatever you call it is woven into our business life like an intricately handcrafted Persian rug. Remove a few key threads, and the whole pattern can be weakened or even destroyed.

Etiquette is another word for "convention" or for "accepted rules." The corridors of business—here in the United States as well as overseas—are replete with both of those. I once surveyed 100 alumni of the School of Business at the University of Wisconsin asking this question: "Now that you have graduated and have been working in the real world for two years, what did you *not* learn about U.S. business at the university that you *wish* you'd learned?" The majority of replies dealt with office conventions, rules, behavior, and protocol. The opening phrase in many responses was "In my college classrooms, nobody ever told me about office protocol and etiquette." No one told them about such things as when to use first names, telephone protocol, office memoranda, clothing, time for personal tasks, the "pecking order," expense reports, business jargon, acronyms, office dating and smoking, how to ask for a raise, getting a haircut on company time, and on and on.

One respondent summarized the role and the importance of office behavior with this grim, seasoned reaction: "That factor that, if ignored, could turn your springboard of success into a ship's plank."

Now, what about protocol with *international* business associates? Can insensitive hosting of foreign guests actually lose business? You bet. John Hill, former government diplomat stationed in Bangkok, relates this true incident:

———— □ ————

A Thai government agency canvased American engineering firms to submit proposals for a giant construction project in Thailand. Narrowing the field to four final candidates, the Thais sent a delegation to the United States to personally interview each firm. The group arrived in Chicago but, due to a mix-up by the engineering firm and its failure to double-check arrival times, the Thais were not met at the airport. Nonetheless, even though the visitors were unfamiliar with Chicago, they found their own way to a hotel in the Loop. They phoned the embarrassed U.S. executive and, after hearing his apologies, agreed to meet in his office the next morning at 11 o'clock. The next day the American was at his desk at the appointed time, waiting. And he waited, and waited. Finally, in mid-afternoon, he received a phone call from the visitors saying "We have been waiting at our hotel—no one has come to pick us up. We are simply not accustomed to this type of treatment. We have booked a flight out this afternoon to our next destination. Goodbye."

———— □ ————

What was the American's explanation for this unintended gaffe? "We did not want to appear over-anxious or fawning," he explained. "Among our clients in the United States, the business proposal itself is what's important. Surely any American could have found his way from the airport to a hotel and then to our office." While he may have been right about fellow Americans, he was wrong about his international guests and, poof!, there went a possible contract, literally flying away to some competitor.

Summary

At this stage, words like *cosmopolitan, statesmanlike, protocol,* and *hosting* should be acknowledged as proper and necessary business skills.

If Lord Chesterfield is credited with coalescing proper behavior into the art of etiquette in the mid-eighteenth century, then his twentieth-century successor in the United States was assuredly Emily Post, whose name has become synonymous with good manners.

Emily Post taught that consideration for others separates the savage from the civilized man. One of her biographers, Esther B. Aresty, in her book *The Best Behavior* (Simon and Schuster, 1970) summarizes Miss Post's teachings as follows: "Consideration for others is not inborn. It is instilled. Though polished behavior and etiquette add grace and flavor to our lives, the greatest personal enrichment lies in mastering the technique of genuine courtesy. The gracious deed, the gracious word, the considerate silence, the polite delay—in the end bring greater rewards and approval than the way we handle our forks."

The word *etiquette* is of French origin. Another French phrase, *savoir faire,* embodies much of what has been discussed here. Literally it means "ability," "tact," "good manners," "good breeding," "knowledge of the world." But the French maintain that *savoir faire* has much deeper meaning that only the French can fathom. That has always intrigued me, so, after speaking at a marketing meeting of an international computer manufacturing firm, I put this question to three of the company's French executives: "What is really meant when the French say they are unique in having *savoir faire?*"

The first, who happened to be the youngest, said "Let me explain it in the form of an illustration. Let's say a man comes home and finds his wife in the arms of another man. If the husband says nothing, turns around, closes the door and departs, that is French *savoir faire.*

The second executive, slightly older, said "You've almost explained it, but not quite. To use your example, the man comes home, finds his wife in the arms of another man, says 'Excuse me. *Please continue.*' Then turns around, closes the door and leaves. That is true French *savoir faire.*"

The third Frenchman was older and wiser. He pondered a moment, then said: "No, you've almost got it, but not quite. There is more. Using your illustration, if the man comes home, finds his wife in the arms of another man, says 'Oh, excuse me. Please continue.' And turns around and walks out. Now, if that other man *can* continue, *that* is true French *savoir faire*."

So, our hypothesis is established: hosting is, indeed, a necessary business skill. It requires statesmanship, awareness, respect, patience, and a whole collection of other words . . . including *savoir faire*.

In the next chapter, we turn to an examination of exactly how outsiders view America, what notions about us they bring here, and what questions lurk in their minds.

=2

HOW OTHERS VIEW AMERICANS

"What the United States does best is to
understand itself. What it does worst is
understand others."

—*Carlos Fuentes, Mexican novelist*

Those are harsh words from Señor Fuentes. But just wait, there are
more portraits to come, both good and bad, of how we Americans
are visualized.

This chapter represents that magical mirror on the wall described in Chapter 1. Remember how the nasty Queen in "Snow
White And The Seven Dwarfs" posed the fateful question "Mirror,
mirror on the wall, who is the fairest of them all?" To her chagrin,
the mirror answered not the Queen but Snow White. As the
British would say, "Hard cheese, old girl," (translation: "Tough
luck, lady.")

If we as Americans stood, internationally, before that honest
and courageous mirror, how would we fare? Would we be viewed as
loveable Snow White or as the ill-tempered Queen? In this chapter,
we will attempt to answer that question using the opinions and
quotations of both American and foreign observers. We will draw
on the opinions of authors, historians, educators, journalists, sociol-
ogists, and just plain common folk. We will learn the views of
everyone from an abdicated British king, Edward, Duke of Windsor,
who observed "The thing that impresses me most about America is
the way parents obey their children," to the more flattering words
of Israeli writer Ehud Yonay who said "One comes to the United
States—always, no matter how often—to see the future. It's what
life in one's own country will be like 5, 10, 20 years from now."

Examination of one's own ethos is not an easy nor always a pleasant task. But, according to psychologists, the ability to laugh at oneself is both therapeutic and endearing. American commentator-humorists from Mark Twain and Will Rogers to their current successors like Art Buchwald, Bob Orben, Russell Baker, Dave Barry, and Lewis Grizzard have entertained and enlightened us for decades by writing about the flawed American anima, assuring that we enjoy goodly doses of both therapy and self-endearment.

Later in this chapter we will recount some questions often asked of and about Americans. We will also provide some tips for responding to the tougher questions. But now, using that magical, insightful mirror combined with a large magnifying glass of truth, let's examine how others perceive the American society.

WE MARCH TO DIFFERENT DRUMMERS

Charles Kuralt has created a wonderfully special and sensitive view of America in his role as roving chronicler of backroads America. In his book, *On The Road* (G. P. Putnam & Sons, New York, 1985) he describes how Americans march to different drummers.

Kuralt talks about "the mood of America" and how it changes from Tribune, Kansas to Haines, Alaska, depending on the richness of the wheat crop and if the lumber mill is hiring. "The mood of New York City," he writes, "is much affected by heat and rain and the percentage of taxis with their off-duty signs lighted at any given time. You can't get your thumb on America's mood."

The eighteenth-century French writer-observer of America, Alexis de Tocqueville wrote "As they mingle, the Americans become assimilated . . . . They all get closer to one type." But in 1854, Henry Thoreau disagreed: "If a man does not keep pace with his companions, perhaps it is because he hears a different drummer. Let him step to the music which he hears . . ."

Kuralt comments, "We admire de Tocqueville, but it was Thoreau we listened to."

America is, first, a land of shifting moods and one perhaps also of contradictions and of different drummers. This is one truth about America that visitors soon discover.

But truth is just one form of realism. Perceptions are quite another. What about perceptions from *outside* America? What about stereotypes?

Jean Cramer, American correspondent in Paris for *The New Yorker Magazine* has this to say about stereotypes: "Europeans view American culture from TV and movies. For example, the French consider our culture as a 'cowboy culture.' That's why they liked Ronald Reagan. So, they're shocked when they come to the U.S. and see poverty and homelessness. When I ask them 'Don't you read your newspapers?' they reply 'Yes, but we don't believe it.'"

Perceptions and stereotypes like that are also seen from the opposite side of the world. Former Tennessee Governor Lamar Alexander spent a six-month sabbatical in Australia. "From abroad," Alexander reported, "America looks like a magnificent, rowdy, boisterous place. From abroad, it looks like we blame the Japanese for more than what's their fault; that we expect our antagonism to the Russians to be the determinate of every part of our foreign policy, and the world is more complicated than that. I recall D. H. Lawrence's description of Americans as 'millions of squirrels in millions of cages,' which from a distance look like they're running in circles."

Kuralt sees Americans marching to different drummers, the French see the United States as a giant Wild West show, and from Australia we appear to be a "rowdy, boisterous place." So, looking at America is like looking into a kaleidoscope—a lot depends on how the viewer peers into the tube.

We also have other sharp reminders that the world does not revolve around the North American continent nor the American nationality. That's called ethnocentrism. Here are two examples. When David Ryan, a college student was visiting Borneo, he was asked "Where are you from?" "America," he replied. "North or South?" was the retort. And they weren't asking if he was a Yankee or a Rebel. An even more striking reminder comes from a Midwest marketing executive traveling with his Chinese sales manager. He tells how, after a few drinks, his Oriental-born manager turned to him and confessed: "Frankly, you round-eye Americans all look alike to me. I can't tell you apart."

FIRST IMPRESSIONS

We discussed earlier that impressions are formed, and business deals possibly won or lost, at literally the first greeting. Therefore, it may be helpful to learn some of the typical, strong first impressions of many international visitors who come to the United States. Some of those impressions are not flattering, but here is an opportunity to employ a few of those intercultural skills we wrote about in the first chapter—like objectivity and "tolerating ambiguity and diversity," both signifying that we must be less ethnocentric and more accepting of what seem like far out and disagreeable views.

Here are perhaps the four strongest impressions, followed by a mixed bag of lesser ones.

1. The first impression noted almost universally by most visitors is the *vastness* of America. A distance of 500 miles means little to the average American—that's merely the distance from San Diego to San Francisco, or from New York City to Detroit. In contrast, if you start in London and travel eastward just 500 miles, you'll find yourself crossing at least four national boundaries and winding up in Warsaw which, to our minds, seems like a gigantic jump. For a visitor to the United States, our vastness is experienced physically by riding a plane or train across the empty spaces of the Great Plains, by staring at the seemingly endless string of mountains in the Rockies, and finally by realizing that we actually stretch across four different time zones. Think on that. Very few other countries have more than a single time zone within their boundaries. Unless they've traversed Siberia, visitors have difficulty comprehending five-hour transcontinental air flights within the same country, much less taking several days and nights for a cross-country train trip. Some visitors, accustomed to comfortably touring all of Europe by bus, come to the United States and sign up for a 60-day Greyhound unlimited travel ticket thinking they can experience all of America via one four-wheeled caravan. All they experience is a permanently numbed bum.

2. The second impression, and this may come as a shock, is that America is *plump*. Nutrition experts tell us we do, indeed, weigh more than most other nationalities on earth. Furthermore, regardless of current health and fitness fads, America is getting heavier. A Louis Harris poll in 1989 reported that 64 percent of those Americans polled were overweight compared to 58 percent in 1983. Also, according to a Louisiana State University researcher, about 20 percent of the adult population in

the United States are classified as "significantly obese," meaning a weight about 30 percent above what would be ideal for a person's age, stature, and gender. The number of overweight and obese people in our cities and countryside is often one of the first observations of international visitors. They assume that this is a result of our rich, plentiful diet, not realizing that in most cases it is probably a result of an uneducated selection of foods with high fat content, plus lack of exercise.

3. The third impression of observant visitors usually deals with our hurried *tempo* of life, especially in business. "Time is money," "Money talks,"—that seems to be our credo. We are proud of it. We work hard, play hard, have "power breakfasts," quick lunches, and employ every electronic gadget possible to increase our pace. In most other countries, the pace and pressure is generally slower and softer. True, the Japanese work longer hours and seem to live for their work, but there, unlike here, patience, contemplation, and even silence are also virtues. In business, Americans think in terms of hours and days plus that almighty business demarcation, "the fiscal quarter." In contrast, the Japanese businessperson thinks in terms of months and years and, yes, even decades. Latin Americans and Middle Easterners prefer a breaking-in period of socializing before hunkering down to business. Americans want to jump right into the fray. We Americans take pride in an attitude of "Let's get right down to business." Allegro is the tempo of America, and visitors feel the beat almost from the moment they arrive.

4. The fourth impression that usually drifts to the top in the foreign visitor's pool of perceptions concerns the easygoing, *friendly nature* of most Americans. Waitresses smile and chat with customers, people wave freely and call each other by their first names, and taxi drivers seldom hesitate to engage foreigners in unrestricted dialogue—something rarely done outside the United States. Americans usually treat foreign visitors with a certain curiosity, respect, and a desire to assist. Americans, it is widely said, want to be liked and this is noted and appreciated my most visitors. Soviet radio reporter Irina Simonova commenting at a Midwestern backyard picnic said "I knew about the style of life (in America) and I knew about the

high standard of living. I didn't know about the friendliness and the attitude—but you can actually feel it here."

Those are four key first impressions. There are many others, of course. The following lesser impressions are single snapshots of scenes and settings stored in millions of visitor memory banks:

> Uniformed police with huge pistols hanging on their hips. Houses with wide open yards surrounding them. The absence of protective fences in front of and between homes. Endless interstate highways. Hollywood movies and VCRs. Houses made of wood instead of brick, stone or mortar. Basements. Different state license plates on autos. Youths riding skateboards in Converse hightops with untied shoelaces. Absence of formal border crossings between states. Orderly traffic. Huge cars. Low gasoline prices. Basketball hoops above garage doors. Gigantic food markets. Store shelves stacked with a hypnotic assortment of packaged soaps and cereals. Mickey Mouse. Outdoor advertising. Baseball and football. Printed T-shirts. An incomprehensible number of TV channels. Fast food outlets. And the list goes on and on. But hovering above all these individual pictures and impressions is the panorama of vastness, of open space, of a country that seems to continually stretch forever over the horizon.

These are the *tangible* impressions, the material things one can see and touch in America. What about the *intangibles*, the ones inside the American national body? What about the values and mores and attitudes of Americans? To examine those, let's dig a bit deeper into the American ethos.

DEEPER IMPRESSIONS

For this examination, we turn to one of our academic explorers— V. Lynn Tyler at The David M. Kennedy Center for International Studies at Brigham Young University, is one of those who looks at horizons near and far. In his book *Intercultural Interacting* (1987), and from a lifetime of other writings, Tyler offers a few stereotypes describing how, at times, various people of the world view Americans. In a segment titled "How Others May See You," Tyler invites readers to seriously consider that:

Initially it may be difficult for you to accept and understand how people from other countries view you, your country, and your culture. Being stereotyped can be annoying to anyone. By understanding how others perceive you as a foreigner, you can better prepare to help them understand you, and you them.

Stereotypes can be used as starting points or "people-maps" to determine what people are really like. The following describes how various peoples of the world view Americans:

—*Careless:* With dress, possessions, time, money, rules, manners, ceremonies, nature, relationships, politics, and more.

—*Generous/Hospitable:* As victors in war, as neighbors, as U.N. benefactors.

—*Self-indulgent:* Pursuing material things.

—*Sentimental/Romantic:* Prone to extremes in emotional expression; open.

—*Materialistic:* Usually honest; ambition and success are paramount; vastness.

—*Confident and Self-Confident:* Even brash, yet demand almost too much of self.

—*Complacent yet Arrogant:* Ethnocentric, embarrassingly so; misunderstand honor.

—*Colonistic:* Ethnocentrically imperialistic; disregard for other systems; overly proud of own systems.

—*Competitive yet Equalitarian:* A paradox to most in children-to-adult varieties; class and rank may be temporary; no real aristocracy.

—*Resourceful:* Combining all of the above; lovers of common sense and results, inventions, innovations, and flexibility; "now" oriented.

—*Independent and Different:* Individually feeling not to "fit others' mold," but fiercely defensive if encroached upon as an American."

Tyler offers this summary quotation:

Stereotypes are most at folly when dealing with individuals, but they are most useful when dealing with peoples in general . . . as in this instance. [Quote adapted from Wu-Kuang Chu]

He continues:

> If you agree with these perceptions, why do you? If not, how are Americans different from this? How can you help others understand your feelings? How can you understand theirs? Search for the keys to effective intercultural understanding in your own experiences.
>
> Just as Americans are so much more than "pizza, tacos, apple pie, and baseball," other people are much more than you may have thought. There are ways of developing accurate perceptions and of building bridges over which you and others considerately can cross.

Tyler concludes with this quotation from Sir Francis Bacon:

> If a (person) be gracious and courteous to strangers, it shows he (or she) is a citizen of the world, and that his heart is no island cut off from other lands, but a continent that joins to them.

Another profile of the American psyche appears in the Harris-Moran text, *Managing Cultural Differences* (Gulf Publishing Co., Houston, 1979). They quote from John Fieg and Lenore Yaffee's book, *Adjusting to the U.S.A.* (Meridian House International, Washington DC, 1977). Here is the list, with explanations paraphrased, of how mainstream U.S. culture is described:

1. *Pace of Life.* The emphasis in America on punctuality and efficiency is often distressing especially to people from Africa, Asia, and Latin countries.

2. *Friendship.* Americans are gregarious on the first meeting, and this is often misinterpreted as an intended deep friendship. "The American comes on too strong too soon and then fails to follow up with the implicitly promised friendship," the authors say.

3. *Service and Egalitarianism.* Because of a general absence of subservience in the United States, visitors find many waiters, taxi drivers, bellboys, and other service employes what they consider as too egalitarian. In their home countries, the relationship would be, by American standards, almost fawning.

4. *Emotional Expressiveness.* Here we seem to stand in the middle of the spectrum: to the effervescent Latins we appear cool, and yet to the reserved Asians we appear too forward and impulsive.

5. *Individuals, Freedom, and Privacy.* Some visitors are deeply impressed by the degree of individual freedom, particularly in the political arena, that an American enjoys. Others are disturbed by what they consider too much freedom, such as the widespread personal ownership of weapons.

6. *Self-Reliance and the Nuclear-Age Family.* Feelings are mixed by, on the one hand, the female's strong family role and the independence of children, and on the other hand the disregard for aged family members and strong family unity.

7. *Informality and Morality.* Because many cultures dress more carefully and conservatively, they automatically relate what we consider casualness and fashion with looseness in morality, even sexual provocation.

8. *Crime.* Our open society and free press, especially the sensational press, cast an image around the world of a country besotted by crime. Many visitors come here fearing their own safety. Others connect Chicago not with the heartland of the United States—indeed, many of them can't find it on the map—and with any mention of Chicago they make a machine-gun motion with their hands, saying "Oh, yes. Bang, bang, bang! Al Capone!"

9. *Tipping, Taxes, and "Sales."* In many countries, tips are included in the cost of a meal or hotel room; the same with sales taxes (often called "V.A.T." for value added taxes). As a result, visiting consumers become wary of our tipping and tax practices. They also are confused by American merchandising in determining when a "sale" is truly a "sale."

10. *Race Relations.* This social problem is well-known to visitors and views are as mixed and confused as our own. Many come here to find the problem less explosive than they imagined, while others cannot understand our apparent impassiveness.

11. *Teacher-Student Relations.* In many cultures, the teacher is not only a firm disciplinary figure but high on the social hierarchy. Therefore, visitors are shocked to see what they consider disrespectful attitudes toward teachers and school administrators by American students and parents alike. Other visitors admire the informality of the student-teacher

relationship here and the freedom of expression and individual growth it encourages.

12. *Lack of Knowledge about Their Countries.* The American's general lack of knowledge about world geography, compounded by our pervasive monolingual society, are great disappointments to most visitors. It hardly creates the need for the "respect" listed atop the list of important multicultural managerial skills in Chapter 1.

QUESTIONS MOST ASKED
ABOUT AMERICA

Foreign business visitors are usually sensitized against asking delicate, difficult questions about America and, wisely, stick to business matters only. However, during informal social sessions and after a business relationship blossoms into a more personal and informal state, it is highly possible your discussions will venture further afield.

To help you prepare, here are the kinds of questions that might—just might—arise. The basis for these questions, incidentally, is borrowed from work conducted by Dr. Charles T. Vetter, Jr. and the book *Citizen Ambassadors.* Vetter served as a senior training officer for the U.S. Foreign Service Institute. More information about Dr. Vetter's excellent work is provided at the end of this section.

American Culture and Society

1. The American wife/mother seems, from the outside looking in, to run the family. Is that true? Why?

2. Over half of American mothers work outside the home; doesn't this threaten the unity and well-being of the family?

3. American women are known for being "liberated." Liberated from what? It seems to us she has more freedom than women in any other society.

4. The American society does not seem to have the respect for the elderly held by most other cultures. This is evidenced by the number of nursing homes for the aged. Is this correct? Why?

5. Why does there appear do be so much violence, so many cults and gang wars in America? What is there about your society that causes these to develop?

6. What about the demand for drugs in your society? You blame other parts of the world—with some justification—for supplying the drugs, but the supply would dry up if the demand stopped. What is the United States doing to fight your drug problem?

7. Why is there this apparent hatred toward minorities: Hispanics, Indians, blacks, Asians? This is difficult for us to understand when we read history and learn that America was founded by dozens and dozens of different "minorities."

8. Americans seem to know very little about world geography— names, places, locations. Why is this?

9. Your newspapers do not carry much international news. How well-informed is the average American about international politics and current events?

10. I am thinking of sending my children to school in America but several things worry me: class demands seem geared to the "average" student; students seem to have so much freedom and independence; alcohol and drugs and sexual permissiveness seem so prevalent. What do you think?

American Government

1. I have difficulty understanding the differences between your Democrat and Republican political parties. What are the basic differences?

2. Your Congress and your President always seem to be squabbling and disagreeing with each other. And it seems to take so long to get things done. Why is that?

3. Your media reports on the power of the military-industrial complex. Does that exist even greater today? Is it a problem in your government?

4. The media in America seem to play a strong role in the conduct of your government. I appreciate that the media helped uncover the Watergate scandal, but now it seems to be trying to

constantly searching for more and more scandal. Is that true? Is that good?

5. What is the U.S. government doing about all the corporate buyouts and mergers? There seems to be a frenzy of corporate raids and what you call leveraged buyouts. Isn't that weakening your system?

6. While your recent administrations seem to favor freer trade, you still have strong pockets and waves of protectionism in America. Don't those people understand the economic interdependence that exists around the world today?

7. You say you don't like socialism. What is so wrong with it? Why wouldn't it be good for America?

Americans in the World Economy

1. America seems to use such a huge amount of energy supplies—big cars, comparatively low gasoline prices, and an endless stream of appliances. That forces prices up for countries like mine. Why can't America conserve more energy?

2. Your huge multinational companies seem to have created great problems around the world—AT&T in Chile, Exxon in Alaska, Union Carbide in India. What is being done to control them?

3. I don't understand how you can have poverty and hunger and homelessness in the midst of such wealth. Why is this the case in America?

American Foreign Policy

1. Explain the sometimes controversial American position on the following issues:

   □ Nicaragua

   □ Panama

   □ The Middle East

   □ South Africa

   □ The military build-up in Japan

□ Gorbachev's *glastnost* and *perestroika*

□ The People's Republic of China

□ A Palestinian homeland

2. What are your views on the role of the CIA and the FBI? How do they differ? Don't they compete, or overlap or even conflict with one another?

3. What is the American government policy regarding the 1992 Unification of Europe?

4. What is the American policy regarding massive oil spills, like the Exxon accident in Alaska in 1989? What would the policy be for similar problems in foreign lands?

5. What is the American solution to the Iran problem? To worldwide terrorism? To the reduction of human rights in so many other nations?

If, after reading this list, you'd like to throw up your hands in frustration, you can't be blamed. This is, indeed, a challenging list of difficult and often embarrassing questions. Take solace that it is highly unlikely you will be confronted with more than a few of them over an evening of social conversation with your foreign visitors. As we said at the outset, most business travelers tend to separate business and politics. They usually do not intrude on personal matters or what they consider to be private opinions.

However, when the questions do surface, here are some general tips on crafting statesmanlike responses to even the most insensitive query. Once again, the basic advice is drawn from Dr. Vetter's work.

TIPS FOR RESPONDING

1. *Avoid arguments.* Solomon said "A soft answer turneth away wrath" and the last thing the international business maven wants is wrath. If, however, your guest insists on being contentious, use these devices: listen, keep cool, ask softer questions, and keep an open mind. Try to avoid allowing a

reasonable discussion to turn into an argument or, worse, a debate that could turn into an injury-prone battle.

2. *Determine what the critic is really thinking.* Good questioning can be an art form and a valuable skill not only when hosting but in all aspects of business. The same applies to being a good listener. Here is a chance to hone those business skills. Uncover the origin and concern of the critic's view. Extract facts, if they in fact exist. Ferret out any hidden agenda. Avoid lashing back by criticizing the guest's home country or personal viewpoint.

3. *Draw on your own experience.* Avoid generalities. Cite your own personal experiences, or, if possible, of a mutually respected third party. If you don't know the answer to a critic's complaint, say so. Your personal experiences make the best possible testimony in any given debate—but don't become bullheaded or angry about them.

4. *Move the discussion beyond the American context.* America is often a "whipping post" when it comes to problems such as prejudice, immorality, and poverty. Yes, these problems exist here, but elsewhere as well. However, don't revert to difficulties in the guest's home country unless he or she brings it up. Even then, avoid unrequested opinions. Find something to praise!

5. *Be reasonable.* Often your guest is using English as a second language and may inadvertently use words that are stronger or harsher than intended. Also, people in different cultures are more emotional with rhetoric than others. "Courtesy is hard to argue against," says Dr. Vetter. "If you must express righteous indignation, express it as graciously as possible." Dr. Vetter observes: "Antagonists often have a very difficult time dealing with calmness and objectivity: two keys for universal exploration."

Finally, Dr. Vetter suggests that many visitors arrive here with questions they would *like* to ask, but dare not. In this case, you might want to help them along. You would show commendable sensitivity plus a willingness to communicate by providing an opening to let those questions spill out. "What do people in your country think about United States/Soviet Union disarmament discussions?" you might ask. Or, "What do you think about America's actions in Central America?" Once you've opened this conversational gate, however, keep the tips for responding well in mind so that the ensuing conversation does not become a runaway torrent.

If this type of question-and-response exercise interests you, I suggest you obtain a copy of the publication titled *Citizen Ambassadors: Guidelines for Responding to Questions Asked About America* from the Brigham Young University David M. Kennedy Center for International and Area Studies, Publication Services, 280 Herald R. Clark Building, Provo, Utah 84602.

Finally, well before any such confrontation, consider and prepare and rehearse your own answers to some of these questions. Ask yourself "How might I reply non-confrontationally to that question some evening over dessert and coffee?" It's a useful question.

SUMMARY

The president of an export management company in Memphis frequently sends his representatives to overseas markets, many of them remote and backward countries. "I always insist that they wait before calling on any customers, though," he explains. "I want them to assimilate and gain a positive attitude. I then call them on the phone and say 'Tell me something that you've found there that you really *like* about that city or country.' My reason is that I want them to be thinking positively and diplomatically before they start calling on a customer. It's very hard to do business with anyone when you are thinking negatively about them."

That's good advice, whether we are traveling abroad ourselves or hosting foreign visitors. If at first your guests seem strange or difficult or, well, truly "foreign," find ways to think positively. First impressions can be both fickle and dangerous. Look beyond fleeting impressions for positive reasons to turn a business relationship into a mutually enjoyable and prosperous business friendship. If we show objectivity and understanding, that's where the fabled magic mirror reappears. Our guests will see this, and react to what they see in front of them, just as we all do when looking into the reflection of a mirror.

In the next few chapters, we delve into the true grit of hosting: some specific ideas for memorable entertainment, plus things you should know about dining and social drinking.

3

How to Entertain

"When foreign guests arrive, there's
a lot more in their suitcases than just
clothes and toiletries."

—*An experienced host*

Visitors do, indeed, arrive here with satchels full of unexpected notions, which make for special challenges when entertaining. This true story, related by Larry Greb, former marketing manager for the S.C. Johnson (Wax) Co, might be titled "Tea and Sympathy."

———— □ ————

Mr. Satish, a native of Pakistan, was paying his first visit to the United States for a training program hosted by Johnson Wax. On the first morning, after a few hours of work, Greb asked if he'd like to take a break for coffee. "Gladly," Satish said, and they headed for the company cafeteria. Satish opted for tea and so his host put a tea bag into his cup. Satish looked at the tea bag for a moment, then tore it open and emptied the leaves into his cup. "No, no, Mr. Satish," Greb gently explained. "Here in the United States we just leave the tea in the bag in the cup and pour hot water over it." "Oh, I see," said Satish apologetically. "I hope I didn't embarrass you." Greb assured him it was no problem, and they moved to the counter holding containers of cream and sugar. Satish looked at the small bags of sugar, pondered a moment, and then with a delighted look of comprehension dropped the whole paper packet of sugar into his cup.

———— □ ————

Entertaining foreign visitors can be as surprise-filled as an adolescent's first date. Further, when visitors arrive in the United

States, they bring along customs and behavior as different from ours as corn-on-the-cob differs from *crepe suzettes.*

Let's examine the verb "to entertain." The *American Heritage Dictionary* defines it as "holding the attention of; to amuse." Synonyms include: divert, beguile, engross, absorb, please, charm, cheer, enliven, host, fete, and even rejoice.

Wow! you say. Talk about a tall order. Here they come, those accent-laden foreign visitors, bearing unspoken customs like "not eating the flesh of any animal with a cloven hoof," and I am expected to charm, cheer, beguile, and fete them. Where do I begin?

As with any complex problem, we solve this puzzle by breaking it down into smaller, more manageable parts; or, in our case, three separate chapters.

This chapter will provide some suggestions for novel ways to provide entertainment for your guest, including a delicate topic—sex. Closing this chapter is a section on conversational taboos and a couple of case studies on business entertaining.

Since food is nourishment for both body and soul and an integral part of entertaining, the succeeding chapter will deal with the subject of *dining.* You will learn what is considered peculiar about *when* we Americans eat, *what* we eat, *where* we eat, and *how* we eat. You will also learn about some of the unusual culinary habits and customs of your visitors.

Next, we will enter the domain of Bacchus, the Greek god of wine and drink, and learn—once again—what is considered peculiar about American habits. In that chapter, you will learn what raises the eyebrows of your guests at an American cocktail hour. You will also discover other national attitudes on social drinking plus favorite alcoholic beverages around the world, country by country.

Most of the information in these three chapters applies equally to both social and business entertaining. However, in Chapter 6 on "Business Protocol," you will find additional, specialized information on certain aspects of business entertainment, such as tax deductibility of entertainment expenses, and specific hints on the protocol of business correspondence, telephone usage, business cards, public speaking, and much more. Chapter 9 provides the do's and don'ts of gift-giving. Chapter 10 deals with entertaining specific nationalities: Canadians, English, Japanese, young people. Chapter 11 contains tips on specific but often overlooked aspects of entertaining: how American hotels are different, toasting, dealing with young foreign visitors, and how using the English language can be like trying to hold mercury in your hand—it slips and slides away so quickly it's easy to spill and make a grand mess. In the Appendix you will also find several resource lists to help you entertain and stimulate conversation regardless of the nationality of your guests. For example, you can locate the country your guest comes from and then learn the predominant religions and the favorite sports there.

As a further aid, beginning on page 168 there is a "Tip List" or quick reference listing, country-by-country, with eight or ten short but key tips you might like to bear in mind when hosting someone from a specific country.

Let's begin with some ideas and suggestions for general hospitality.

IDEAS FOR GENERAL HOSPITALITY

Ideas for places to go and things to do are limited only by your own imagination. Here, to jump-start your creative battery, is a list contributed by seminar audiences around the country. They were asked "What are some novel ideas you found successful when entertaining international visitors?"

□ Rodeos, or anything having to do with cowboys and Indians, are very popular opportunities for entertainment. You can bet that nearly every foreign visitor has seen an American wild west movie. The French and Germans are especially captivated by that period and actually have cowboy roundups and rodeos in their own countries, attempting to replicate that lusty period in American history.

□ State and county fairs—animal judging, sulky racing, crafts and dress-making, country western music—the list of unique sights for a foreigner at a fair is endless.

□ Boat tours on major rivers and lakes, such as the mighty Mississippi, for example. This is just as exotic to visitors as the Amazon and Yangtze are to us. In the minds of visitors, paddle steamers create visions of Mark Twain and "Gone

With The Wind." As for lake tours, when tour boats traverse a U.S. shoreline announcing who lives where and how much the properties are worth, British visitors, for one, are amazed by this "invasion of privacy" but still delight in this insight into American life.

□ Fall colors—only a few countries can rival the annual coloramas that stretch across the northern half of the United States each Autumn. Consider this simple form of entertainment, especially for Middle Easterners who may never have seen this Fall display.

□ A local grocery store—while the giant supermarkets are perhaps the best, whatever the size of the store, visitors love to compare packaging, sizes, assortment, and prices.

□ A local courtroom is an unsuspecting attraction that often catches the interest of business visitors because law, justice, and order are important in every country. It also shows you aren't hiding anything.

□ Sporting events—baseball and football are the logical candidates—but be prepared for the almost impossible task of explaining innings, outs, downs, scrimmage line, and why there are three strikes, yet four balls. Tennis is played all over the world and with its simplified scoring system, you don't have to know your opponent's language. The Japanese enjoy baseball, golf, and skiing, and of course swimming is another universal sport. Basketball is also growing in popularity and because games are plentiful at all three levels—high school, college, and professional—it becomes a good candidate. Showing your guest a local or incompany health and fitness spa is another idea. Sports new for visitors might be racketball, bowling, water ski competitions, horseshoes, curling, ice hockey, lacrosse, or even sailing. (Refer to the Appendix of this book for a list of the most popular sports country-by-country; this will prep you in knowing which sports your guest is likely to know or not know.) Americans are known as sports enthusiasts and if our games are foreign and complex to visitors, "Don't worry," advises one British publication dryly, "any one of 200 million Americans will be glad to explain them."

□ The cultural attractions—such as your local history and art museums, concert halls, theaters, and so on. One veteran host added, "Skip churches, though, unless you live in Salt Lake City. Not because ours are unworthy, but because religion can be a touchy subject and also because we can hardly compare with the cathedrals of Europe and South America and the temples of the Orient." On the other hand, if your visitor expresses interest, by all means take them to your local church service. Bear in mind that American museums are often vastly different from museums in other parts of the world. The reason is that American history is so comparatively new and recent and visitors marvel that only 100 years ago native American Indians roamed much of this continent. Our historical museums also demonstrate how much progress has been achieved in the United States in a relatively short period of time.

□ Potluck dinners at local churches or clubs is as American as you get—everyone streaming to the community hall with a favorite "dish to pass." For some visitors, it may even conjure visions of pioneer Americans circling the Conestoga wagons for the evening meal.

□ Attending live television shows is still, for most, a novel experience that represents an important part of the American cultural scene. Make certain, though, that your guests have a reasonably good command of English.

□ Regional food harvests—fish boils at lake and seashore sites, crawfish boils, barbecues, pig-picking in the Carolinas, corn boils, crab harvests, catfish broils—the list is endless.

□ Bingo games—while the game itself might already be known to your visitors, the prospect of "people watching" might produce a memorable evening.

□ Demolition derbies have been described as "bumping-car rodeos" or, less kindly, as typical American "conspicuous destruction." Auto races are another option.

□ Auto shows—Europeans are usually very automobile conscious and knowledgeable about horsepower, displacement, and design features. In many European countries, the type of car driven by a company executive is a direct reflection of his (or her) status within that company. This is particularly true in West Germany and Great Britain. Therefore a chance to examine the latest U.S. auto models can be both entertaining and informative.

□ State Capitols help emphasize the traditional separation in the United States between federal and state's rights. The capitols themselves also have a rich and varied history.

□ Local amusement parks like Disneyland and other major national theme parks.

□ Local schools—a visit to a typical American classroom might have special appeal to any visitor with children back home. Almost everyone likes to compare common and essential institutions like schools.

□ Any American holiday—spend the day in typical American fashion, whether it be attending a Labor Day parade, or a Fourth of July picnic and fireworks display complete with pony rides for children and mud volleyball for grownups.

□ Tours of local factories, whether they make pens or power generators, it is possible your guests will enjoy seeing the inside of a typical U.S. manufacturing plant and observing how products we all take for granted are fabricated and assembled.

□ Local colleges and universities are usually scenic as well as historic. Also, just observing typical American college students can be fascinating to some guests. You might also check with campus officials to learn if foreign students are enrolled there from your visitor's country and then maybe even arrange for a chat over coffee.

□ A typical American ranch or farm is a good idea, if your guests have any interest whatsoever in agriculture. A local farmer will usually be willing to give your guest a tour of his buildings and land.

These are just a handful of idea-starters. More will come to you as soon as you look around you. Visitors are curious and interested in what *you*, personally, do for entertainment, so don't be afraid to consider your own everyday pastimes and entertainments.

Formal Business Entertaining

There will be times that call for more formal entertainment, such as when your visitors are foreign government dignitaries. For these occasions, obtain a copy of *Practical Protocol* by James E. Lott, Gulf Publishing Co., Houston, 1973. The author is the former protocol officer for the City of Houston. This is an excellent guideline to everything from table seating arrangements to motorcades and press releases. Lott writes: "For most entertainment activities an informal approach is often most congenial and personable." He quotes Longfellow "In character, in manners, in style, in all things the supreme excellence is simplicity."

As a sampling, for more formal entertainment occasions Lott lists these bits of simple courtesy: place cards at a luncheon table, a list compiled beforehand of those attending, including titles and responsibilities; a clear indication of who is the host; and finally, don't feel obliged to cater only to the best restaurants. President Lyndon Johnson delighted most foreign potentates with outdoor, Texas-style barbecues at his ranch. These always produced an opportunity for relaxation as well as a sampling of Americana.

Your local library will also have a collection of books on etiquette for more formal business occasions with advice on: proper forms of invitations, cocktail receptions, selecting wines, receiving lines, choice of foods, head table seating, national anthems, national flags, table styles, seating diagrams for different styles and sizes of tables, and a explanations of the pecking order of importance among dignitaries. Emily Post and Letitia Baldridge are just two of the more popular authors of these wonderful reference books on rules of etiquette.

Be prepared, though, for an occasional boomerang—a seemingly good entertainment idea that comes whizzing back to haunt you. Mine occurred with our Danish distributor. I decided to take him to a typical social event of our company's men's club. Our group met monthly at a rustic cabin without running water. We cooked on grills, played softball, drank a few beers, and then had a speaker or demonstration. On this night, the program was a men's hair stylist who gave an actual demonstration using one of our members. Many months later, I learned the Dane's version of the evening was this: "Those Americans are strange. They have every type of modern convenience known to man, yet they meet in a broken down shack, cook outside enveloped by smoke, urinate behind trees, and finally—for entertainment—they sit around and watch some fellow get his hair cut."

WHAT ABOUT THE "S" WORD—SEX?

How to deal with sex? That's a double-barreled question, by the way. The first half of the question pertains to sex as in sexual entertainment. Where and how does it fit within business hosting? The second half of the question is how to deal with that subject in a book like this without offending someone?

First, in over 30 years of hosting scores of business visitors from all over the world, not once did one of them request or show any expectation for a hired sexual partner. My company was headquartered in a quiet, Midwestern city. Circumstances could have been quite different if we had been located in a large metropolis where escort services are advertised in telephone directories.

This incident pertaining to sexual entertainment actually happened in my home city:

——————— □ ———————

During a visit by one of our European distributors, I was hosting a casual lunch when suddenly my guest turned to me and asked rather matter-of-factly, "I've been meaning to ask—are there any ladies of the night here in your city?" Not realizing that he was joking, I found myself answering quite factually and forthrightly: "No. She's in the hospital. She was recently involved in an altercation with her husband." For my cosmopolitan European friends, this answer became legendary—that there would be only one shady lady in town, and that her every move was known. I'm certain the story was told again and again throughout Europe.

——————— □ ———————

The next point to remember in business entertainment is that in other countries sex can be, and often is, an *expected* part of business entertainment. There is a case study involving an American business executive and his South Korean business partners in Chapter 7. Also, Chapter 6 on "Business Protocol," contains a segment titled "Women in International Business" and offers some advice on what American businesswomen should do when hosting international businessmen.

In my own case, while traveling overseas I have several times been confronted with "sexual" hosting gestures. In all cases, I was able to convey to my host that, while I was appreciative of such thoughtfulness, I was quite happily married and practiced fidelity with my spouse. However, on one occasion in a Southeast Asian capital, my distributor's salesmen conspired and insisted that I have a "date" for the entire evening. And it was clear they meant the entire evening. During our dinner, I turned to the distributor and covertly asked "How do I handle this? I don't want to be rude or offend your men by refusing their 'gift.' Nor do I want them to consider me unmasculine. But frankly I cannot in good conscience accept." He smiled and said, "Don't worry. Just carry on. It will work out." The sales team dropped me and my hired companion at my hotel, grinning and laughing at my discomfort. Inside the lobby, out of sight of the departing salesmen, my "date" turned to me with a lovely smile, primly offered her hand and said, "Good night." And left. The distributor had obviously rescued me with a few whispered instructions to the young lady. The overall result was that we had *all* "saved face," which is absolutely vital in the Far East. The salesmen were not embarrased by my refusal; the young lady was not embarrased in front of the group; and, most importantly, I did not have to overtly reject their special gesture of entertainment, and so my personal honor was preserved.

Dick Primm of Charlotte, N.C. was not as fortunate. While traveling throughout Japan, he telephoned his wife to report that nude bathing with mixed sexes was common in some areas there, and he wanted her to know that he was only showing respect to local customs. She replied, "Well, if you do, another custom in Japan is *hari kari*, so why don't you try that custom as well."

James Bostain, a popular lecturer on cross-cultural communication who also provides training to U.S. Department of Commerce officials, tells us that to "Be Prepared" is more than just a motto for the Boy Scouts of America. It applies, he says, to both business and social situations. His message is that, as with my own experience, certain other cultures view extra-marital sex as more common and accepted than here in the United States. Bostain illustrates by telling of an American businessman in the Orient who had just completed long and arduous negotiations with his Oriental counterparts only to hear his host announce, in effect, "Good. We have all labored long and hard. Now that we are finished, let us all go to the nearest house of prostitution to celebrate." The American was dumbstruck. Turning to the leader, he stammered "But . . . but, what about your wife?" The Oriental businessman turned to the American with an incredulous look, more so because of the irrelevancy of the question than anything else. Finally, with a sudden burst of comprehension the Oriental replied to the American "Ohhhhh! I see what you mean. No, no. She not want to come along."

All this is fine, but what about the macho foreign male visitor who "comes on strong" to an American businesswoman? Let one such victim provide an answer: "My Latin customer was pretty obvious about his interests. He kept saying how he was so attracted to my bushy eyebrows—which, I must admit, was a novel opener. But he kept touching me and, throughout his visit, he became more and more forward. My response was simply firmness with a smile. I just kept pushing him off and let him know politely but clearly that our relationship was strictly business, and that I was there because of what was behind my eyebrows."

The lesson in all this is that in international business we must learn to expect the unexpected. If, as Charles Kuralt posed in Chapter 2, Americans "march to different drummers," then it is also important to recognize that other cultures march to sitars, flutes, bagpipes, cymbals, and other strange and unconventional types of accompaniment. Be listening for such counterpoint. Be understanding. Be flexible. Consider it "dancing" and not necessarily "dirty dancing."

CONVERSATIONAL TABOOS

Conversation is called, contradictorily, both the "lost art" and the "art of the civilized and genteel." Certainly in America the incursion of TV-watching has not improved our skills in managing intelligent, entertaining conversation.

To improve your conversational skills, you might learn six magic questions—who, what, when, where, how, and why? Memorize them. Then, when stuck for conversation, pull one out and simply begin a sentence. For example: *What* is your climate like at home compared to here? *When* did you leave? *How* long will you be gone from home? Or, *how* was your flight over? *Where* have you visited in the United States before this? *Why* have you come here—business or pleasure? *Who* is accompanying you on your travels? Then, depending on the answers, do the circle once again, keying off the information that is being revealed with each answer. Questions are extremely important because the artful host gives the guest center stage by merely listening. Polite questions flatter and draw out your guests.

Watch out for unconventional forms of questions, though. One hostess in Dallas, curious to know her visitor's impressions of her city, politely inquired "And how did you find Dallas?" The visitors answered, "I didn't have any problem at all. The airplane delivered me here." Another example of routine questions being misinterpreted is given by famed Danish comedian Victor Borge. He relates that a Danish friend of his entered an American airport, walked to the ticket counter and requested a round-trip ticket. "To where?" the ticket agent asked. "Why back to here, of course," said the Dane.

Turning from questionable questions, there are numerous other conversational areas that probably should be avoided. Here is a short but important list of conversational no-no's:

□ *Religion.* This is usually considered a very personal subject, and probably best avoided unless your guest raises it first, or unless you have become very well acquainted. The Salman Rushdie affair in 1989 demonstrated to the whole world just how volatile religious convictions can be. Iran's Ayatollah Khomeini ordered Rushdie assassinated because of his writings which devout Muslims considered as blasphemy. Another important aspect of Islamic teaching is that only God knows the future. With devout Muslims it is silly to try to predict the future. As a result, be cautious about asking for forecasts or predictions about crops or oil prices or even travel agendas. Muslims punctuate their conversation with the word "Inshalla," meaning "If God wills it." So, if you should ask where your guest is traveling to next week, he might reply "To New York," and then tack on "Inshalla." (In the Appendix, you will find a list of predominant religions, country-by-country, to help you know in advance something about the prevailing religions in your international guest's home country.)

□ *Politics.* While this is often a tough area to skirt, a proper host should *never* say anything that might be construed as critical of the politics of another country. True, after guest and host become well acquainted, it may be possible and proper to discuss world events and foreign policy but be certain to do it in a thoroughly statesmanlike and diplomatic manner. If your guest wishes to discuss politics, one indicator might be if he or she initiates the discussion by asking questions about the American political scene.

□ *Highly personal questions.* While this may seem obvious, what may seem personal to us is open game for others, and vice versa. For example, among the British, one's personal privacy is sacred. Therefore, even the customary American conversational gambit "What do you do?" becomes forward and impolite in proper English social circles. We in the United States are identified by *what we do;* the British are not. On a scale of rudeness, it would be comparable, I suppose, to someone asking us "How much money do you make each year?" Or, "How much did your house cost?" Incidentally, among some cultures those exact questions might be popped at you and considered perfectly proper. In that case, a polite answer might be "Those are questions we here in America often wonder about among our neighbors and colleagues, but it is considered a personal matter and so that information is usually kept private." The questioner will get your message. Orientals also dislike frank, personal questions. Frankness and outspoken expressions are usually considered rude in the Far East. Peace and harmony in relation to other people prevail. "Face," meaning self-esteem and reputation, must be preserved at all times.

□ *Saying "No."* Many cultures have difficulty coming out with a straightforward negative statement, or rejection of something. Westerners say the Japanese are most noted for this, with a dozen or more ways of avoiding a flat "no" in conversation. In written form, where no one can be offended, it might occur. Accordingly, a response like "That would be very difficult" probably means "no."

When a Japanese would *like* to say "no" it might come out as "I will do my best to comply, but if I cannot, I hope you will understand." This reluctance to say "no" stems from an unwillingness to disrupt harmony. It is true of the Indochinese (Vietnamese, Cambodians, Laotians, and Hmongs) as well. Among all these cultures, it is important to ask questions in the "right" way. For example, instead of asking "What do you find difficult about the United States?", which automatically implies criticism and therefore possible loss of face to Americans, it is better to ask "In what ways do you wish you could have been better prepared before you came to the United States?" Or, offer alternatives: "What things have Americans done that have been most helpful? Which have given you the greatest concern?" Another trick is to phrase your question so it can be answered in the positive. For example, instead of asking "Would you like to visit my factory?" (which calls for a "yes" or "no" answer and where the guest might reply "yes" just to maintain that all-important harmony), you might ask "Is it correct you would like to visit our factory, or perhaps your time is too limited?" That type of question allows an affirmative answer to either option: "Yes, we would like to visit your factory." Or, "Yes, our time is too limited." But if you think all this is complicated, wait until you try to sort out geographic questions, like national borders and national designations.

□ *Geography.* Gilbert Grosvenor III of the National Geographic Society, tells this story. When Anwar Sadat presided as leader of Egypt, he learned that a very influential U.S. Senator had often voiced strong interest in visiting Egypt to learn more about that pivotal Middle Eastern country. Sadat therefore extended a personal invitation which the Senator eagerly accepted. The reddest of carpets was rolled out, with Sadat personally escorting the Senator on a tour of the Pyramids, the Aswan dam, and other treasures of his country. Standing on the shores of the Red Sea, the Senator turned to Sadat and said: "This is wonderful. I've always wanted to see the Persian Gulf." As Grosvenor later commented, "I'm certain Sadat concluded that any U.S. official who was so ignorant about basic geography could not be worth much in the halls of Congress."

The moral here is: A basic knowledge of geography, and especially the geography of your guest's country, can be exceedingly important. One gaffe can bring frostbite to a budding relationship. Following are a few basic geographical nuggets that you should store away in your mind's safe deposit box to help you in international conversations:

1. Taiwan is officially called "The Republic of China" and should *never* be confused with "The People's Republic of China" (often shortened to the PRC), or what is often called Mainland China, or Red China. Taiwan is the island originally called Formosa, where Republican forces fled to escape Mao Tse Tung's communist army in 1949.

2. There are two distinct Irelands: the Republic of Ireland, which is the largest segment of the island with Dublin as the capital, and Northern Ireland which is part of the United Kingdom and has Belfast as its capital.

3. Belgium also has two important components, although not politically divided as in Ireland. The *Flemish* reside in the North and speak a language related to both German and Dutch; the *Walloons* live in the south and southeast and speak French. In temperament, actions, and culture, each group reflects either the Dutch or French heritage, which are quite dissimilar.

4. The terms *Scandinavian* and *Nordic* are often muddled or used as synonyms. Nordic refers to a subdivision of the Caucasoid ethnic group most predominant in Scandinavia. The Nordic or Scandinavian region stretches from Greenland, to Iceland, Norway, Sweden, Denmark, and Finland. Finns are different racially and linguistically but customs and lifestyle are more Scandinavian than anything else. Swedes, Norwegians, and Danes readily accept being lumped as Scandinavians but are also touchy about retaining their separate identities and languages. Remember, too, that both Norway and Denmark were occupied by the Germans in World War II, while Sweden remained neutral. Some hard feelings still linger, so it is helpful to step carefully on these cultural eggshells scattered along the shores of the North Sea.

5. It is extremely important to distinguish between *East* and *West Germany,* which are unofficial designations. The Eastern part is officially known as the German Democratic Republic, or GDR

for short; the Western part is the Federal Republic of Germany, or FRG for short.

6. *North and South Korea* fit the same mold. The official name in the North is the People's Democratic Republic of Korea, and the South as the Republic of Korea. Relations between the two are still strained and tense.

7. As pointed out earlier, the word *Indochinese* refers to Vietnamese, Laotians, Cambodians, and the Hmong (pronounced "mong").

8. *Australians* and *New Zealanders* become vexed when they are mis-identified. Americans often try to cover up by saying "Well, you all sound alike." That's not good enough. Take pains to make the right designation. To untrained American ears, the *South African* accent also sounds like the Australian or New Zealand pronunciation. But that is like saying Gary Player is Australian and Crocodile Dundee comes from Capetown.

9. Even with our good, old friend the *United Kingdom,* most Americans do not know the difference between Great Britain, Britain, and England. Here is the formula: Great Britain refers to the island that contains three separate political divisions— England, Scotland, and Wales. When you throw in Northern Ireland, the designation becomes United Kingdom.

10. *Moslems* (or Muslims) are people who abide by the *Islamic* religion. Even though the dictionary refers to the religion as "Mohammedanism" because of the founder Mohammed, it is impolite to call it that. Remember, too, that the Arab or Islamic region of 19 countries clustered around the Mediterranean Sea ranges from "moderate" to "extreme." This can refer to either their political stance or their religious zeal. Egyptians, Saudis, and Jordanese, for example, are considered on the moderate side both religiously and politically.

11. Canadians dislike being called "Americans." (See Chapter 10 on Canadians.)

12. The full and correct name of our neighbor to the south, *Mexico,* is "The United States of Mexico."

13. Finally, *avoid all ethnic jokes.* This may seem like an obvious piece of advice until you find New Zealanders telling Irish

jokes, Belgians telling Dutch jokes, the Dutch telling Belgian jokes, and ad infinitum. It is amazing. Ethnic jokes just materialize, no matter the size of a country. In Italy they tell jokes about the people of Cuneo, a city outside Milan. Canadians tell them about "Newfies," the people of Newfoundland. And before civil war ravaged tiny Lebanon, they actually told the same basic ethnic jokes told around the world but there the butt of the stories were people from a small village called Homsey. But while such jokes may seem universal, and while it may be tempting to haul out your own list of ethnic jokes—don't.

CASE STUDIES

Here are two true life examples of hosting international guests provided by some experienced business managers from around the country:

Moroccans in the Kitchen

A Charlotte, NC, business host had the task of entertaining a Moroccan customer. The American detected that his guest was tiring of American restaurants, so one evening he gambled and invited the Moroccan to his home. "He arrived with his two wives and five children in tow," the host explained. "None of us in my family spoke any Arabic or any French but even so they managed to make themselves right at home. We all ended up in the kitchen cooking *couscous* (a Moroccan favorite) and it worked. They had been on the road a couple of weeks and enjoyed cooking their own food again. Frankly, they made a mess of everything in the kitchen, but my family and his had a wonderful time. I'm certain that one evening in my home cemented the relationship between us because we have been good friends and good business associates ever since."

Italians at a Fish Boil

A Port Washington, WI, manufacturer of construction equipment learned that his Italian distributor had visited both coasts of the United States but never America's heartland. So, he was promptly invited to Wisconsin. As the plane landed at the Milwaukee airport, the Italian was amazed to see Lake Michigan, never realizing such a large body of water existed in the middle of the United States. The American host had chartered a fishing boat to take the distributor and his 17-year-old son angling for lake trout and salmon, so they traveled immediately from the airport to dockside. The fishing trip was documented with both still photographs and video tape and the group returned to the American's home where the host had arranged for a fish boil, a special custom of the area. This involves placing whitefish and vegetables in a huge metal kettle over an open fire. When the pot comes to a boil, the chef throws fuel oil on the fire. The result is a spectacular fireball which also causes the pot to bubble over, thus removing the fish oils. "We substituted other fish, but I think my Italian guests believed we were actually cooking their catch of the day," the host explained. "I also arranged for some other Italian guests to attend so my distributor would be more comfortable socially. And I arranged for a 17-year-old daughter of a business associate to take the son for a ride so they could listen to their kind of music and drive around the countryside. The day and evening were obviously a grand success. I think the reasons were that, first, it was a unique experience for my business guests but secondly because we took care to add special little touches, which were not unnoticed by this important customer."

SUMMARY

The art of entertaining foreign visitors deserves research, thought, and a touch of courage. Done well, it brings a warm reward akin to finding the perfect gift for your closest earthly friend. Done poorly, you may risk losing an important business contract.

No one can possibly memorize all the nuances and rules of entertainment suggested in guidebooks like this. What you can do, though, is become more sensitive, more aware, and more conscientious about your responsibility. Do some research and planning. Don't take things for granted. Learn and laugh at the same time. And remember that for our visitors even the *simplest* acts in our country—like Mr. Satish and his tea bag—may be totally new experiences.

Having learned all this, your guests still may bring more surprises out of their behavior baggage. Let John and Freda Gibb, a charming and gregarious American couple, tell their story:

——— □ ———

While on a Mediterranean cruise, John and Freda struck up a close acquaintanceship with a fellow passenger, a widow from Europe. As is so common with shipboard friendships, at the end of the cruise they said to the woman, "You must come and visit us in America some day." Several months later, the widow wrote and advised she was planning a trip to the United States and would enjoy seeing them again. John and Freda immediately renewed their invitation and the lady arrived on the 1st day of May. As it happened, John and Freda were known for their warm congeniality so they threw themselves into a memorable entertainment schedule for the lady who was clearly delighted over such hospitality. Finally, after three weeks of nonstop partying and touring with the month of June approaching, the American couple was near exhaustion and so they ventured to ask, "Well, is there anything else you would like to see?" Pausing just a beat or two, the matron replied, "Yes, there is. I think I would like to see the Fourth of July."

——— □ ———

=4=

DINING DIFFERENCES

Corn-on-the-cob may be as American
as pumpkin pie, but *both* could send your
visitor searching for the Pepto-Bismol bottle.

Breakfast, lunch, and dinner—sounds simple, but it isn't. Ethno-centric Americans are inclined to think the act of eating is so elementary that everyone does it exactly the same way. But it's not all that simple, not all meat-and-potatoes. No matter how well-intentioned we are, a visitor to the United States might well be retreating to his hotel room every night to gulp down stomach soothers simply because of the upsetting ways—and times—we Americans eat.

This chapter will take this relatively simple ritual, dining, and dissect American habits to compare them with the customs of other cultures. We will begin with *when* we eat, the times of day we like to ingest our food, and compare them with other time-clocks around the world. Then we'll look at this curious corn-on-the-cob quirk, and learn not only *what* American foods are strange (even repulsive) to our visitors, but which of their favorite foods we might consider equally stomach-turning. From there we'll turn to *where* and *how* we eat. Even our restaurants and our knife-and-fork handling may seem peculiar to our esteemed visitors. You'll learn that American cafeterias can be confusing to visitors, and also that when your mother told you to keep one hand in your lap while eating, German mothers were telling their children just the opposite.

Hungry? Good. Take some imaginary international guests in tow and we'll head out for dinner on a journey examining just how the American culture compares with others when it comes to when, what, where, and how we eat.

WHEN WE EAT

Dawn appears exactly the same way every place in the world, but from that moment on, eating patterns and customs around the world may vary as much as the weather. At one extreme, for example, in the Western provinces of China a routine daily greeting is "Have you eaten today?" Note that the question is not "Have you had breakfast or lunch or supper today?"

Throughout history we have not always eaten three meals per day: morning, noon, and night. In the Middle Ages, the custom was to take two meals per day plus a period of fasting.

However, for extra nourishment the very young and the very old were allowed to "break the fast" by having a third meal, hence our word "breakfast." In the United States, we have added a unique modification called "brunch" which is not generally known nor practiced overseas. In fact, it's hard to even find the word in some American dictionaries. So, an American-style brunch might be one new custom to propose when entertaining your visitors.

We in the United States customarily call the midday meal "lunch" and it is normally a light meal. Again, throughout history it was not always so. In early agricultural America, the main meal was taken at midday. That changed as the faster pace of an urbanized and industrialized America emerged. Today, many Americans seem to breeze through light lunches, preferring instead to linger at the dinner table over a large meal in the evening.

Here is an extremely important point to remember when entertaining international visitors: For most overseas residents, the main meal of the day is served at midday, not in the evening. For visitors, eating a heavy meal before retiring for bed could be just as upsetting as for us to consume, say, British "kippers" for breakfast.

This matter of how much is eaten and when presents a number of unique problems when hosting foreign visitors. Here are some examples:

□ Letitia Baldrige, former Chief of Protocol in Washington DC, once arranged a luncheon honoring President Mitterand of France. At the luncheon, Baldrige asked her lunch partner, a senior French official, what bothered him most about doing business with Americans in this country. Without pausing he proclaimed "Doing business at breakfast! You Americans with your endless meetings at the breakfast hour—it kills us!"

□ The American propensity for a quick "soup 'n sandwich" at lunch is also not shared by most other cultures. I once had a Latin American salesmanager tell me he was so confused by that term "soup 'n sandwich" (which he thought was one word) that he looked it up in the dictionary, but couldn't find it.

□ As a host, the considerate gesture is to *ask* your guests if they prefer their main meal at midday, or if they would like to experiment with the American way. Even then, at midday take them to a restaurant where both fares—light and heavy—are offered so the guest has a choice.

□ Next, keep in mind that "midday" does not necessarily mean "noon." In Mexico, for example, the midday meal begins at, say, 1:30 P.M. or later and can last until 3:30 or so. Once again, the considerate host will ask when the guest normally has his or her midday meal.

□ For language purists, the word "dinner" in American-English means the *main* meal of the day, which can be either at midday or in the evening. "Supper," on the other hand, is an evening meal, especially a light meal. Different languages may use different words and connotations. You, as a conscientious host, might inquire not only about midday meals versus evening meals in the home country of your guest but what the proper terminology is as well.

□ When a foreigner does take his major meal of the day at midday, what does he or she have in the evening? The answer is usually a light meal—so light that it might be only cheese and a bit of fruit. Again, ask your guest what is customary.

□ The dinner hour in America is somewhere around 7 P.M., plus or minus an hour. In other countries, it is often later, with Spain being notable. There dinner is often not taken until 10:00 P.M. or even later.

□ When entertaining the British, you might hear the phrases "afternoon tea" and "high tea." According to Judith Martin, who writes as Miss Manners, "The event at which one has tea, little sandwiches, and cookies in the late afternoon, is called 'tea' or 'afternoon tea.' High tea is not a spiffy occasion; it is an informal replacement for supper, with food such as eggs and tinned meats."

WHAT WE EAT

Following is a list of foods, common in America, that many foreign visitors find unusual, maybe even to the point of being repulsive:

Marshmallows

Grits

Watermelon (and seed spitting contests)

Commercial, white (preservative-filled) bread

Popcorn

Pecan or pumpkin pie

Sweet potatoes

Catsup

Cheeses (to most Orientals)

Roast turkey

Hot dogs

Crawfish

Corn-on-the-cob

Take corn-on-the cob—most Americans are totally unaware that in virtually every other country around the world corn is considered a food for animals only. But we Americans shuck the ear, boil it, lather it with butter, add salt, and consume it like a typewriter gone amok.

Just picture how we look: butter dripping down our chins, bits of corn wedged in our teeth. At that point we turn to our foreign guests, smile, and say "Isn't this good!" No one can blame our visitors for silently thinking: "He not only serves animal food, but he looks like an animal when eating it."

Another surprise may be that the so-called Italian, Mexican and Chinese food we eat in America is not necessarily the same type of food eaten in Italy, Mexico, and China. Our pasta dishes are a world apart from what appears on tables in Italy. Here you get a little pasta and a lot of sauce; there the ratio is switched. As for Mexico, we eat *fajitas* in America but you won't normally find them in Mexico. And our Chinese food is mostly an American creation and unlike the three distinctly different styles in China: Cantonese, Mandarin, and Szechwan.

Would you believe that Chinese fortune cookies are purely an American invention? It's true. Most Chinese in Hong Kong, Taiwan, and Mainland China have never heard of them, much less eaten them. The origins may go back to the twelfth century in China when messages were slipped into mooncakes, but the fortune cookie as we know it was probably invented here around 1912 by a Los Angeles noodle maker. Whatever the case, don't force them on your Oriental guests in the belief that you are giving them a taste of home.

This list above is hardly all-inclusive. Be prepared to find other surprises. In fact, a recurring theme throughout this book will be to encourage you to discover new and different cultural quirks such as these. (The Appendix provides a case study on how to go about collecting these important oddities.)

We Americans also have our own cultural quirks. For example, why do Americans have a taboo about eating horse meat? It's nutritious and tasty, but in America it's absolutely not eaten, knowingly at least. This taboo has nothing to do with taste or hygiene or even the sacrilegious thought of eating the cowboy's best friend. Instead, according to Tad Tuleja in his wonderfully informative book *Curious Customs* (Harmony Books, 1987), the prejudice toward horse flesh dates back to the year A.D. 732 when Pope Gregory III ordered horse flesh banned from Christian tables because horse-eating was a ritual in the pagan Germans' religious rites. And that cultural bias continues with us today.

Now let's reverse these tables laden with strange dishes. When it comes to surprise foods, our international visitors are not without guilt. Here are some international delicacies that cause at least some Americans to grimace in undisguised disgust:

Japan	Sushi, or raw fish
Hong Kong	Shark's fin soup
South Korea	Dog meat
Mexico	Ant eggs, toasted grasshoppers, flying bedbugs

People's Republic of China	Bear's paw soup, fried yak, raw monkey brains, sea slugs, anteater, bats, or stir-fried bees
England	Kippers (smoked herring)
Netherlands	Raw herring
Scotland	Haggis (sheep or calf innards)
Jordan	Sheep's brains (they look like orange Brussels sprouts)
Norway	Reindeer
Saudi Arabia	Sheep's eyeballs
Latin America	Octopus

Speaking of *sushi*, the Japanese word for raw fish, I once took my Latin American marketing manager (the one who couldn't find "soup 'n sandwich" in the dictionary) to Japan where I introduced him to that expensive Japanese delicacy. He studied it for a moment and said, "What do they call this? " I explained that the Japanese called it *sushi*. "Sushi?" he said. "Well, in my country we call it bait."

For further exotica, visitors to Hong Kong might be treated to a visit to special stores where, before your eyes, a live snake is removed from a container, an incision made into the gall bladder and the liquid gall removed. You, the guest, are then expected to drink it. Reason? It is considered an excellent aphrodisiac.

What to do when faced with, to your palate, bizarre foods? Here is some advice from various worldly travelers—guests and hosts alike:

□ My policy is I simply tell my foreign friends "don't tell me what it is."

□ Swallow it quickly.

□ Cut it up into thin slices. Then pretend it's chicken.

□ (In Oriental cultures, say) "Oh, I couldn't eat that. I am not worthy."

□ Pretend to eat by pushing the food around. And by all means do not turn green.

Archbishop Rembert Weakland of Milwaukee estimates he has visited at least 35 foreign countries and during those visits has been confronted with eating deep-fried caterpillars, fish eyes, and a fertilized duck egg. His advice is to fix something more familiar and palatable in the mind. For instance, he thought of pretzels when faced with the caterpillars, and jelly beans when looking at the fish eyes. But he admits with the fertilized duck egg he failed. "I thought of everything in my culture that would help me," he said, "but nothing came."

Returning to more American oddities, at least in the eyes of visitors, two American staples—ice water and coffee—are frequently cited. Foreigners coming to the United States often comment on the ubiquitous glass of water, loaded with ice, which is served almost religiously at every restaurant table. Many other countries simply do not have this practice, or omit the ice, or serve bottled mineral water instead.

Then there's coffee. The increasingly popular decaffeinated coffee habit here in the United States has not spread overseas as rapidly or extensively. This is especially true in coffee cultures like Italy, Brazil, Colombia, Turkey, and the Middle East. There they prefer strong, thick coffees, so thick that when you tip the cup to drain the liquid, you are suddenly confronted with a glob of muddy sludge slowly creeping toward your eyeball. For those nationalities, our coffee is considered anemic. So when an American waitress asks "Decaff or regular?", the reaction from your foreign guest might be total, blank-look confusion.

Foreigners to American restaurants are also startled to be offered coffee at the beginning of a meal. And while coffee at the end of a meal is almost universal, certain coffee terminology can also cause consternation. Ian Kerr, a British-born public relations executive, once visited the headquarters of his client in a small Midwestern city. Dining at the local hotel one evening, he finished his meal and the waitress politely asked "Coffee?" "Yes," he nodded, "but I'd like a demitasse, please." Without missing a beat, the waitress responded "Oh, I'm afraid all we have is Sanka."

Even American **breakfast** menus can be a travail to many visitors. For Europeans, for example, breakfast is typically a hard roll, jams, and an assortment of cold meats and cheeses. The traditional American ham and eggs, plus sweet pastries, are as unwanted to them as, say, rice would be at an American breakfast. In Australia, hearty breakfasts of meat and eggs are popular, but not with the sweet pastries we Americans may serve. To impress your next guest from West Germany, here's a little-known fact to tuck away and use: Germans are the greatest users of honey per capita than any other single nationality, and strongly favor it at breakfast time. Therefore, placing honey on the table before a West German guest is showing extra-special consideration and fulfills author Martha Stewart's injunction that "The great host is one who treats his guest with the same special considerations as he treats his family."

What is the most common fare on American **dinner** tables? When a distinguished importer from Hong Kong was asked that question by his American host, he swiftly but diplomatically replied, "Well, you do eat a lot of beef, don't you." The lesson here is that while most visitors to the United States crave and relish our thick prime ribs, steaks, and hamburgers, they can also get too much of our rich beef. In fact, some, like the Argentines, consider our beef inferior to theirs, while others are simply unaccustomed to it.

Consider entertaining your visitors with a typical American outdoor barbecue, whether it be barbecued hamburgers, steak, or barbecued chicken. For them our grills, charcoal briquets, fancy fire starters, and other implements are an unusual and often delightful accompaniment to the food itself. Remember, though, that cooking over open fires predates Homos Erectus and variations can be easily found in other countries. Brazilians are noted for their *chariscos* where a variety of meats are cooked over barbecue grills. In the Middle East, an unforgettable sight is the open fires on the banks of the Tigris River in Iraq where fish are hauled from the river, splayed on sticks which are then stuck into the ground canted toward a blazing fire. Be proud of American traditions (baseball, hot dogs, apple pie, and barbecues) but remember we didn't necessarily invent all of them. Hot dogs, as just one example, originated in the German city of Frankfurt, which explains why they are called frankfurters. (The American term "hot dog" originated, according to The Oscar Mayer Co., in 1900 at New York City's Polo Grounds one cold evening when a concessionaire offered "dachshund sausages." He hawked them as "red hot" and the next day a newspaper cartoonist pictured a dachshund in a roll, thus giving birth to the term "hot dog.")

Dietary rules around the world are too esoteric and complex to cover here, but a few tips and guidelines may be useful.

□ Muslims are increasing as guests in America and it is important—even critical—to respect their dietary rules. For strict Muslims, pork is absolutely forbidden. To be more precise, any animal that scavenges (pigs, goats, dogs, various birds, and, among some Muslims, even lobster and crab) is forbidden to be eaten. The same applies to any animal with a cloven hoof or foods cooked in the oils of any of these animals. This taboo list includes all forms of pork (ham, bacon, sausage, etc.). Nor may food be prepared by using pork products (bacon grease, lard, etc.) This also includes pates, terrines, and frankfurters if any pork is used in them. The same applies to foods cooked in alcohol. A considerate American host will review the menu in advance, even to the point of questioning the chef, and then reassuring the Muslim guest which dishes are absolutely safe to eat. So important is this abstention among devout Muslims that one veteran American international businessman reported that when his Middle Eastern devout Muslim guest learned, *after* the fact, that he had inadvertently eaten a piece of bacon wrapped around a filet mignon, he abruptly jumped up and raced to the bathroom to vomit.

□ Visitors from India, Pakistan, Bangladesh, and so on, are often vegetarians. Buddhism has no dietary restrictions, however, since it is a personal and individualistic religion; restrictions may be self-imposed. Because Buddhists abhor killing, some do not eat meat. Most American restaurants can easily accommodate this preference and vegetarians are accustomed to making this habit known to hosts in advance, so it is usually not a problem.

□ Orthodox Jews do not eat pork or shellfish, nor do they eat certain parts of the cow. "Kosher" means "ritually clean" so meat and poultry may be eaten if the cattle or fowl are ritually slaughtered. Milk and meat should not be served together.

□ There are no stray dogs in Hong Kong or South Korea. No need to say more.

□ In Japan, the *appearance* of food on a plate is just as important as the quality and the taste. In restaurant windows there, not only is the menu displayed, but full-size replicas of the dishes as well. (Ironically, many of these plastic replicas are produced in America and exported to Japan.) To help you remember that style and appearance are important in Japan, envision the ballet-like Japanese tea ceremony. The act of serving tea could be mundane, but the Japanese lift it to truly artistic levels.

□ In Italy and France, salads are often served and eaten *after* the main course rather than before.

□ Visitors to the United States are usually overwhelmed by the *quantity* of food served on each plate here. In most other countries, smaller portions are the norm. Moreover, in continental restaurants, the food is often cooked or carved alongside your table. Small portions are then served, with second helpings later, if desired. At a typical Oriental meal, smaller portions are also the rule.

□ Japanese visitors particularly welcome beef of all kinds, but especially steaks. They also relish fresh melons. This is because both are scarce and terribly expensive commodities at home.

Finally, it is important to take *nothing* for granted at the dining table. Take the basic word "entree," an essential part of any menu. For Americans, the entree is the main course of the meal—the *plata fuerte* (literally, strong plate) as the Latins call it. But in Europe and many other countries, the entree is the starting course—what Americans would call the "appetizer." Not knowing this fact could create considerable confusion when you ask your guest "What would you like as an entree?" He or she believes you are asking which appetizer they wish, while you are asking which item they prefer as a main dish. The resulting confusing dialogue could rival an Abbott and Costello "Who's on first?" routine.

WHERE WE EAT

Fortunately, restaurants in America are a cornucopia of variety. With diligence, every national menu can be found, especially in large cities. Even in medium-sized cities, the choice can be delightful. For instance, on the picturesque Capitol square in the center of Madison, Wisconsin, summertime lunchers can sample Chinese, Mexican, Indochinese, Vietnamese, Indian, German, French, English, and, of course, McDonalds cuisine.

Once inside a restaurant, dining practices around the world can differ as dramatically as menus may differ. For example, in France it is customary for patrons to bring pet dogs into restaurants. It is also common in France for those pet owners to ask the waiter to take the dog into the kitchen to be fed a treat of some snacks. Nancy Dowd, a travel agency owner in Albany, NY, reported that she once accompanied a French couple and their pet poodle on a trip to Japan. Inside a Japanese restaurant, the couple gestured to the waiter to take the dog to the kitchen for such a treat. The waiter complied and later returned . . . with the dog on a platter, cooked.

If American restaurants are symbols of our culture, then over-seas visitors must think of America as the land of cloned ponytailed waitresses who say "My name is Buffy, and I'll be your waitress." Then, when serving the food, Buffy invariably says "Here ya' go." A visitor with limited English might wonder "Go where?"

These Americanisms inside restaurants can create confusion for our international visitors. Ann Lang, a program director at Chicago's International Visitor's Center, recalls that one young international visitor who knew a smattering of English entered a cafeteria, sat down and waited to be served. Someone finally told him that this was a "self serve" restaurant. So, he got up and went into the kitchen to cook himself a meal.

Here are some other American restaurant customs that may surprise your visitors:

□ Dividing restaurants into smoking and nonsmoking sections, as we do in the United States, has not become as common outside the United States, so make certain your guests are aware of this growing custom.

□ Even the arrangement of our tables and booths is unusual to some cultures. In Oriental countries, for example, the practice is to sit at large round tables, usually with what we would call a "Lazy Susan" in the center from which all food is served. Among West Germans in a crowded restaurant, if only one person is seated at a table it is quite proper to ask to sit at a vacant spot at the same table. Also, food might be served at different times among a party of four or six or more.

□ The seating arrangement at a restaurant may be important to some nationalities. The safest measure is to seat the guest of honor to your right or in a prominent central spot. In China, for example, the guest of honor sits at the center, facing the door, flanked by a descending order of subordinates. Among the Danish, the guest of honor sits next to the hostess.

□ Our "theme" restaurants may also be an oddity to visitors. From fast-food to pizza, and from cowboy motifs to houses of pancakes, the United States is known for its variety of franchised eateries with McDonalds and Kentucky Fried Chicken outlets thriving in such disparate places as Moscow and Tokyo.

Where are the best dining spots to take international visitors? That's a good question, and worthy of careful thought and advance study. Here are some suggestions:

□ For Japanese visitors, try your golf club. By now almost everyone knows that the Japanese love golf, mainly because their tightly packed islands have little space available for golf courses.

□ Restaurants specializing in steaks, prime ribs, or barbecued ribs are usually winners with Europeans and Orientals because those cuts of meat, especially in the amount and quality customary in the United States, are uncommon in those regions. Middle Easterners eat large quantities of lamb, which is difficult to find in many U.S. restaurants. For Latin Americans, good beef is often freely available and therefore not a rarity. In fact, when it comes to huge, succulent steaks, Argentines consider our beef inferior.

□ Good seafood is enjoyed by most every culture, and therefore in United States coastal areas where fresh fish is available this is usually safe fare to offer a visitor. In the Midwest and other regions where Friday night fish fries are the custom, that can be a novel and amusing way to entertain your visitors, especially if it is a neighborhood restaurant with local atmosphere.

When choosing places to eat, the most unlikely choice can sometimes become the most memorable. I once had the challenge of entertaining my largest customer, a husband-and-wife team who represented just under $10 million in annual purchases from my company. She was British, he was a Pole who had lived in the Orient most of his life, and they currently lived and worked in Japan. Coincidentally, my wife and I had promised our young children we would go to the local 4-H County Fair. We announced to our distinguished guests that we were all heading for the local county fairground. It turned out to be a huge success. They had never eaten in church dining tents nor enjoyed bratwursts, beer, and homemade pie set among prize-winning flower assortments and country crafts. At one of the carnival booths, the husband won (or bought) a huge stuffed tiger for my daughters that became a long-remembered memento on both sides.

It's a natural inclination to take foreign guests to restaurants specializing in their national food: Germans to the best available German restaurant, the Chinese to an Oriental restaurant, and so on. Personally, I avoid doing this. First, the American version is usually not what they are accustomed to at home; and second, they can enjoy that cuisine any time they wish. The only time I take international guests to a restaurant of their own nationality is when I detect they are tiring of strange menus and might appreciate a taste resembling home.

Speaking of home, when it comes to selecting a novel place to entertain foreign visitors, that choice seems to rank above all others. As I travel the country presenting seminars and workshops on this topic of hosting international visitors, I often ask those in the audience with successful experiences to relate the best single location to entertain. "Your own home" is always the winner.

It is pandemic, apparently, that visitors enjoy seeing another person's home, especially an American home. The reasoning is that taking your guests to first class restaurants is easy, almost expected. But we should remember that most foreign business guests usually come from major cosmopolitan cities—London, Tokyo, Vienna, Geneva, Caracas—where first class restaurants abound.

So, if not a classy restaurant, where then? The answer, as movie alien E.T. would say, is "Go home."

There is always a natural curiosity in every nationality to see where and how someone else lives. Your home will produce memorable experiences for visitors. For example, in countries where maids and servants are prevalent, your guests will be fascinated to see their American hostess doing the cooking and serving. One American businessman reported that his Korean guest watched the man's wife cooking the meal, turned to him and said graciously: "We hope you will permit your wife to join us for dinner." In Korea, a woman's place is not only three paces behind a man, but also squarely in the kitchen.

To give your guests another revelation, just look toward the basement of your home. Many, many other homes around the world simply don't have them. I once took a British guest to my basement where, first, he was fascinated by the central heating and air conditioning system, and then he asked the purpose of the extra sink and stove where my wife canned fruits and vegetables. I said it was for canning. He looked around and asked "Where is the tinning machine?" I explained we didn't put them into cans. "Well why do you call it 'canning' then?" he asked. When I showed him the jars from past seasons of canning, he shrugged and sniffed, "Oh, you mean *bottling*, don't you," which I quickly learned is the British term for canning. So, you see an innocent trip to the basement can produce new learning experiences for host and guest alike.

One veteran hostess of diverse international guests reports that her most successful at home menu was either *shish kebab*, or fried chicken, cold potato salad, and homemade pies. The kebabs create an air of informality with each guest personally stabbing items for his or her skewer and then cooking it on an open barbecue grill, while potato salad and homemade pies are usually new to many foreign guests. "Then," she advises, "for a spirited dinner conversation all you have to do is introduce the subject of the World (soccer) Cup competition and you're guaranteed a spirited and maybe even rousing evening."

How We Eat

How we Americans eat our food is, surprisingly, filled with oddities that fascinate, and sometime confuse, our visitors.

Just look at our "zigzag" style of eating. Probably more than any other affectation, that distinguishes Americans from many other nationalities. Hollywood even recognized it by including episodes in war movies where American spies, working undercover in occupied Europe, were betrayed when they accidentally lapsed back into the American zigzag style of eating. Europeans and many Latins eat with the fork firmly fixed in the left hand, never switching back and forth as Americans do. We Americans marvel at how the British can hold a fork in the left hand, pile meat, potatoes and even slippery peas on the back of the fork with a knife, then balance the whole pyramid of food perfectly on the journey upward to the mouth. On the other side of the table, for "Continental Style" eaters with those forks firmly fixed to the left hand, the way Americans eat is equally fascinating. We appear juggler-like, cutting food with the fork in the left hand, dropping the knife, flipping the fork to the right hand, holding it like a pen, and finally eating.

Exactly how those two distinct styles of eating developed is unclear, but there are several theories:

☐ The British style may have originated a hundred years or more ago in their famed "public" schools, which we would call "private" as well as "posh" schools. The story goes that schoolboys there were required to completely finish every morsel on their plate before they could ask for seconds. This meant eating swiftly, and the act of shifting the fork over to the right hand lost valuable time. Therefore, they developed the style of keeping the fork constantly in the left hand.

☐ A completely different theory holds that in American frontier days knives were common but forks were scarce. Prior to the advent of forks, eaters would grip meat with the teeth and cut portions off with a knife. When the fork came along, it was used to hold the meat for cutting and then passed from person to person. Since the majority of people are right-handed, they would cut with the right hand and then drop the knife, shift the fork to the right hand, and eat.

☐ A third proposition is that the European style was simply a fanciful bit of fashion never adopted in the United States. In 1853, a French etiquette book advised Europeans "If you

wish to eat in the latest mode favored by fashionable people, you will not change your fork to your right hand after
you have cut your meat, but raise it to your mouth in your
left hand."

Incidentally, while dining and entertaining, this business of how
we hold forks can be a wonderful conversation starter and clever
method of gathering cross-cultural trivia. Most people are aware of
the differences in eating styles, but never paused to consider the
origins. Put the question to them: "Do you know the origins of our
different style of eating?" See where it leads you.

Perhaps the most ancient utensils, and the most difficult for
Americans, are chopsticks. There is no quick way to learn. Being a
good host and also a good sport, however, you might choose to
emulate your chopstick-using guests some evening. If so, here are
some hints on protocol provided by Dr. Cheryl Brown of the fac-
ulty at the University of North Carolina who lived and studied in
China:

□ When using chopsticks, especially for eating rice, Orientals
customarily hold the chopsticks and bowl close to the mouth, and
appear to be scooping and shoveling the rice into the mouth in a
style American mothers would never approve.

□ Another strange sight for us, but a common after-dinner
custom in the Orient, is using toothpicks while still seated at the
table, one hand picking and the other covering the mouth.

□ When using chopsticks, placing them parallel across your
bowl or plate says "I've had enough, thank you." However, an
Oriental host will still offer more since the custom there is you
must refuse at least *twice* to get your message across. So, when
hosting Orientals, be sure to ask twice.

□ Don't worry if you drop a chopstick on the floor. It is not an
embarrassment. In fact, some Chinese believe it means you will get
an invitation to dinner.

□ Don't point with your chopsticks or use them for any other
purpose, like scratching your ear.

□ Don't suck on your chopsticks.

□ Don't stick chopsticks upright in your rice. Among some Chinese, this is a superstitious act bringing bad luck.

□ Dr. Brown advises that you might at first be shocked to see your Chinese guests spitting bones on the table, even on the floor. This is an accepted custom among many Chinese.

□ Among the Indochinese, chopsticks are standard but most are familiar with western utensils. They hold the spoon in the right hand and the fork in the left and push the food onto the spoon with the fork. A knife is generally not used when eating Indochinese meals, because the food is already cut into bite size pieces.

Did you know you can also send subtle signals with your Western eating utensils? For Americans, to signal we have finished eating we normally place knife and fork in parallel across the plate. For the Swedish, placing the utensils criss-crossed atop one another on an empty plate does *not* mean they are finished but instead signals they would like another helping. Among Egyptians, it is impolite to eat everything on one's plate. Once again, as grist for a conversation mixer, ask your guests if there are any special table customs or signals in their country that we should know.

One custom you may encounter is this. Offering a napkin to your guest would seem a harmless enough act, but for the British and Canadians, the word napkin means a diaper. Imagine how it sounds asking your guest if he or she would like a diaper before eating. For them, the proper word is *serviette.*

Even the simple act of passing the salt can convey meaning. In Finland, when passing the salt, it is bad luck to pass it hand-to-hand. With Finns, you should place the salt down on the table for the next person to pick up.

And what about the alignment of the utensils? In American social circles and indeed in most places in the world, the rule-of-hand is to start at the outside of the line-up of utensils and work inward. That means the outermost fork is intended for the first course, the next fork for the second course, and so on. As for knives, Americans customarily have only two: a bread knife and a cutting knife. In Europe and some other regions, a special fish knife is added, or takes the place of the cutting knife. Finally, in Europe they also usually place a fork and spoon at the twelve o'clock position at your place setting. They are intended for your dessert.

Speaking of how we eat, here's another good question to draw out your guests and amplify your cross-cultural research: "When I was a child, my mother taught us not to put our forearms or elbows on the table. In fact, I was taught that we should keep our hands in our lap when not eating. I understand in other countries, such as West Germany, it is just the opposite: it is considered impolite to keep your hands in your lap at the dinner table. Is that true? What is the custom in your country?"

I have tried this gambit numerous times and it always sparks a lively and informative conversation. Everyone seems to have a strong conviction on what is correct: one elbow only, forearms only, one wrist only, both hands resting on the table, or both hands in the lap. A Swiss diplomat told me with great confidence that in regions like Germany and Switzerland the admonition to *not* put your hands in your lap originated in the sixteenth century. In those days, he claimed, hands in the lap suggested some form of sexual action was going on under the tablecloth.

What would be your reaction if your guests slurped soup or smacked their lips loudly or even gave out a table-shaking belch? Among the Indochinese and some Mediterranean cultures, these are all not only common but can be considered complimentary to the hosts, indicating pleasure.

SUMMARY

You would think that one cultural common meeting place would be the dinner table, but as we have seen here some startling surprises can easily be served up along with the food. An anecdote that seems to typify this whole chapter was related to me by a woman from Rockford, Illinois. She and her family reside near a large community college there and often host foreign students as a way of helping them acclimatize. On one of these occasions, they invited a student from Iceland to stay at their home and while helping him unpack she noticed that he had a collection of forks, each pattern different from the other. "Do you mind me asking why you have all those forks?" she said. "Well, it's a curious thing," the student replied, "Whenever I am invited for dinner in an American home, when the hostess serves dinner and then clears the plates, she says to me 'Keep your fork.' So I do."

In this chapter, we have inspected the seemingly simple act of eating in America. As we have learned, what we regard as common can actually be considered strange and peculiar by our guests. Such idiosyncrasies—on both sides of the table—also exist when it comes to the so-called "water of life," meaning wines and other spirits. Now that we have learned about the when, where and how of dining, let's raise our glasses to toast—and learn about—the social drinking habits of our thirsty guests.

5

SOCIAL DRINKING

"In Japan, they call social drinking
'the water business.' In my terms,
it's neither 'water' nor a 'business.'
It's downright two-fisted drinking."

—*An American manager in Japan*

The national drink in Peru is called a "Pisco Sour." This is an innocent looking, limeade-tasting drink found, to my knowledge, only in Peru. It slides down easily, even innocently, but hits bottom and bounces back to the head with the force of an Incan war club. A distant relative of this drink might be margaritas in Mexico. The manager of the American Chamber of Commerce in Lima, capital city of Peru, tells this story about Pisco Sours:

——————— □ ———————

An American businessman attending a large, formal event in Lima downed one too many Pisco Sours. After dinner, he staggered out of the dining room into the ballroom. As the music began, the American turned to a distinguished-looking person with flowing grey hair, wearing a long, bright red robe, and asked for the first dance. "Thank you, *señor*," the person responded, "but the orchestra happens to be playing the Peruvian National Anthem, and I happen to be the Archbishop of Lima."

——————— □ ———————

Business entertaining and hosting almost invariably lead to the bar. So, before you put your foot up on the brass rail, it is wise to recognize that drinking habits in other countries can vary dramatically from those in the United States. As in Japan with "the water business," Americans are often unaware of the differences. This chapter will put the mirror to Americans and reveal how we are different when it comes to libations. It also lists favorite foreign drinking practices. Having views from both sides of the looking glass may help you avoid "slips 'tween cup and lip" like the one our Pisco Sour-drinking American friend experienced in Lima. We start with a self-examination.

HERE'S LOOKING AT YOU, AMERICA

For the first round, we shall examine some common imbibing habits in the United States that your international visitors may find new and strange.

America is identified with the cocktail hour—this hour-long, before-dinner ritual—more than any other country. In fact, many foreign visitors are curious to know what is meant when they see American cocktail lounges advertising "Happy Hour," "Two-for-one Time" or "Double Bubble Huddle," or—according to one sign—"Animal Hour."

The American cocktail hour, according to writer Lowell Edmunds, stems from the Roaring Twenties and Prohibition when Americans began drinking in their own homes because it was the only legal place they could drink. The designated period between the arrival of guests and the formal sitting down for dinner was named, logically, the cocktail hour. After the repeal of Prohibition, the custom continued as a ritual in itself: cocktail lounges were born, and people staged cocktail parties (no dinner) as a separate entertainment form.

Judith Martin, also known as "Miss Manners," waspishly defines the American cocktail party as an event when you get to meet "all the people your host didn't like well enough to invite to dinner."

Letitia Baldridge reports that when she asked an Italian industrialist what bothered him most about doing business with Americans he replied, "The length of your cocktail hour before dinner. I meet my American friends in a restaurant, and they keep ordering drinks before we can order the meal. It exhausts us all. One cocktail before dinner is enough; otherwise no one makes sense in our discussions."

Here are some other "Americanisms":

□ *Ice cubes.* In probably no other country is ice so plentiful nor plunked in so many glasses as in the United States. As the British are fond of saying, "I can't think of a faster way to ruin a good glass of Scotch."

□ *Bourbon.* It's unique to America. Made from distilled corn, the name comes from the locale where it originated, Bourbon County in the state of Kentucky. For a wonderful narrative portraying the unique American distilling industry, read Henry Morton Robinson's 1960 novel, *Water of Life.*

□ *Whiskey.* Order a whiskey in the United States and you'll be served bourbon; order a whisky in England and you'll be served Scotch. One difference is in the spelling: English scotch whisky is spelled without an "e." Scotch is also different in that it is distilled from malted barley, the malt having been dried over a peat fire.

□ *Cocktails.* The names of American cocktails, as well as their potency, can drive your visitors dizzy. Some peculiarly American cocktails (and their origins) are: Harvey Wallbanger (named after a 1960s California surfer); Gibson (from the American illustrator Charles Dana Gibson); a "Coalminer's Breakfast," or "Depth Charge" (when a shot of whiskey is dropped into a glass of beer); and while the infamous Martini apparently originated in the United States, bartenders around the world have slowly added it to their repertoire. In Italy, though, a specific brand of white vermouth is called Martini, meaning you'll likely be served that brand of vermouth sans gin. For more on this subject, refer to John Mariani's very helpful book, *The Dictionary of American Food and Drink.*

□ *Beer.* This fermented malt beverage is found all over the world, but American beers have several differences. Compared to, say, Australian beers, American brews contain less alcohol. American beers are always served cold, while English beer is normally served at so-called room temperature (more like 50-degrees F). American "pilsner" beer, named after the city of Pilsen in Czechoslovakia, where it was first brewed, is milder than the European version. Ales, porter, and stout beers are not as common in the United States as, say, in Europe. And the most popular beer in England is called "bitter" which does have a slightly bitter taste but for Americans is more distinctive for being less carbonated. Dark beers, such as "bock" beer which is served in the United States in Spring, result from longer roasting of the barley until the kernels are actually burnt. This not only produces the distinctive dark coloration but makes the beer heavier and more filling. (It was originated by the monks in Germany who fasted during Lent. To compensate, they learned to brew this heavier, more nutritious brew.) Finally, the world's most popular style of beer is "lager," from the German word "to be stored," which has a gold color and distinctive hop flavor.

□ *Brandy.* Hollywood's image of brandy involves dinner-jacketed men in the drawing room after dinner swirling and sniffing brandy from warmed, balloon-shaped glasses. Nothing wrong with that, except that it's not the way to drink brandy. First, American brandies differ greatly from continental brandies. Fruit brandies are more and more popular in the United States. Also, straight brandy is often served in mixed drinks here, as in brandy-and-soda or a brandy Manhattan. The so-called "fine brandies" are usually imported, with Cognac and Armagnac the most familiar examples. Wine critic Ronn Wiegand advises that one rule-of-thumb is that $15 per bottle marks an appropriate cut-off mark between fine brandy and "less complex" brandies. Warming brandies either over a low flame or with cupped hands, is a tradition debunked by Wiegand. "For the same reason you don't want to use a big glass," he says, "you don't want to warm it because the spirit in the glass is already high in alcohol and warming it up just allows it to evaporate faster, which means you get more effect of the alcohol and less of the flavor." The ideal temperature, he concludes, is about 60 degrees. So, Hollywood has created still another myth.

□ *Wines.* American wines have established a credible reputation around the world and, with only a few exceptions (see the next section), you can offer them to your cosmopolitan guests with confidence. Some customs to mind: it is not necessary to allow white wines to "breathe" before drinking since that only applies to red wines and then only for reds over 10 years old; it is pointless to smell the cork after removing it because what you're really looking for is moistness; what you really want to smell is the wine itself. The recent rise in popularity of white wines in the United States meets with much approval from visitors, but they are shocked to see them poured over those ubiquitous ice cubes.

FERMENTED FAVORITES FROM FARAWAY LANDS

Now, let's turn to your guests. What are some of their favored national spirits you should know about? Here, in what we might call "hops-scotch" fashion around the world, is an assortment of fact and lore about certain countries and what they prefer to quaff, sip, and gulp:

□ *Argentina.* Since almost 50 percent of the Argentine population has roots extending back to Italy, it is not surprising that the most popular spirit here is red wine, or *vino rojo*, in Spanish. The wines of Argentina are especially tasty and a source of great national pride. Never pour wine back-handed or with the left hand, however. To an Argentine, that's considered rude.

□ *Australia.* Beer is the most popular national drink there, and as indicated earlier, it is more potent than here. In fact, according to the Beer Institute, in 1987, 1123 liters of beer were consumed per person in Australia compared to 90 liters of beer per person in the United States. Next on their list would probably be Scotch whisky. Incidentally, resist emptying a glass of beer in front of an Australian and then thumping it on the bar upside down. If you do so, you have just signaled that "I can lick anyone in the place!"

□ *Austria.* White wines probably head the list here, along with hearty beers. A favorite delight in Austria occurs in the Fall months when the first, young and "raw" white wine is harvested and is a hallmark of the famous "Oktoberfest." The stereotypical scenes of beer houses with serving maids, long wooden tables, and singing revelers is very accurate for Austria.

□ *Chile.* Like Argentina, preferences can be traced to the emigration of Germans to Chile. As a result, excellent white wines are produced and consumed in goodly quantities in Chile.

□ *Canada.* Rye whiskey is indigenous to Canada, but beer, wine, and Scotch whisky are also very popular.

□ *England.* Here the preference is for English beers, Scotch whisky and then at lesser levels of consumption, gin and wines. Sherry, a fortified wine that comes from dry to sweet, is often favored by ladies. Incidentally, the "proof" content of spirits, meaning the amount of alcoholic content, is measured differently in Great Britain. In the United States, the standard is 100 proof, or 50 percent ethyl alcohol by volume. In England, the proof measurement is determined by an archaic formula involving how much gunpowder can be soaked before it will ignite. But the result is almost identical, so this is useful only for conversational trivia. Cider is also drunk in the United Kingdom, but it is not the innocent apple derivative known in the United States and is, instead, an alcoholic drink popular in most British pubs.

□ *France.* Wine, wine, and more wine is the national drink in France, with a considerable amount of nationalism distilled into every bottle, so be cautious about praising U.S. vineyards. Also, the French do not like to be reminded that in the late nineteenth century offshoots of French vines were transplanted in California and that soon after a blight destroyed virtually all French vineyards. Because the California descendants of the French roots had developed an immunity to the blight, the West Coast sprouts were shipped back to France. Thus, Californians can claim that French vineyards owe their very existence to The Golden State. But, *attencion!* To a Frenchman, those are fighting words. The French insist that their unique soil and climate are what produce their incomparable product and reject the California root argument. Aside from wine, for Americans a curious but popular French spirit is Pernod, a licorice-tasting clear liquid that turns bright yellow when water is added and can be drunk before or after a meal. As for the harder stuff, Scotch whisky is also popular. Finally, the French strongly favor bottled mineral water and may sniff with suspicion over using common tap water as a mixer.

□ *Greece.* An aniseed-flavored liqueur called *ouzo* is much favored here and is usually served with water. Also, *retsina,* a wine with resin, is popular. Beer and wine are commonly taken with dinner.

□ *Italy.* While everyone knows that Italians relish wines, especially red wines, business travelers also order beer and Scotch. Incidentally, there is also one powerful, bitter-tasting liqueur found in Italy called Fernet Branca. So potent is it that a warning must be printed on the label. The English version says, in effect, "Caution—large quantities can be dangerous to your health." With a touch of Italian *dolce vita*, the Italian language version of that same message reads "Consume until the desired effect is reached."

□ *Japan. Sake* is the traditional, well-known drink in Japan. Made from rice, it is served slightly warm and in small portions. However, the Japanese also commonly drink Scotch whisky and beer. A fine Napoleon brandy or Cognac is considered a special treat, therefore it makes for a welcomed gift for Japanese. The Japanese believe that you cannot truly get to know someone unless you drink—seriously—with them. That is why it is called "the water business." (More about specific drinking customs in Japan is found in Chapter 10.)

□ *Mexico.* Most Americans are well aware that tequila is regarded as the national drink of our Southern neighbor, with beers and margaritas following close behind. For business travelers to the United States, however, Scotch is a favorite. Wines are not common in Mexico because vineyards do not thrive there and so all good wines must be imported. Incidentally, it is the *maguey* worm that is found in bottles of some brands of tequila and is regarded as such a delicacy in Mexico.

□ *The Middle East.* There are 19 countries in the Middle East commonly called the Arab countries. First, it is important to know that there is no separate, distinct Arab nationality and, second, that the so-called Arab bloc is bound together by three ingredients: language, religion, and oil. The Muslim religion forbids the consumption of alcohol, so most of your Middle Eastern guests will probably prefer fruit juice, colas or mineral water. Alcohol is forbidden to be imported into countries like Saudi Arabia. However, you will encounter numerous Middle Easterners who nonetheless imbibe Western liquors. So, when entertaining, be prepared with plenty of soft drinks and juices, but you might mention that alcoholic drinks are also available.

□ *Southeast Asia.* Many of these nations imported their drinking habits from their colonial occupiers. Thus, scotch and gin are known and are popular in places like India. Buddhists do not have any religious laws about alcohol because it is a religion based on individual choice. Therefore, some Buddhists will take alcohol and others will not.

☐ *The Netherlands.* Once again, our old friends beer and Scotch whisky are popular here. You should also know that each European country seems to have a unique, local white spirit (vodka in the U.S.S.R., schnapps in West Germany, *ouzo* in Greece, and so on) and The Netherlands are no exception. Here it is called *genevre*, a unique cousin to vodka or gin, but with an incomparable taste. Try it, especially with beer or with raw smelts.

☐ *People's Republic of China.* While scotch and beers are commonly served here, the national drink is a clear, white, and wicked, 120 proof, sorghum-based wine called *mao tai.* And with toasting so common at formal banquets in the PRC, it can become the villain of the evening. Watch out for *mano a mano* duels during these toasting bouts. Shouts of "kam-pie" start the action, which literally mean "bottoms up" and you are expected to do just that—swallow the full contents and turn the glass upside down as proof you have not cheated. (More on this in a section on Toasting in Chapter 11.)

☐ *Peru.* As described earlier, the national drink here is Pisco Sour. Treat it respectfully and you'll never be guilty of asking the Archbishop of Lima to dance.

☐ *Scandinavia.* In all three countries, Norway, Sweden and Denmark, the national drink is *aquavit,* from the Latin, *aqua vitae,* meaning "water of life." This strong, clear liquid comes from potatoes, is usually served Arctic cold, and is usually sipped alternatively with beer. The Swedish are especially proud of one of their versions, a golden aquavit that is aged by storage in tanks of ocean vessels that make long, rocking journeys across the seas and then back to the Swedish bottler. In fact, printed on the inside of the bottle label is the ship's name and the dates of the actual voyage.

☐ *South Korea.* It is said the South Koreans are the Irishmen of the Oriental world, with drinking a popular recreation. The most popular drink here is *soju,* a clear, white liquid made from sweet potatoes. Another is a drink derived from cabbage called *kim-chee.* Beer is also very popular, along with Scotch whisky, especially at banquets. Accompanying the drinking, incidentally, is very active singing and dancing with special emphasis on solo performances. So, to give your Korean guests a touch of their homestyle hospitality, strike up some singing after dinner.

□ *West Germany.* The famous *gasthaus* of Germany and Austria is a national symbol and institution and one would expect this birthplace of modern fermented malt beverages—beer—to excel in brewing. And that's exactly what you will find. Beer, followed by excellent white wines, are the two most popular drinks in this country. The world-renowned white wines that come from the sunny slopes along the Rhine River have made that name synonymous with fine wines.

SUMMARY: ADVICE FOR THE ROAD

You can hardly go wrong offering your guests either wine, beer, or scotch plus, of course, mineral water, soft drinks, and fruit juices. And you could easily add vodka and perhaps gin to that list. Brandy is another choice that is well-known around the world. Bourbon, however, is new and often distasteful to most people outside the United States.

After-dinner liqueurs, or "cordials" as they are called in England, are popular among Europeans and Latin Americans. Not so among Orientals, with the exception of the Japanese who favor Cognac or some comparable fine brandy.

Running cross-current to all this advice is the fact that many well-traveled international business types have slowly developed worldly tastes and habits. Many of them have learned American customs and may want to impress you with acquired tastes for, say, bourbon on the rocks. It is still helpful to be prepared with a bit of knowledge and respect for their ways.

What if you, as a host, don't drink alcohol of any kind? That question arises frequently in my workshops and seminars. There are several solutions at hand:

□ If you wish to minimize questions, hold a glass of tonic water with a slice of lemon or lime, or a glass of ginger ale. Both resemble a mixed drink.

□ If you believe an explanation is necessary, just tell your guests that for personal reasons, you do not drink alcohol, but you have no objection whatsoever if others do.

□ Another option is to explain that, for medical reasons you do not drink alcohol; a variation on that is that you are currently taking a certain medication that does not permit mixing with alcohol. The problem with this gambit is that some of your guests may then want to know what type of medication you are taking or what type of illness you have.

□ When toasts are offered, there is no discourtesy to use water for a toast or to merely lift the wine to your lips and no farther.

When entertaining people from Europe or possibly Latin America, two words are helpful to memorize and use. The first is "aperitif" (pronounced a-PEAR-a-teéf) which generally means any drink taken before a meal; the second is "digestif" (pronounced dee-jes-TEEF) which is any after-dinner drink, that word suggesting that it will aid the digestive process. Therefore, as host, your invitation becomes: "Would you care for an aperitif (or digestif)?" While these are French words, the Spanish cognates are very similar, so they are quickly understood in both languages and quickly give you a touch of worldliness.

And speaking of drinking before and after dinner, Americans are stereotyped for belting down two or even three mixed drinks before dinner. Europeans and many other nationalities, however, are more tuned to only one cocktail before dinner. Then they usually shift to one or perhaps even two types of wine with the meal, followed by the very civilized aid to digestion, the "digestif," after the whole procession.

No matter how well you prepare, though, when entertaining with liquid spirits, as a host you will undoubtedly encounter some hiccups—not the stomach kind, but instead hiccups meaning mistakes and surprises. Here is an example of what I mean:

———————— □ ————————

I once took two Argentine executives to a carefully selected country roadside restaurant that resembled a scene from a Norman Rockwell painting. Even though they spoke no English, the Argentines were clearly delighted with the novel atmosphere and menu. When the time came for the gum-chewing waitress to take our drink order, the Argentines loyally ordered *vino rojo*, red wine. When I translated this to the unschooled waitress, she quickly countered with "Straight up or on the rocks?" As I translated back, my guests could not believe their ears. For them, red wine over ice was a sacrilege. I quickly ordered "straight up." Then, after dinner they asked for cognac, expecting of course to be served brandy ala Hollywood-style in large balloon snifters. Not so. I covered my eyes as I saw the waitress present each of them with a typical Midwestern jigger of brandy accompanied by a beer chaser. I have been told that in Buenos Aires they are still telling the story of that American roadside inn that poured red wine over ice and served brandy with beer chasers.

———— □ ————

6

BUSINESS PROTOCOL

"We're running a $170 billion trade deficit
essentially because the captains of
American industry don't know how to deal
with people who are different."

—*Former United Nations Ambassador
Andrew Young*

An aging baseball player last year decided to complete the final innings of his career with a season or two playing in baseball-happy Japan. Since this was his first time outside the United States, it was not surprising when he commented "It's a big change. Everything is so different." Then, his follow-up comment spoke volumes about American insularity. "The only American names I've seen in Japanese stores," he said, "are Sony and Nikon."

By a bevy of different measurements, the United States is not faring well in the competitive international marketplace. Why? There are many reasons. Governor Thomas H. Kean of New Jersey explains it this way: "For more than a century, Americans enjoyed unchallenged superiority in virtually everything we turned our hands to. We could afford the luxury of ignoring the seers who urged us to learn the tongues and ways of other lands. But those days have gone the way of leaded gas and nickel phone calls."

According to Governor Kean, doing business successfully with people from other lands requires learning ". . . the tongues and ways of other lands."

Supporting that view is Philip Caudill who handles intricate relations between Phillips Petroleum Co. and its many foreign customers. "Do your homework, know your audience, and don't take yourself too seriously," says Caudill. Research is important, and Caudill offers this simple example:

———— □ ————

Phillips learned through its research that residents of European countries prefer being addressed as French, German, Spanish, etc.—instead of as "Europeans." "There is indeed a Europe but there are very few Europeans," he said. "It could be catastrophic . . . for an American business person to approach (people from) the European Continent as if (they) were all the same."

———— □ ————

Sondra Snowdon offers an additional, supporting view. She is president of her own New York consulting firm specializing in educating executives in the art of international business protocol. Snowdon advises "The first and greatest mistake, I feel, is that Americans fail to recognize the importance that rank and status play in negotiations with foreign executives." Other examples of protocol pratfalls noted by Snowdon: In the United States, it's business before pleasure, but in many other countries it's pleasure before business; in Saudi Arabia, for example, you would never discuss business on the very first meeting, and in Japan a lot of elaborate entertaining may be done before serious business talks begin. The reason, in all cases, is they want to establish a level of trust.*

I frequently have the question asked: "Must American business managers learn the most basic of all protocol—to speak one or more foreign languages—before attempting to compete in the international prize ring?" My answer is: While knowing other languages is a wonderful and valuable skill, it is not absolutely essential. Fortunately for us, English has become the language of business around the world.

Again, the words of Snowdon: "Foreigners understand that Americans generally do not speak languages other than English. That doesn't bother them. What upsets them is that Americans don't take the time to learn even the most rudimentary forms of introduction and greetings, simply as a show of respect. That baffles them."

* Reprinted with permission from *Industry Week*, July 8, 1985. Copyright, Penton Publishing Inc., Cleveland, Ohio.

Finally, Snowdon adds this profound fact: "The Japanese, for example, won't let any executive do business in the United States until he's spent at least a year studying our customs and business practices."

This chapter will hardly substitute for spending a year in some distant country just to learn customs and business practices, but it will help you avoid a profusion of peccadilloes—small sins—when it comes to protocol and other behavior in business.

We will begin by listing fundamental differences in the general styles of doing business, comparing U.S. methods with Latins, Asians, and Europeans. Then we will move into some very specific areas of protocol: handshaking, attitude toward time, phone etiquette, letter-writing, first names, gift-giving, speech-making, and more.

Two other pertinent subjects—protocol for women in business, and the rules for tax deductibility when entertaining business guests—are also discussed.

Concluding this chapter is a special section on the highly important art of *negotiating* with businesspeople from different cultures. As experienced hosts know full well, negotiating, entertaining, and protocol are so interwoven it's difficult to separate them.

ARE EXECUTIVE MANNERS IMPORTANT?

Is protocol important between Americans in their own offices? Do we have our own set of rules? The 500 pages of Letitia Baldrige's *Complete Guide to Executive Manners* (Rawson Associates, 1985) argue emphatically "yes."

Baldridge was former social secretary to United States Ambassadors David Bruce in Paris and Clare Booth Luce in Rome. She was also First Lady Jacqueline Kennedy's chief of staff. In the business world, she was Tiffany & Co.'s first public relations director and Burlington Industries' first consumer affairs director. She speaks from experience having committed, she confesses, just about every social blunder imaginable. For example, on one occasion she staged a diplomatic reception and seated a top foreign government official next to his wife's lover, precipitating a challenge to a duel.

"Good manners are cost-effective," she says. "They increase the quality of life in the workplace, contribute to optimum employee morale, embellish the company image, and hence play a major role in generating profit. On the other hand, negative behavior, whether based on selfishness, carelessness, or ignorance, can cost a person a promotion, even a job."

In the broader field of international business, the cost-effectiveness of proper protocol is elevated to the second or even third power. The reason, quite simply, is because there is so much more room for error. Let us begin by studying basic differences in style between different national groups.

DIFFERENCES IN STYLE

"Most people think that culture is manners, food, dress, arts and crafts," says international consultant Clifford Clarke. "They don't realize that how you *motivate* a guy is (also) culturally determined. Every managerial task is culturally determined."

Here are some examples of how management and culture and style merge, as reported in a *Wall Street Journal* article titled "American Culture Is Often a Puzzle for Foreign Managers in the U.S.":

□ Arab oil workers sent to Texas for training found American teaching methods impersonal.

□ Japanese workers at a U.S. auto plant had to learn to put their ingrained courtesy aside and interrupt conversations when there was trouble.

□ Executives of a Swiss-based multinational couldn't understand why its American managers demanded more autonomy than their European counterparts.

□ The Japanese are so shy about criticizing anyone that when a Japanese manager had to criticize his American subordinate it took five practice runs before he was direct enough that the American could realize he was being criticized.

As for basic differences in style, read these paraphrased excerpts from Professor Susan S. Holland in *The Annals of the American Academy of Political and Social Sciences*:

The American Manager is conditioned to value objectivity and to depersonalize decision-making. He or she thrives on accuracy, directness and openness of communication. Americans value pragmatism, practicality, egalitarianism, problem-solving, competition, self-advancement, individual responsibility, and initiative.

Management systems delegate authority and expect subordinates to assume responsibility and to make decisions. We are expected to work in team or group relationships. Promotion is based on the demonstrated ability to assume responsibility and achieve goals.

The Latin American Manager has a hierarchical culture with these characteristics: authoritarian, paternalistic, socially stratified, family-oriented, humanistic, intuitive, personalistic, and not necessarily achievement oriented. Where an American business person believes in a "cards on the table" relationship, the Latin tends to keep business dealings more shrouded in order to retain tactical advantages. One can quickly see how these contrasting styles can clash.

The Asian Manager is more similar to the Latin style than the American style. That culture has these features: the family is more often the central social unit rather than the individual; paternalistic and rigid hierarchical relationships prevail; the elderly are highly respected; formal authority as well as seniority, loyalty and obedience are respected; formal rules and procedures are valued; indirect or circuitous dialogues are common and acceptable; and there is a general dislike for disagreement or any type of confrontation.

The Western European Manager cannot be easily type cast because of the *un*common composition of the so-called Common Market: the Belgians will never be like the Italians, the Scandinavians will never mirror the Spanish, and so on. Here a mixture of the traditional and the new is found. Enterprise, productivity, ambition and competitive self-advancement are valued. Counterpoints are a greater orientation to leisure, public service-oriented activities, and the family. Less value is placed on the profit motive.

How does all this conceptual stuff translate into actual day-to-day behavior between different business cultures? Here are two examples provided by Dr. Robert Shuter who teaches intercultural communication at Marquette University and is an international business consultant.

A corporate headquarters sent a telex to its subsidiary in Taiwan with the concise instruction to "Send blue box as soon as possible." Somewhere en route, the urgency of the message was lost and the Taiwanese interpreted the phrase "as soon as possible" as meaning "at your earliest convenience." Three weeks passed. Back in the United States, irritation grew into anger. Then, when they finally did send the blue box, the hierarchical conscious Taiwanese sent it to the boss of the person originally requesting it. As Shuter explains, the Taiwanese culture deals with time in specifics and "as soon as possible" was vague and meaningless. And, being leader-centered, they sent the box to the leader, not the subordinate. Result: culture clash, disharmony, and inefficiency all due to attitudes and office protocol.

The second illustration involves a Swedish owned firm in the United States with American managers and Swedish employees. Chaos developed because the Swedes continually violated the corporate chain of command. "Swedes tend to be a very efficient group," Shuter explains. "They don't like the American notion of going to your manager before you go anywhere else. The Swede is accustomed to going to anybody he pleases to get information—even *above* his boss. The Americans thought the Swedes were starting a revolution, and the Swedes thought the Americans were crazy."

SPECIFIC EXAMPLES OF OFFICE PROTOCOL

First Names

When NBC's "Today" Show host Bryant Gumbel interviewed Judith Martin, author of the book *Miss Manners' Guide to Excruciatingly Correct Behavior,* he opened by asking if he could call her "Judith." Her firm but friendly reply was "Not yet."

While this may be excruciatingly correct, her advice is not practiced that much in the United States. We Americans appear to be in love with first names. We like to be instant friends. We wear friendship and informality on our sleeves. When meeting people we immediately use the person's Christian or so-called "given" name—with two exceptions. The exceptions are when the person is, (a) elderly or, (b) clearly very senior in rank. In those cases most people show respect by attaching "Mister" or "Mrs." or whatever. Overseas, the practice of immediately jumping to first names is generally frowned upon. The rule in most countries overseas is, when first introduced, use "Mister" or "Miss" or "Mrs." or "Doctor" or whatever formal appellation applies. The next rule is that what *appears* to be the first name often is not. When hosting people from China, Korea, and certain other Southeast Asian countries, for example, you will be confronted with three names: Lee Kwan Ho. In that case, he is "Mr. Lee" because his family name comes first, and his so-called "given" names follow. In Latin America, a man named Juan Hernandez Garcia is actually "Mr. Hernandez" because "Garcia" refers to his mother's maiden name and is attached to distinguish and identify him from all the other people named Hernandez.

Yes, it gets confusing. Just bear in mind two bits of advice: first, if confused, just politely *ask* the person what is the proper way of addressing him or her, and second, don't jump to first name basis *until invited.*

Business Cards

Ask any seasoned international executive "What is the single most important piece of business protocol?" and the answer will be "Your business card." One reason is that in international circles the innocent-looking business card is also your personal shingle, your logotype, your label, your identity card all in one and, topping it off, it explains your niche in your firm's pyramid of power. Here are four basic rules to consider when dealing with international guests:

- □ Rule Number One: Have plenty of cards at hand and be prepared to exchange them liberally.

- □ Rule Number Two: Make certain your title is clearly stated and understood; avoid such obscurities as "Associate Deputy Manager," and also avoid the temptation to upgrade your title because if you are discovered your integrity will be lost forever.

- □ Rule Number Three: For nationalities where English is not commonly taught, have the card translated into the language of the people you are hosting and printed on the reverse side; make certain the printing is of equal quality lest you imply their language is second-rate. (The Appendix contains a list of those countries where English is the official, unofficial, or widely studied language.)

- □ Rule Number Four: Exchange cards with respect: hand it over with care, lay it in front of you, and avoid scribbling notes on the card.

In Japan, the exchanging of business cards is almost ceremonial; the full pantomime is described in Chapter 10, which also explains other special business customs when dealing with the Japanese.

Greetings

This aspect of protocol can be varied and complex. Perhaps the quickest solution is to suggest you refer to Chapter 12 beginning on page 168. There you will find thumbnail advice on key bits of protocol for each country. In almost every case, those capsules of advice begin with the *proper greeting* for that nationality. Bear in mind that your guests may already be attuned to American customs and therefore greet you Yankee-style: firm handshake, direct eye contact. Nonetheless, it is a mark of grace and courtesy to show your visitor you are also aware of his or her customs. Greetings can vary from firm handshakes to limp handshakes, from bowing (in Japan) to placing the hands in a praying position (in Southeast Asia), and from hugs (Latin America) to bussing cheeks (Soviet Union), and even to nose rubbing, the customary greeting of Maori tribes in New Zealand. For the specific greeting in the nationality that interests you, see Chapter 12.

Time

Punctuality is a word honored by many around the world and ignored by probably many more. Once again, the "Tip List" later in Chapter 12 tells you which countries honor it and which ignore it. As just one example, almost everyone has heard of the "*mañana*-attitude" so prevalent in most Latin countries. That attitude of what-I-can't-do-today-I'll-do-tomorrow usually infuriates and frustrates time-conscious Americans. Well, if that bothers you consider that Saudi Arabians reputedly have a word in their language, *bukra*, that is considered similar to *mañana* but ". . . without the same sense of urgency." In the Arab culture, they have a beautiful concept of time as not being the precise metered segments we live by in the West. There, time is a continuous flow of events in which past, present, and future tend to blend. The Arabic word *inshallah*, meaning "If God is willing," also punctuates conversations and simply implies uncertainty about any future event. According to their beliefs, only God can foretell the future and direct what gets done. Parenthetically, within Saudi Arabia, time is marked by the lunar cycle meaning that days and hours are determined by the revolution of the moon. That means a Saudi may actually wear two wristwatches: one with Greenwich-based timekeeping and the other with Saudi lunar time. But because of their casual regard for time, as one oil company executive quipped: "Arabs have clocks, two of them in fact, but it often seems to a Westerner that neither clock has hands." With such high levels of self-imposed stress in the West, maybe that's not such a bad idea. In fact, one American colleague of mine boasts of having such a watch, without hands, because he claimed he was so independent he "wanted to make his *own* decisions."

Letter-Writing

Correspondence in American business has many conventions and traditions. For example, we sign off our letters with such phrases as: "very truly yours" (which we often don't mean literally), and "sincerely" (how many *in*sincere letters do you write?) Similar conventions apply for other cultures. The Latins, for example, have a standard closing paragraph in correspondence with flowery language which, when translated directly into English, sounds archaic. Even the British have unique phrases. For example, they tend to close letters with "faithfully yours," which to many American eyes sounds a bit Victorian, almost religious. These variations pop up everywhere. American businessmen report that letters from Philippine business associates have arrived with the salutation "Dear Boy," which sounds condescending but apparently derives from "houseboy" meaning "one within the family." It is intended as a friendly, family-like greeting and not a subservient relationship. Arabic-speaking correspondents tend to write letters with what we might regard in English as a syrupy almost gushing style. That is because Arabic can be such a dramatic, emotional language.

When American businesspeople write to foreigners, it is not necessary to copy those conventions or styles. But there are several rules for letter-writing that can be helpful. First, use simple and direct language. Abide by the rule that "good writing is clear thinking made visible." Second, remember that the written word does not smile. That means that humor or tongue-in-cheek references are difficult to convey via letter. Also, remember that when we converse face-to-face, we can accompany our words with facial expressions—smiling, questioning, friendly, worried, sincere, attentive, or inattentive expressions. But that is not possible with harsh, black-and-white, impersonal written words.

Smoke Signals

Attitudes about smoking vary from country to country and continent to continent. As a general rule, industrialized nations are waging anti-smoking campaigns while developing countries are puffing more furiously. Smoking is heavy and increasing in Latin America, but declining in Western nations. Many European countries have banned smoking in public places. Yet in the Middle East, Asia, and Africa, Western cigarettes are valued commodities. Countries with high consumption rates (comparable to the United States): Canada, Cuba, Greece, Hungary, Poland, Cyprus, and Japan. Low consumption countries: Peru, India, Netherlands, Norway, Portugal, Sweden, Hong Kong, and the Philippines. A pack of 20 cigarettes can cost (at 1989 prices) over $2.50 in Great Britain, $4.00 in Norway, but only 80-cents in France.

Protocol tips: If you smoke, always ask your guests if they mind if you puff away; if you *don't* smoke, politely explain why so your guests are forewarned, but also provide places and times for them to light up.

Automobiles

Some foreign cultures, and indeed some segments of American society, carry on love affairs over autos. When hosting international visitors, this can extend into the business culture. In Great Britain, for example, executive status is reflected directly by the make and cost of the company-supplied auto. A Rolls Royce goes to the tippy-top corporate mogul. Bentley's come next in the hierarchy, then Jaguars and so on down the corporate plateaus. For British executives, the automobile is an extremely important business status symbol, much more than, say, titles that seem to rank high on the status priority list in American offices. Switzerland is more like Britain. The top man in a Swiss firm drives, say, a Mercedes 500 and the number two man drives the next Mercedes downward on the numerical scale. West Germans are also great *aficionados* of automobiles. As most of the world knows, most Germans seem captivated by the engineering and speed of a car. The message is that, when entertaining here in the United States, it is important to be aware of the role autos can play. For example, hiring a stretch limousine might be an adroit move when hosting visiting Japanese or Middle Eastern businessmen, but it might be considered ostentatious by the more frugal Northern Europeans. For some status-conscious European cultures, if you are president of your firm and you drive a five-year-old economy car, your visitors might consider that a contradiction or perhaps an example of American egalitarianism. Incidentally, for these auto-loving visitors, a trip to an American antique auto museum or exhibit might be a wonderful choice for entertaining.

Dress

On your home ground, you can probably wear loafers and jeans in the office if that's important to you. If you've traveled abroad extensively, you know how you can encounter all types of national garb. But when hosting here, if you want to make your guests comfortable and be conventional as well, it is wise to dress in traditional styles. That means dark suits and ties with modest colors and patterns. Women should dress just as conservatively. Furthermore, be certain to inform your guests precisely what you mean when you issue an invitation and add "dress informally." To some visitors that phrase could signify "Switch from a suit to a sports coat with tie" when you really mean "Wear a golf shirt and blue jeans." In fact, if the occasion is a boat ride or county fair or company picnic, or whatever the situation, it is just good courtesy to advise "At this event, we normally wear . . ." and then describe the type of recommended clothing. Your guests will appreciate your thoughtfulness.

Gift-Giving

This topic is examined in detail in Chapter 9. Suffice it to say gift-giving in business is much more important than many Americans realize. There are definite rules, so it is wise to be aware of them.

Telephones

As with the other office protocol reviewed here, even the om-nipresent telephone can have its special quirks. For example, German businesspeople normally answer the telephone by stating their name; to do otherwise is a breach of custom. Americans are usually very comfortable conducting business by phone; many Europeans are less comfortable and prefer face-to-face discussions. American businesspeople traveling abroad do as they do at home: pick up the phone and seek to discuss business or make appointments. They soon learn, first, that business appointments are customarily made long in advance and, second, that Europeans are shocked by Americans who phone from their hotel rooms to sell their product. Moreover, according to travel writer Neil Chesanow, Europeans dislike conducting business over the telephone with *anyone* they haven't met personally.

Here are examples of good telephone etiquette: take a moment or two for social chit-chat; speak slowly and clearly; avoid American colloquialisms; summarize from time to time; at the conclusion, review what has been agreed. Also, when conversing with some-one with limited English, consider using a conference phone speaker and have someone present who is fluent in the other language to help you glide over bumpy words and phrases. Be certain to inform your telephone partner that his or her words are being amplified and that others are present. Then, it is always a good idea to confirm important points made during the conversation in a follow-up letter, both as a permanent record and also to buy a touch of comprehension insurance.

Public Speaking

If you find yourself addressing a business audience from different cultures, here are a few tips on protocol: Your first words should formally recognize each senior person present; remember that jokes have difficulty crossing cultures; avoid telling stories that depend on word plays or strictly American punchlines; avoid political com-ments and try to bone up on sensitive issues in the homes of your audience; get advice in advance from a confidante of the culture represented in the audience—in fact, try out some of your major points in advance to assure that you are not inadvertently offending in any way; and finally, probably the best way to measure your effectiveness will be in the question-and-answer period—in fact, it's always a good idea to have a few "planted" questions to get the process started.

Talk Metric

Let's face it: we don't measure up. The majority of the world now marches in terms of centimeters, meters, and kilometers. If your business discussions will involve measurements, it would be a noticeable courtesy, maybe even a requirement, to convert your data into metric in advance. Even with common English phrases, like "an inch of protection" or "missed by a country mile," the result may be confusion rather than clarity. You should also know that the U.S. Trade Bill of 1988 contained an obscure clause that will greatly encourage the switch to metric. Henceforth, U.S. government agencies are to use metric in procurement solicitations and bidders are to bid in metric. Most big U.S. companies— like the auto industry—have already switched to metric, but this law should stimulate medium- and small-sized companies to follow.

Work Hours

Visitors usually know and respect U.S. practices and observe our five-day week, 8:00 to 5:00, or 9:00 to 5:00 system. However, you might like to know that in Islamic countries, Friday is the day of rest and Saturday and Sunday are normal work days. In many Latin countries with fabled long lunch hours (perhaps 1:00 to 3:30 P.M.) the day begins late (say 9:00 or 10:00 A.M.) but also ends late (7:00 or 8:00 P.M., or even later.) And speaking of the clock, businesses in many countries have adopted the 24-hour clock system of stating time, so that 9:00 A.M. become 0900 hours and 3:00 P.M. becomes 1500 hours. (A trick for making this conversion quickly is to remember that A.M. hours remain the same—you just add a "0" in front—and the P.M. hours can be converted by adding 12 to the time. Thus, 9:00 A.M. becomes 0900 and 9:00 P.M. becomes 9 + 12, or 2100 hours.)

Titles

Just in case your hosting involves hobnobbing with heads of state, ambassadors, cabinet officers, or high-ranking clergy, here are some helpful tips. It is proper to address each of those as "His (or Her) Excellency." The Commonwealth nations, however, do not use that and prefer instead "The Right Honorable." An exception to these rules is with, say, an ambassador where we write him as "His Excellency" but to his face we call him "Mr. Ambassador."

Respecting titles is not only for the exalted. In countries like Germany and Italy, executives and other professionals are very proud of the titles preceding their names. These often reflect their education or profession. In Italy, anyone with a college degree is entitled to be called "Doctor" ("Dottore" in Italian). The same applies to architects and lawyers. In Germany, what Americans would call the president or managing director of a company is called "Herr Direktor," a medical doctor "Herr Doktor" and an engineer as "Herr Ingenieur." In Mexico, a lawyer is addressed as "Licenciado," an appellation that is considered *very* important there. Also, if you wish to show special respect to a senior man of influence and power in traditional Latin countries like Colombia, you might add the title *Don* to the person's name. *Treat all of these titles with respect.*

In England, separate books exist on the protocol surrounding the addressing of Royalty, Peers, clergy, and others. For business purposes, though, here are a few important facts. First, look for letters *following* a British person's name. These refer to special honors bestowed by the Crown and signal special prestige and respect. Second, a "Director" of a British firm has a much loftier meaning than "Director" in the United States. In the United Kingdom, it means he or she has not only been appointed to the firm's Board of Directors but is usually also an important officer within the company as well. The "Managing Director" is usually the top official, equivalent to our corporate president.

The term vice president in the U.S. business hierarchy carries clout and symbolism, but it is not as common in most business ranks abroad. Savvy business visitors from overseas have learned the significance and rank of a U.S. corporate vice president but, even so, many find it strange. Numerous jokes are made in many foreign languages about "that American who is President in charge of vice."

Arrivals and Departures

It is fitting to conclude this section on business protocol with perhaps one of the most important single pieces of advice: Arrange to have someone meet and greet your visitors at the airport.

Having personally debarked from hundreds of airplanes in countries all over the world, I can attest that no gesture of consideration quite compares with walking off an airplane in a strange country and seeing someone there to meet you and personally escort you to the office or your hotel.

If you cannot do it yourself, send a reliable designate. Make certain the greeter is absolutely reliable and responsible. On one occasion when I had extremely important guests from Buenos Aires arriving in Chicago on a weekend, I entrusted that job to a hired limousine service. My guests spoke very little English, were unacquainted with O'Hare airport, were arriving after a tiring overnight flight, and had no idea how to find public transportation to take them the 100 miles to my offices. So, it was essential to have someone meet them. Even though the hired driver had the flight and gate number and arrival time, he came back empty-handed saying weakly, "I just couldn't find them." I learned later that my guests sat in the baggage area for three hours assuming the driver had been delayed. Since it was a weekend, they could not telephone our office, so they finally located someone who spoke Spanish who helped them find the correct public bus service to our city. Topping off this misadventure, I learned later that the day of their arrival also happened to be the birthday of the senior visitor. It was a hosting nightmare.

ENTERTAINING: A BUSINESS TAX DEDUCTION

All entertaining, whether it be for domestic or foreign business purposes, is generally subject to the tax laws of the Internal Revenue Service. These laws are complex. When in doubt, the best advice is to consult your tax specialist for advice.

Here, however, are a few basic rules you should know when entertaining:

□ The keystone standard for tax deductibility of any expense connected with entertaining is that it must have *a direct and demonstrable business purpose.* However, entertainment expenses directly proceeding or following a substantial and bona fide business discussion need only be associated with the active conduct of the trade or business.

□ For business meals, as of the 1986 tax-reform act, only 80 percent of the cost is deductible for tax purposes.

□ A key factor in determining the deductibility of any entertainment expense is *intent.*

□ To claim any deductibility, you should have clear and concise records of those expenses. You must have validation.

□ Deductions are not allowed for what the Internal Revenue Service terms lavish or extravagant entertainment. However, the IRS provides no specific standards to help define those terms.

□ Test your situation by asking these questions: Was the transaction of business the central focus of the entertainment? Do you expect to earn income or other benefits in the future from those you entertained? Did you engage in business with those you entertained while you were entertaining them? Do you have records, receipts, and documented evidence showing the amount, date, place, and reason? In addition, written notes of explanation are recommended.

WOMEN IN INTERNATIONAL BUSINESS

Ten years ago, there probably wouldn't have been a section in a book like this on the topic of "women in international business." Until the last decade, the attitude was that global business was strictly a man's world. Thank goodness that attitude is changing, and rapidly—at least in the United States.

Women represent over 35 percent of the students enrolled at the American Graduate School of International Management, also known as "Thunderbird," in Glendale, AZ, one of the best jumping off spots for a career in international business.

Whenever I speak to groups on college and university campuses, I encourage young women to consider careers in international business. International trade is a growth market. The United States is losing market share in the global marketplace and needs all the new vitality it can muster. Moreover, as visiting foreign businessmen come to the United States and observe the contributions American women are currently making in business, it causes them to return home and rethink their debilitating male chauvinistic traditions.

Certain cultures are well-known for male chauvinism and the subservient role of women. When traveling to the Middle East, for instance, especially to traditionally conservative countries like Saudi Arabia, a visiting U.S. businessperson will be in a man's world. It would be extremely difficult for an American woman to do business there. The wives of Saudi businesspeople are kept in the background. On the streets, most still wear the traditional veil and long dress. Yet, interestingly, more and more Saudi businessmen have their wives accompany them on business trips to the United States where, dressed in Western styles, they accompany their husbands to social engagements. Happily, among other Mid-East countries, women are emerging to take on more and more business responsibilities.

Japan is another culture known for keeping women in the background. Japanese businessmen, traveling to the United States, are rarely accompanied by their wives. Yet, even in Japan, women are now advancing in business careers because of shortages in the technical and professional areas. As just one example, companies there are actually sending recruiters to college campuses seeking women for jobs such as computer software engineers.

Jumping around the globe, in China and the Philippines and in Latin America, women can be increasingly found managing important business responsibilities. Of course, in Europe women are following the path set in the United States and moving with positive persistence and deserved recognition throughout the corridors of business.

Patricia M. is the marketing manager for a South Carolina textile firm and frequently travels to South America while also hosting Latin customers in this country. "I am finding less and less prejudice because I am a women," she reports. "In fact, if there is any trace of reluctance it is more because of my youth than my sex."

For other American women interested in a career in international business, a helpful book is *The International Businesswoman, A Guide to Success in the Global Marketplace,* by Marlene L. Rossman (Praeger Publishers, 1986).

What should the American woman business manager do when hosting international visitors? Here are some suggestions:

□ Be "gender neutral" and keep invisible antennae up and quivering to all incoming vibrations.

□ Do nothing that can be interpreted as flirtatious or sexually provocative.

□ Dress conservatively and avoid situations where intimacy might arise—like frequent touching or a cozy dinner for two.

□ If your international guests insist on opening doors, lighting your cigarette, or holding your chair at the dining table, let them do so without protesting. They may be acting naturally, according to rules they think apply, and any demurring on your part could cause them personal public embarrassment.

□ When entertaining in your home, be natural and act as you would with any guest. Don't think it necessary to emulate the woman's role in the home country of your visitor. Be yourself. Your guests will usually like and respect that.

□ If you are single, don't entertain at home alone unless the visitor is female or someone you have known for a long time. Sally Wecksler, New York literary agent who often travels abroad and often hosts international business guests, suggests that you entertain with another colleague, go to restaurants, have a dinner party, go to the theater, opera, and so on.

□ In the office, be totally professional with your foreign visitors. Listen carefully, ask good questions, know your facts before venturing forward, and watch for the same silent signals you would in any business relationship. But, always be gender neutral and keep those invisible antennae quivering actively.

It should almost go without saying that these *same* suggestions apply to American business males when—and if—a foreign woman is being hosted. Be gender neutral, grow invisible antennae, do nothing flirtatious—the whole list.

BUSINESS NEGOTIATING

If the act of negotiating in any U.S. business is a complex subject, then negotiating between different cultures in international business is doubly complex.

Here's a simple example. My good friends Dr. Paul Odland and his wife Barb travel frequently to South America where he provides free surgical orthopedic procedures for crippled children. One day, while buying mementos in a local bazaar, Paul spotted a carving that he liked and wanted to purchase. The non-English speaking vendor was asking 500 pesos for the carving. With Barb acting as interpreter, Paul offered 300 and the vendor proposed 450. The haggling in the noisy market became spirited, even intense, with Paul stepping up his price slightly and the seller retreating slowly. The pace increased so fast Barb could not keep up with the back-and-forth interpretation until—suddenly—all three parties realized that Paul had gone *above* the vendor's last stated price, and the vendor had gone *below* Paul's last offer. After a moment of embarrassment, they compromised, laughed, and settled the deal. Moral: in cross-lingual negotiations, proceed cautiously, especially when relying on interpreters.

Communicators call this interference *cultural noise.* By noise they mean the sideline distractions that clutter and confuse a message. These could be confused translations or gestures or behavior or clothing or office surroundings or interruptions or even a poor telephone connection.

Common mistakes made by inexperienced American negotiators include:

- □ Ignoring the etiquette of the culture across the table.

- □ Not negotiating face-to-face.

- □ Ignoring the importance of rank.

- □ Jumping right into business without a period of socializing.

- □ Assuming American ways are the only ways to do business.
- □ Lacking patience.
- □ Assuming "yes" means "I agree" when it could very likely mean "yes, I hear you."
- □ When hitting a roadblock, failing to retrace steps and examining if, perhaps, one misunderstood word or a phrase was the cause.
- □ Failing to review, affirm, confirm key points.
- □ Assuming an interpreter is always 100 percent accurate.
- □ Putting too much emphasis on speed and quick action.
- □ Failing to have the authority to make decisions on the spot.
- □ Assuming that, as in America, all cultures view a final agreement as fixed in cement.

This last point is especially important. Americans tend to be what anthropologist Edward T. Hall calls "low context" people, meaning we like our agreements spelled out in precise detail. We expect others to abide by the letter of the contract. This is not so in other cultures. The Japanese, for instance, are "high context." That means, according to Hall, ". . . most of the information is already in the person, while very little is in the coded, explicit, transmitted part of the message." Twins who have grown up together have high context communication, whereas two opposing lawyers in a courtroom have low context communication, Hall explains.

In addition, the Japanese have the attitude that "Any subsequent disagreement can be easily resolved by honorable and well-intentioned parties." In the Middle East, the preference is to talk in allegories and symbols. There it is difficult to remain pragmatic for a long time. An ideology is needed to bring people together.

Negotiating in international business is, indeed, a large and complex subject. It is, frankly, too large for a volume on hosting the international business visitor. For that reason, if you wish to do further research on the deeper skills of negotiation, here are three recommended books:

- □ *National Negotiating Styles,* edited by Hans Binnendijk, issued in 1987 by the Center For the Study of Foreign Affairs and published by the Foreign Service Institute, U.S. Department of State, Washington, DC. This excellent resource book contains separate chapters on negotiating with China, The Soviet Union, Japan, France, Egypt, and Mexico.

□ *International Negotiation, a Cross-Cultural Perspective*, by Glen Fisher, Intercultural Press, 1980. This handy booklet covers culture and social psychology, the "players" and styles of decision-making, coping with cross-cultural "noise," and trusting interpreters and translators.

□ *Getting Your Yen's Worth, How to Negotiate with Japan, Inc.*, by Robert T. Moran, Gulf Publishing Co., 1985. This provides a wonderful insight into what most Americans consider the most enigmatic of all cultures. All aspects of negotiation are covered, from entertainment to a delightful exposition titled "Never Take 'Yes' for an Answer."

SUMMARY

Everyone in business has heard about "Board room dramas." Today's business office has, indeed, become something of a stage, and the business people/players are the *dramatis personae*. This should not be too surprising to any politically seasoned, theatrically sensitive American business executive. What we have done in this chapter is taken that same stage, and the scenes that unfold on it, and introduced other cultures and other customs.

Today's worldly business manager must not only be a student of these dramas but a journeyman actor (or actress) as well, learning many different scripts and many different roles. I call it "chameleon" management. That means we must adapt our external appearances and actions to the environment at hand.

The State of Wisconsin's international trade expert, Dr. Rolf Wegenke, explains it this way:

Many Americans wonder how far they must go when acting as host and, yes, trying to impress important foreign decision-makers. Most Americans are disturbed by having to set aside carefully learned roles and rules of behavior from our society. Americans dislike any sense of what they consider play-acting or fawning in order to cater to important guests. Well, I'll tell you my rule. My rule is "We fawn." We go that extra mile. By my book, it is almost impossible to go too far in catering to what may seem like peculiarities of our guests. Even among the most self-deprecating cultures, those that on the surface suggest that such attention is unimportant, we find that strong measures of personal care, sincerity, attention, and genuine interest are extremely important.

So, each time a foreign visitor enters your office, imagine a stage curtain rising and the words "Let the play begin." You are the playwright and the outcome of the script may well depend on the key stage directions—the protocol—which punctuate the unfolding story.

=7

"HOME-AND-HOME" BUSINESS ENTERTAINMENT: A CASE STUDY

To bring some specifics into the many generalizations about entertainment in this text, here is a true-life illustration of business entertainment as done home-and-home—meaning how hosting is done in one specific foreign country and how one American business manager then reciprocates in the United States.

BACKGROUND

Mr. A. is president of a U.S. construction equipment firm that exports $2.5 million in parts and components to a division of a major industrial company in South Korea. The Korean company adds about $7.5 million in parts and labor. The final products are shipped back to the United States for sale here, but a large portion is also sold directly to Australia or to European end markets. The net results: about $12.5 million in total sales, a favorable balance of trade for the United States, and both partners share in a mutually satisfactory piece of business with neither entirely beholden to the other; each is both customer and source.

When Mr. A. goes to Korea, he is invariably met at Seoul airport by a driver and interpreter. If he wishes to shop in Seoul's famous Itae Won shopping area, the driver and interpreter accompany him. The next morning, he is accompanied by a company official on the air flight from Seoul to the home city of his host. The guide helps Mr. A. through various security points, made necessary because domestic flights have a greater threat of hijacking due to the continuing tensions with North Korea. Depending on rank and importance to the Korean company, a guest is accommodated at either a local hotel or the corporate guest house, with the more honored guests hosted at the guest house. In this case, Mr. A. is taken to one of several dozen suites at the guest house where all expenses are paid by the host company. Flowers and a fine bottle of Scotch whisky also await him in his suite. If he has been accompanied by subordinates, they stay at the local hotel where they will pay for their own accommodations.

The first evening starts at 6:30 or 7:00 P.M. with a dinner in Mr. A.'s honor at the guest house. Dressed in business suits, everyone removes their shoes at the door and stands around in stocking feet enjoying cocktails and hors d'oeuvres. Female hostesses dressed in traditional Korean garb are positioned discreetly at the elbows of guests and hosts alike, although Mr. A. notes that his hostess is the youngest and most attractive. Everyone is then seated at a long rectangular table, open in the center, with Mr. A. carefully placed in the middle of the long side of the rectangle, directly opposite his senior host, Mr. Y. The menu is printed in both Korean and English. After the first toast, the food is served. Six or eight courses follow, each course modest in size, and eased down with more Scotch plus tea. A string of one-on-one toasting is done throughout the meal using a communal shot-size silver cup. In between these toasts, the cup is cleansed in a bowl of water with lemon slices floating on top and then refilled and passed on to the next pair of toasters. "Not very sanitary," thinks the American, "but after a few rounds of toasts, nobody seems to care."

After dinner, a three-piece band enters (one instrument is a Western-style guitar). The senior host begins and sings two or even three songs, two in Korean, one in English. Then, in turn, each of the other Korean hosts sings—one song in Korean, one in English. Then Mr. A. is invited to sing. (Mr. A.'s advice is to sing anything. Sing "God Bless America" or "You Are My Sunshine" or any silly tune that comes to mind. It is just bad form to refuse.) The hostess, usually a good singer, accompanies him for support. Both she and the band know an amazing variety of American songs to help accompany him. After his performance, to shift the onus, the hostess sings in Korean. Mr. A. makes a short but flattering speech: "If you, Mr. Y. (the senior host), were not so successful in business I am certain you would be a highly successful professional entertainer."

Throughout the evening, all the participants address each

other as "Mr." . . . *except* for Mr. A. and his counterpart, the senior host. After 18 months of doing business with one another, they are now on a first name basis.

But the evening is hardly over. Now comes the dancing. The drinking continues, the hostesses demonstrate a few traditional Korean dances, and there is even group dancing à la American square dancing. At the stroke of 10:00 P.M., the band plays the equivalent of "Goodnight Ladies" and the social event concludes. But it is not yet *completely* over.

Now comes the delicate moment. The hostess whispers to Mr. A. that she will be pleased to meet with him privately in his suite. There are several ways of anticipating and dealing with this dilemma, Mr. A. counsels. One way is to quietly and covertly explain to the senior host that, while the hostess is most charming and attractive, you adhere to American monogamous customs and vows; thank him profusely but explain that you must regrettably decline. The second option is to actually allow the young woman to come to the room. "If she is rejected in any way, I have been advised on good authority that this can be recorded negatively on her personnel file and is considered quite a serious matter," Mr. A. explains. "There are always two beds in the room, and if you like you can plead fatigue from jet lag."

In contrast, when Mr. A. hosts Mr. Y. from Korea, the scenario is a little different.

Mr. Y. is dutifully met at the nearest airport, this time by Mr. A. himself to show special attention and respect. They go to Mr. A.'s country club for lunch or dinner, and the offer of golf is always tendered, but usually not accepted. The menu is carefully planned: two or three appetizers, the best entree the chef can provide, a huge trolley of desserts, and a tray of after-dinner drink choices. Accommodations have been arranged at the finest local hotel with flowers and a fine bottle of Scotch whisky in Mr. Y.'s room and slightly lesser choices for his subordinates.

The guests are picked up the next morning, Mr. Y. in one auto, the subordinates in another, and business discussions ensue, perhaps with Korean flags and Korean language signs to decorate the setting. Later in the day, there is a visit to Mr. A.'s residence. "How many families live here?" one of Mr. Y's subordinates asks. Photographs are taken throughout the day and evening and later mailed to Korea as mementos.

Mr. A. realizes that he can hardly match the sumptuous hosting he receives in Korea, so he carefully watches for other opportunities and ways to extend his hospitality.

One of those opportunities arises soon after when the construction equipment industry staged a major trade show in Las Vegas. Mr. A. decides this is the equivalent of his home ground, so he arranges the following: two stretch limousines meet the five Koreans at the airport; a private dining room is reserved at the hotel; American delicacies are served—lobster, choice cuts of beef; finished off with a dazzling assortment of after-dinner cordials. Respecting Korean customs, solo and group singing follow. Since most of the other trade show participants fought for taxis and ate in public dining rooms, this show of thoughtfulness and care earned Mr. A. an abacus full of good marks for hospitality among his Korean business friends.

8

How to Use Interpreters

"The girth of thy donkey's saddle is loose."

—·*A mangled toast in China*

Visiting Poland in 1977, former President Jimmy Carter's interpreter mauled Carter's official arrival message in at least three ways. First, when attempting to say Carter had "left the United States that day" he said Carter had "abandoned" the United States. Next, he translated Carter's phrase about the Poles' "desires for the future" as their "lusts for the future." And, finally, he pulled the biggest whopper of them all by saying: "The President says he is pleased to be here in Poland grasping your secret parts."

Interpreters are often absolutely necessary but, as President Carter learned, translated words are not necessarily absolute.

Fortunately for Americans, English is the *lingua franca* of international business. As a result, when most international visitors come to the United States, they usually arrive carrying a working knowledge of our language. This is lucky for us, but unlucky for them. For our part, we are saved from having to learn other languages. On their part, visitors must learn to cope with one of the most complex, prodigious languages in the world. That's where translators play key roles.

The job of interpreting or translating American-English is demanding. It is made doubly difficult because American-English is filled with colloquialisms, acronyms, idioms, slang, lingo, jargon, and buzz words. Adding to that deviltry is that our visitors from overseas, or their translators, may have learned the Mother Tongue: English-English. Most Americans are unaware that there are dangerous differences between American-English and English-English. So dangerous are these inconsistencies that, to quote Sir Winston Churchill, "long and acrimonious debate" and misunderstandings can—and do—result between the British and Americans.

More on that subject in Chapter 11 that documents how using the English language in international discourse is like tossing around a sensitive hand grenade. Handled carelessly, it blows up in your face.

This chapter deals with how to use translators and interpreters effectively. Translators generally deal with the written word while interpreters deal with spoken or oral communication.

There are about 5,000 different spoken languages. With the ever-increasing number of foreign visitors coming to the United States each year, odds are steadily growing that at some point in your lifetime you are going to need the services of one or the other.

The cost of translation services can be a major expense for many American businesses. When the Chrysler Corporation decided to re-enter the European market, for example, it cost $6 million just to translate service manuals.

This chapter will offer a number of useful tips on how to use interpreters and translators effectively. You will learn: how to find them, how much they charge, how to treat them, how to work comfortably with them, and most important, how to avoid communication clinkers. But first, here are some true anecdotes involving interpreters and translations.

EXAMPLES AND ANECDOTES

For this section, we set the stage with this apt and ancient Chinese proverb:

> We get sick from what we put in our mouths,
> but we get hurt by what comes out of them.

Here are some examples of what actually came out of the mouths of some interpreters and translators that not only hurt, but maimed or even killed the complex process we call communication.

□ A U.S. executive in the metals business visited West Germany and, using an interpreter, was describing a chemical-treating process called "pickling." The interpreter asked for time to locate that word. Finally he decided on "gurke" and consequently told the prospective German customer that the process apparently had something to do with vinegar and cucumbers.

□ The word *gosses* is colloquial for "kids" in France, but one interpreter used it in French-speaking Canada where it means "testicles." So, when in Quebec be careful about inquiring in French-French "how the kids are."

□ Early in the 1970s, a Japanese president of a company that manufactured electronic medical measurement devices visited several cities in the United States. He was accompanied by a hastily hired local translator. At one stop, the Japanese executive was received by two American managers of a competitive company in the United States. At lunch, the Americans asked rather bluntly when Japan would lower its tariffs and allow more imports into Japan of American medical measurement equipment. The Japanese executive launched into a long-winded monologue that extended through the soup course, past the salad, and well into the entree. At long last, he finished. The interpreter turned to the eager Americans, shrugged his shoulders, and simply said: "He doesn't know."

□ Make certain your interpreter knows the colloquial usage for the country in question. For example, there are many vocabulary and pronunciation differences between, say, Mexican Spanish and Argentine Spanish. The word *coger* for instance in conventional Spanish means "to catch." But in Argentina, Uruguay, and Paraguay, *coger* means "to fornicate." I once said, in Spanish, to an Argentine that I was going "to catch a taxi" (using the word *coger* which is perfectly acceptable in Mexico). The Argentine looked at me oddly and simply replied, "It's impossible."

□ An educator from Clinton, Wisconsin traveled to Japan for the first time and told his first audience that he was "tickled to death to be there." He found out later that his Japanese interpreter had described him as "scratching himself until he died."

□ Ask an American for a mental picture and word-association he or she has when you say "Nikita Khruschev" and the answer will probably be: "I see him sitting at the United Nations pounding his shoe on the table, and I hear him saying 'We will bury you.'" Kenneth Frook, a Russian specialist at Diplomatic Language Services in Arlington, Va., explained to *USA Today* that back in 1958 translation was not the art it is today. "Now, when you go to inter-preting school, you learn language equivalents rather than word-by-word translations. The sense of Krushchev's comments was actually 'We'll overtake you. We're going to surpass you Americans in economic growth.'" Frook, incidentally, served as a translator at the U.S. Embassy in Moscow in 1984–85. To avoid major misad-ventures like "We will bury you," the head of the United Nation's team of 58 translators explains that today interpreters always translate *into* their mother tongue.

□ Even semi-professional interpreters can put both feet into their mouths. A Midwestern company sent one of its executives to Mexico City to head its subsidiary there. Fortunately, the execu-tive's wife had been a Spanish teacher in American schools. So, when one of her first tasks was to buy furniture for their new home, she felt comfortable heading for a bedding store to buy a mattress. The Spanish word for mattress is *colchon*, but she inadvertently used a very similar-sounding word, *cojon*, which means "testicle." Just picture the reaction of that Mexican salesman when the Spanish-speaking American entered asking to see "a cojon." To make matters worse, she followed up with the explanation that she wanted to see "a big, firm mattress." I expect the sales staff is still laughing.

□ Nike, the running shoe manufacturer, used a Kenyan in a TV ad for its new hiking shoes. A Samburu tribesman looks into the camera and speaks Maa, his native tongue. The message appears as a subtitle: "Just do it"—the Nike advertising slogan. The film crew later admitted they never really knew what the Samburu actually said. It turned out he said: "I don't want these. Give me big shoes."

□ A Philadelphia wife accompanied her banker husband on a tour of duty in Tokyo. Being conscientious, she attempted to learn some Japanese. She was doing fine with light, social conversational Japanese, she reported, and so one day while shopping she built up her courage and approached a Japanese man asking "Pardon me, but do you have the time?" The man looked startled and backed away. When she returned home, she asked her bilingual maid what had gone wrong. The maid listened to how the phrase had been presented in Japanese and then politely explained that the innocent question had come out sounding like a seductive Mae West saying "Come up and see me some time."

□ Imagine the plight of foreign visitors to the United States who try their rusty English on, say, New Yorkers. The Big Apple may be America's most cosmopolitan city, but it is not known as the friendliest metropolis. I once observed a foreign gentleman with halting English at a subway station asking passersby for the correct time. He was repeatedly rebuffed by brusque New Yorkers. Edging closer, I heard the patient, but tiring, visitor finally say to the fifth or sixth passerby, "Pardon me, sir, but do *you* have the correct time . . . or should I go screw myself, as the others have suggested."

□ Dimitry Zarechnak is the senior Russian translator at the U.S. State Department. He was once in the middle of translating for a delegation of U.S. senators visiting Mikhail Gorbachev in Moscow, when suddenly Gorbachev turned to him and asked, "Where are you from?" "Nobody had ever asked me this in the middle of my interpreting," Zarechnak explained. "When I told him my father was from the Carpathian Mountains, he said his father died in the same area during the war. I was beginning to get rather nervous. The senators were waiting, and here I'm having a private conversation with Gorbachev." Zarechnak is so adept at translating from Russian to English that he can adopt either an American or a British accent as the situation dictates.

□ Translations of classic literature is a field unto itself. For example, if you studied Chaucer or Dickens in school, translators did you a big favor. Chaucer in his original Middle English is inaccessible to the average English reader, but in a good modern rendition he changes into a readable entertainer. "In the case of Dickens, his 19th century diction loses most modern day readers, but a good contemporary translation revives the original freshness," says Josef Skvorecky. On the other hand, Mark Twain was so upset with the French translation of one of his essays that he offered his own re-translation. Thus Twain's original ". . . but it warn't no use" became a stiff "to what good?" And finally writer Eudora Welty had her sonorous sounding phrase "crash of a cymbal" translated into Czech as "crash of the dulcimer." This occurred because the original word "cymbal" happens to be homonymous with the Czech word meaning "dulcimer."

□ Professional translator Jo Ann Church, Nashville, TN, reports that a Swedish company that makes Electrolux vacuum sweepers produced new advertising copy in questionable English saying "Nothing sucks like Electrolux." As Church pointed out, even though it's a bit crude, it does rhyme.

□ And finally, a senior vice president of one of the largest insurance companies in America reports that a New York colleague frequently traveled to Japan on business. There he often made speeches using a translator. On one of these occasions, he later learned that the Japanese interpreter's actual version of the speech's opening went something like this:

> American businessman is beginning speech with thing called joke. I am not certain why, but all American businessmen believe it necessary to start speech with joke. [Pause] He is telling joke now, but frankly you would not understand joke so I won't translate it. He thinks I am telling you joke now. [Pause] Polite thing to do when he finishes is to laugh. [Pause] He is getting close. [Pause] Now!

The audience not only laughed, but in typical generous Japanese style, they stood and applauded as well.

After the speech, not realizing what had transpired, the American remembered going to the translator and saying, "I've been giving speeches in this country for several years and you are the first translator who knows how to tell a good joke."

Translation goofs, like an ill-timed rabbit punch, can sneak up behind any of us. What do we do about them? How can they be avoided? Read on.

TIPS FOR TRUSTWORTHY TRANSLATIONS

The business of interpreting and translating comes in many forms: simultaneous interpretation, consecutive interpretation, technical translations, advertising translations, foreign language film dubbing, legal language translations, and freelancers or full-time corporate translators. This section will tell you how they work—sources, fees, etiquette, preparation, working relationships, and also provide common sense tips to make your translations trustworthy and trouble-free. Bear in mind that "interpreting" means the spoken word; "translating," the written word.

Simultaneous interpretation is just what the term implies—

conversion from one language to another as a person speaks, words marching along slightly behind but apace with the speaker. This is, of course, the most demanding of all types of interpretation and more prone to possible error. It is also the highest paid of the two since translators can linger over written words.

Marjorie Smith, a former diplomat with the U.S. Information Agency, contends that simultaneous interpretation from some languages into others is relatively easy. Converting from Japanese into English is one of those because the Japanese language is designed for saying the expected. Verbs come at the end of a sentence in Japanese and so the speaker can watch the reaction of the listener and choose the action word carefully. In the Japanese culture, ending a Japanese sentence with a surprise is considered rude. But reverse the process—go from English into Japanese—and watch out! What is needed is not someone who translates words, but rather someone who can translate thinking. Rhetoric in English tends to be more lively and surprise-filled, which goes against the grain of the ivory smooth Japanese tongue.

"Similar hazards exist when interpreting Russian and English," Smith warns. "In Russian (and German) the most important word often takes the final position in a sentence, and ideally, the interpreter should not begin his English version until he's heard the whole Russian sentence."

And then there is Finnish. A Danish friend is fond of declaring "Finnish is such a difficult language, no one, and I mean no one, can possibly learn it." To provide just a taste, if you ever studied Latin you will remember that a Latin word often takes on a different ending—five possible endings, in fact—depending on where that word appears in a sentence. In Finnish, there are *nine* possible endings. That means a word's ending can change many times, depending on where it's used. That must be a simultaneous interpreter's nightmare.

Consecutive interpretation is, as the phrase implies, like a tennis match: first you speak, the interpreter converts your words, then turns it back to you, and so on. While this is undoubtedly safer than simultaneous interpretation, the obvious disadvantage is that it doubles the time to communicate a message. However, some people who use consecutive interpretations consider that delayed time factor an asset. They say that it gives you more time and allows you to think in between each bundle of words.

Advertising translations are probably best done very slowly, and with allowances for great freedom and flexibility. In fact, verbatim translations in advertising can be disastrous. Here are just a few of the "mistranslations" we know of:

☐ A General Motors auto with "Body by Fisher" became "Corpse by Fisher" in Flemish.

☐ A Colgate-Palmolive toothpaste named "Cue" was advertised in France before it was realized that Cue happened to also be the name of a widely circulated pornographic book about oral sex.

☐ In French-speaking Quebec, a laundry soap ad promised users "clean genitals."

☐ One of the most famous gaffes was Pepsi Cola's "Come Alive With Pepsi" ad campaign. When advertised in Taiwan, it turned out as "Pepsi brings your ancestors back from the grave."

☐ Parker Pen could not advertise its famous "Jotter" ballpen in some languages because it came across sounding like "jockstrap" pen.

☐ Finally, an American airline operating in Brazil advertised that it had plush "rendezvous lounges" on its jets, unaware that in Portuguese (the language of Brazil) "rendezvous" implies a special room for making love.

Turning to the task of translating advertising copy, Larry Greb, former international marketing manager for the S.C. Johnson Wax Co., offers this advice: "The best way to work with foreign advertising agencies is to supply them with a general description of what you want to say, the gist of your message, and let them turn it into the vernacular. Never, never insist on direct verbatim translations," Greb warns.

An example of how verbatim ad translations sound was reported by author Neil Chesanow who found a box of pasta imported from Italy with this recipe for cannelloni:

1. Bring in cannelloni, as they are, a stuffing baked with beef, eggs, cheese parmigiana, pepper or spices, as you like, all well amalgamated and juicy.

2. Besmear a backing pan with a good tomato sauce and after, dispose the cannelloni, lightly distanced between them.

3. At last, for a safe success in cooking, shed the remnant sauce, cover the backing pan, and put her on the oven.

Where do you find interpreters and translators? In searching for translators, the first impulse is to find a bilingual friend or local teacher of the needed language. That might be a high school teacher or an instructor or professor at a nearby college or university. For fairly quick, simple translations this is probably a good expedient.

However, for a professional job it is wise to seek out professional translators. These may be as close as the nearest telephone directory. Most large cities in the United States have numerous professional translation agencies.

There are two national professional translation associations. The **American Association of Language Specialists** is located in Washington DC, telephone (202) 298-6500. **The American Translators Association,** located in Ossining, NY, telephone (914) 941-1500, has some 2,800 members across the country. The latter group estimates there are some 10,000 translators in the United States. Most are freelancers, others have formed small- and medium-sized businesses, while others are employed by large corporations.

Fees schedules run as follows: For written material, most translators charge by the word. Their charges might be expressed as 7.5-cents per word, or $75 per 1000 words for fairly long jobs. For short jobs, the per-word rate might run higher, as much as 15 or 20 cents per word. Those rates might be appropriate for general written material in a common language. Fees rise for semi-technical work and go even higher for highly technical work. Languages like Japanese and Arabic also command higher rates. Conference interpreters charge about $280 per day, or from $25 to $35 per hour. For shorter seminars, the fees run around $200. Those are 1989 rates and apply to consecutive interpreting. Rates are higher for simultaneous interpretation.

In case you are wondering about hiring a full-time interpreter/translator for your company, Erica Meltzer, a volunteer for the American Translators Association, says "Salaries (in corporations) are difficult to pinpoint because they depend on whether the person is a freelancer or full-time translator, how many languages they're proficient in, how difficult the language is and what his or her educational skills are. A ballpark figure for the average salary for a full-time worker with three or four years' experience would be about $25,000 per year with a top salary going to $40,000 for a translator with 8 to 10 years of experience and a master's or doctorate degree."

Following are some specific tips on everything from translating your business cards, to where the interpreter should sit, to the special problems of using interpreters at large meetings.*

Before Meeting with Foreign Visitors

1. Have your business cards printed in other languages, English on one side and the other language on the reverse side. Use equal typesetting and printing quality lest your foreign counterpart thinks you consider his language second class.

2. When writing letters, if you have any suspicion whatsoever that a recipient of your business correspondence is not proficient in English, take the time to have your letters—especially introductory letters—translated by professionals.

3. The same applies when you are hosting foreign visitors and making any type of presentation. It is not only a courtesy and makes a good first impression, but the material then tells your story in, literally, a language they can understand. So, flatter them by having the carry-away literature, visuals, or audio portions converted in advance into their language.

4. If you are going to employ an interpreter for face-to-face discussions with international guests, or even for overseas phone conversations, meet with the interpreter in advance. Get to know one another. Explain the purpose of your forthcoming meeting. Allow time for him or her to become acquainted with your voice, speech, mannerisms, usage of complex words,

---

*Thanks go to experts Rudy Wright and also to V. Lynn Tyler of the David Kennedy Center for International Studies at Brigham Young University for contributions in this section.

accent, and your speaking pace. Acquaint the interpreter in advance with technical terms you may use. If you will be discussing your service or your product, go over them in advance because certain terms and designations will surely be new and strange to the interpreter. Ralph Graner, 30-year U.S. State Department veteran, gives this example: "We wanted to promote and sell our cherries. We told our interpreter we grew 'tart cherries' but found out later our interpreter referred to them as 'cherry tarts.' Think about that. There's a big difference between tart cherries and cherry tarts."

Also, make certain your interpreter knows something about the geographic background of your foreign contacts—for example, which region of their country they come from. That helps prepare your interpreter for regional differences in languages, or for special accents and dialects within that language.

How to Treat the Interpreter during a Meeting

Here is advice on the most efficient use of an interpreter at a meeting, plus some common courtesies:

1. Seat the interpreter between and slightly behind the two principals who should be able to see each other clearly in order to convey body language and gestures.

2. Make certain the interpreter is treated as courteously as any other guest.

3. Brief the interpreter in advance on dress code.

4. Make certain the interpreter is properly fed some time during the evening, perhaps even offered wine or a cocktail. Most interpreters can't work and eat, so it's not a bad idea to offer food in advance.

During Meetings

1. Rank, title, and position in business are usually very important to overseas visitors. Make certain that introductions are translated slowly and thoroughly and that your foreign guests understand titles, rank, function, and so on of each guest. Pay

special respect to titles such as doctor, professor, lawyer, engineer. Among many foreign cultures, these designations are used more freely than in the United States but they are no less important in conversational and written usage.

2. Try to avoid lingo, jargon, and buzz words. Any play on words, topical references, or technical lingo merely become roadblocks for the flow of good communications.

3. Humor is hard to translate. Think about that for a moment. Try explaining a New Yorker magazine cartoon to a foreigner. Most American humor is based on either twisted meanings, a play on words, or on current events. Our punch lines often come from our culture or lingo. Examples: "Play it again, Sam," or "Whatever you say, Kemosabe," or "How'd ya like them apples." Each of these is difficult if not impossible to translate. But just because you can't tell jokes freely is no reason to avoid smiling or laughing. In fact, do both as often as appropriate. They are a universal language in themselves.

4. Never tell dirty stories or risque anecdotes. Never use profane language. It may be insulting or result in your foreign guests picking up your blue words and inadvertently coloring their own vocabulary with them.

5. Pause between sentences. Speak in short, compact phrases. This allows the interpreter time to convert your words. You might even try to agree in advance with the interpreter about the length of phrase to use between pauses. Some interpreters can handle a lot by taking notes. Others cannot and will summarize rather than translating verbatim.

6. Remember that speeches to an audience will take twice as long when using consecutive interpretation. Also, arrange for a separate microphone for the interpreter—that avoids the awkward situation of having to pass a single microphone back and forth.

7. Whether speaking to a single person or a large audience, speak to your audience and *not* to the interpreter.

8. If you are flashing charts or visual graphics on a screen, give the interpreter time to explain each one.

9. Don't be afraid to use facial expressions, body language and other signs of emotion. Edward T. Hall, the famous social anthropologist, claims that over 60 percent of our communication is nonverbal. When appropriate, vigorous body language will be remembered long after the actual words which accompanied the gestures or motions. I have heard audiences at an interpreted speech comment "That speaker was really serious about his message, wasn't he. You could tell by his actions and emotions."

10. Learn at least a few, short phrases in the local language to work into your presentation: "Thank you for your patience in listening to me," or "You have been a very gracious audience; thank you." It's a nice touch that helps endear you to the listeners.

11. Rehearse. Even if this means hiring a stand-in interpreter before the actual speech. This will help you smooth out bumpy spots, become acquainted with the back-and-forth pace, and encourage short but complete sentences.

12. Agree with your interpreter on prearranged signals so he or she can indicate if you are going too fast or too slow.

13. Find a way to thank your interpreter, either publicly or privately. After the presentation, evaluate the results with the interpreter so you can be even smoother the next time around.

How to Handle Translations at Large Conferences

1. Professional meeting planner Rudy Wright of San Diego counsels that when staging international meetings the first step is to designate in advance the official language for the congress, convention, or meeting. Then advise what provisions are being made for other languages.

2. Simultaneous translations are often used for plenary sessions, and consecutive translations for workshops or smaller groups. Facilities for simultaneous interpretations are not common in the United States but can be available anywhere in the country if planned for in advance and for a price. When they are available, meeting planners must assure that proper equipment is available, functioning, and extensive enough for the expected audience.

3. Program managers should warn speakers and presenters well in advance that they will be addressing multinational audiences so that they can prepare their material accordingly.

4. Hotels should be alerted to the multinational nature of the attendees and be prepared to accommodate them with signage, bilingual desk personnel, and other such courtesies.

5. Registration forms should be multilingual, and personnel staffing the registration desk should be able to provide language help. In addition, program agendas and other hand-out materials for the meeting should be available in other languages.

6. Special care should be taken when translating and reproducing name tags, titles, and company affiliations.

7. When possible, simultaneous interpreters should be provided with a text of a presentation in advance.

SUMMARY

A West German business visitor to the United States turns and says in halting English: "Please send me your know-how detailed and your idea of price per piece. If is possible, please send me your offer in German. Especially for this I would be very thankful."

For an alert American marketing manager, these are the kind of words that instantly pump adrenaline through the system and create visions of a new, major customer. But at this point, warning lights should also flash menacingly. Most American individuals and corporations are poorly prepared to respond professionally in another language.

"American . . . businessmen are inexcusably negligent in handling their (international) communications," writes Richard Sherer, publicizing the book *Commercial Translations: A Business-Like Approach to Obtaining Accurate Translations*, by Godfrey Harris and Charles Sonabend (Americas Group, Los Angeles, 1985). "When a misinterpreted word or phrase can mean millions of dollars, translations are often handled by secretaries with dictionaries or supply clerks who may recall how people talked in the old country but probably have no idea of law, finance, or global politics."

When hosting or dealing with the increasing waves of foreign business visitors, Americans would be wise to, first, endeavor to learn more languages and, second, whenever appropriate turn, to professional interpreters and translators. Using the advice in this chapter will make that experience more effective and more enjoyable.

Homemade attempts at interpretation are laudable, but they can blow up like the proverbial exploding cigar, leaving soot all over your face. I learned that lesson well in 1976 during my first business trip to the People's Republic of China. I went with a group of Midwestern business executives, the first such mixed group to be permitted into China up to that point. Accordingly, we wanted to be on our best behavior as well as observe every particle of proper protocol. "They make toasts a lot in China," one of the more experienced hands in our troop advised. "Let's impress them by presenting our toast in Chinese."

I certainly didn't speak Chinese, but I happened to be the only one equipped with a Chinese phrase book (albeit an Army Air Corps issue from World War II). So, I was chosen to make the toast. "What do you want me to say?" I asked. "Something polite but informal," they decided. They directed that I should say "Thank you very much for this wonderful dinner. I have eaten so much I must loosen my belt."

Several in the group helped me work out the phonetics for those two sentences, and I spent hours memorizing the Chinese sounds.

At the dinner, I rose confidently and presented the toast in my newly acquired Chinese. I could see that this obviously startled the audience since I had not spoken a word of Chinese prior to that point. The next morning, a bilingual friend said "Would you like to know what you actually said last night?" I said, yes, of course. He then advised that what I said was "Thank you very much for this wonderful dinner. The girth of thy donkey's saddle is loose."

=9=

GIFT-GIVING

"Beware of Greeks bearing gifts?
Nonsense! Instead, beware of
being *unprepared* when the gifts are
brought."

—A government protocol official

Dallas journalist Jeffry Unger writes that former President Lyndon
B. Johnson once embarrassed a president of Mexico by offering him
a gift when the Mexican had nothing to offer in return. From that
time on, LBJ made it a habit to have his Secret Service agents carry
Accutron watches in their pockets so that *he* would never be caught
similarly empty-handed.

Another former President, Jimmy Carter, and wife Rosalynn,
visiting Cairo, Egypt, in 1988, asked to view the local camel market.
Camel trader Abdel-Wahab Waguih was so honored he not only
gave the Carters a tour but also presented them with two silver
daggers, several Sudanese camel whips and a 6-year-old camel
with a pink ribbon tied around his neck. He also wanted to further
honor his guests by slaughtering a sheep at Carter's feet, a traditional Moslem act of welcome, "But the American Embassy people
told me not to," Waguih said. "They said Carter would not like it."
What the trader was doing was typical of *Saeedi*, the effusive hospitality shown by Southern Egyptians.

In international business, you'll soon learn that you need not
be the President of the United States to be on the receiving end of
such acts of munificence. Furthermore, *refusing* the gift may equate
to a slap in the face, and giving the *wrong* gift may kill a promising
business deal.

So important is gift-giving as an act of protocol and hosting
that the wise manager will develop a well-considered policy to

govern it. First, there is the policy of deductibility. As we learned in the earlier chapter on business protocol, there are Internal Revenue Service laws involved when entertaining and deducting the cost of gifts as a business expense. Next, there is the policy of what to do with a gift once it is received. Many companies have policies regarding the disposition of highly valuable gifts presented to their executives. For example, some allow the executive to keep the gift while other firms require the executive to deposit the gift in a corporate repository. Whatever the policy, as with all business matters, the bywords in gift-giving are "we want no surprises—be prepared." That raises the need to define, in advance, corporate policies versus corporate protocol.

POLICIES VERSUS PROTOCOL

Dr. Rolf Wegenke, the State of Wisconsin's senior advisor on international business, tells of this incident:

> While in Japan, his Japanese host presented him with an extremely valuable painted screen. Anticipating Wegenke's protests, the Japanese said "I know in America you have corporate or government rules about accepting gifts. I want you to know that this gift is *not* in recognition of your title or position. It is, instead, a gift from me to you, as a friend."

How can one refuse such a gracious gesture? This type of dilemma is common. Can you accept? Do you accept? If so, how do you reciprocate?

The quick answers are these: Yes, accept if your company policy permits; to refuse could cause greater problems. How do you reciprocate? That's more difficult to answer. Let's review all the options:

- □ Your company may ban the receipt of all gifts, or gifts over a specified value, and in that case you must tell the giver that because of that policy you cannot accept, and then suffer the consequences.

- □ Accept the gift on behalf of your employer and then turn it over to be kept in a corporate collection bank.

□ Your company may permit reciprocal gifts but limit the cost to the amount allowed by U.S. tax laws.*

□ Reciprocate with an *equally* expensive gift and *not* submit the additional cost over the amount allowed as a deductible business expense for tax purposes.

□ Accept the gift and then attempt to reciprocate via *other* actions: small concessions in your negotiations, favored treatment in service or deliveries, helpful gestures to friends and associates of the giver, and so on.

Another form of gift-giving is entertainment and American business managers may find it difficult to reciprocate or repay the sometimes lavish entertainment provided when they travel overseas. There are several reasons for this. First, we are often limited by federal laws and corporate policies. But second, many overseas business hosts tend to provide entertainment that is far above and beyond what we are accustomed to, and the scales of obligation suddenly dip heavily toward our side. This is just one more reason for treating the art of hosting with care and diligence.

Richard E. Brewer, veteran American business executive, once managed both the Far East and Middle East regions for his company. Both areas are known for excessive (by our standards) gift-giving and entertainment. Brewer offers this solution to the dilemma between corporate/government limitations on the one hand and the traditional generosity of, in this case the Chinese, on the other:

> Let's say a Chinese business person presents you with a valuable Oriental antique. If you refuse the gift, he or she would lose face and that is the worst offense possible in the Oriental world. So you must accept. But then, how do you reciprocate? The answer is "with thoughtfulness." You must search for other ways—remembering birthdays, something special for the children, awareness of that person's avocations—some gesture that demonstrates that you have been both sensitive to and aware of the life and interests of the

---

* (Note: IRS rules are complex when it comes to deductibility: $25 is the limit on an ordinary gift, but there is no limit if the gift is imprinted or marked because then it is considered advertising; and gifts to employees can go as high as $400. The best advice is to check with your tax adviser.)

other person. And, don't necessarily limit it to a one-time gesture. Show your personal interest and sensitivity in many ways over a long period of time.

———————— □ ————————

An example of this "personal interest and sensitivity" is provided by an American executive stationed in Hong Kong. His chief customer, a Chinese, had often presented the American with expensive gifts and entertainment. Now the Chinese scheduled a trip to the American's U.S. headquarters and the American executive recognized that this might be his opportunity to reciprocate in some fashion. The American knew that his customer was an extremely devoted family man with four daughters. Moreover, the American happened to learn that the visit would coincide with the man's wedding anniversary. So, to help lessen the loneliness of the occasion, the American secretly arranged to place in the visitor's U.S. hotel room a giant poster-size photograph of the man's family, along with flowers and a pre-arranged telephone call with the family back in Hong Kong. Nice gesture—but it didn't just end there. There were small gifts to take back to each daughter, helpful information on colleges for the eldest, and V.I.P treatment throughout the visit. But that wasn't all.

On a later occasion, when the same Chinese executive brought his entire family to the U.S. headquarters, the American made a point to personally accompany them. He arranged to have the children feted and hosted in grand style. In the middle of this happy event, unpleasantness suddenly struck. One of the daughters became ill. The American reacted swiftly. Knowing the family might be frightened by an American hospital emergency room, he located a local doctor to make an immediate visit to the girl's hotel room. The American knew that among many Chinese women there is great sensitivity about being examined physically by a doctor. In fact, in some Chinese medical offices there is found a small ivory or plastic figurine of a reclining woman. The female patient discretely points out on the figurine where her areas of discomfort are located. The American explained all this to the local physician who then handled the situation smoothly. The diagnosis was made and the daughter was soon cured. Through his actions, the American business host cemented a solid business relationship in a manner far more impressive than any tangible gift could have possibly achieved.

Moral: There are perfectly effective and legal ways to respect both corporate and U.S. government limitations and still repay and reciprocate for the generosity of a foreign business contact. The answer is "sensitivity and thoughtfulness."

——————— □ ———————

If that is the first law of business gift-giving, the second law must assuredly be: to collect a variety of tangible gifts and have them on hand for appropriate or unexpected gift-giving occasions. And the third law, then, is knowing which gifts might be taboo for a particular culture.

SUGGESTIONS FOR GIFTS

Before offering specific gift suggestions, here are some general tips:

□ Make certain your gifts are portable and easy to pack in a suitcase.

□ If you must give something large or bulky, offer to ship it to your guest so that he or she doesn't have to backpack it on the rest of the trip.

□ Check to make certain yours is a gift "Made in the U.S.A." It is obviously embarrassing to give a Japanese a gift that is "Made in Hong Kong."

□ Whatever you give, make certain it is of high quality. For example, if you choose a bottle of wine, make it the *best* wine available. Also, favor internationally known, prestige brand names.

□ Try to avoid perishable or breakable gifts.

□ Do some homework on taboos. Example: President Kennedy's staff prepared six dozen photos of the President as gifts for a trip to New Delhi. Fortunately, before the gifts were presented, U.S. officials realized the pictures were framed in cowhide—a major blunder in a Hindu nation where cows are sacred.

□ Be cautious about *when* you present the gift—probably at the end of a visit is best. And if your guest has not presented you with a gift by that time, make your presentation very casual and label it a memento of his visit, so as not to embarrass your guest.

- □ Try to make gifts comparable in value: if the guest presents you with a key ring, don't reciprocate with a gold watch, and vice versa.

- □ The more personalized the gift, the better. Therefore consider engraving or stamping the recipient's name or initials on the gift. Or, best of all, have it related to some known hobby or avocation of the guest.

- □ Gifts can fall into several categories: practical or useful gifts (alarm clock), commemorative gifts (a corporate anniversary medal), personal gifts (perfume), indigenous gifts (local art), cultural gifts (history book), consumable gifts (a box of candy), or gifts with intrinsic value (commemorative stamps or coins).

The following is a list of diverse gifts covers all of these categories. One of these may spark an idea that will be perfect for your particular need:

- □ A travel robe (one size fits all).
- □ An American cowhide briefcase.
- □ A book of Norman Rockwell paintings.
- □ A compact, high-quality folding set of binoculars.
- □ A small travel alarm clock/radio.
- □ A book of Ansel Adams photographs.
- □ A tin of Vermont maple syrup.
- □ Native American jewelry.
- □ Original Indian arrowheads from your state.
- □ Wood carving from wood native to your state.
- □ A high-quality, collapsible carry-all bag.
- □ A battery-powered reading light.
- □ A high-quality small flashlight.

☐ A light, quality-made, folded rain poncho.

☐ A money belt or vest.

☐ A Paul Revere silver bowl (historic yet useful).

☐ The newest electronic toy for children (if it's made in the United States).

☐ Something you have made yourself: a carving, jewelry.

☐ Disney World T-shirts for the children.

☐ Photo or history books about your city or state.

☐ An atlas of the United States.

☐ Musical tapes or records (if you know their tastes).

☐ American magazine subscriptions.

☐ Books about cowboy and Indian history.

☐ Western-style belt buckles.

But, to repeat, the best choice for a gift is one that shows you *listened to* and *observed* your guests comments and personal interests. While visiting his distributor in Taiwan, Paul Culp noted that the distributor's wife obviously favored a certain brand of American candy. He also overheard her say it was difficult to obtain. When Culp returned to the United States, he searched for the candy. He finally learned it was made in only one spot in the United States, Grand Junction, Colorado. On each and every subsequent trip to Taiwan, Culp had a large box of that special candy under his arm. It is that type of small but special treatment that is remembered.

SOURCES FOR HELP

Professor Kathleen K. Reardon is an expert on persuasion theory and communication sciences. In 1981, The Parker Pen Co. commissioned Dr. Reardon to conduct research on international gift-giving practices. She surveyed some 125 seasoned international travelers and business executives. The results of this research were incorporated into the book *Do's and Taboos Around the World*, (Wiley, 1986).

Specialized service firms have sprung up around the country to meet this need for locating and buying tailor-made gifts for international business visitors. Look under "gifts" in the Yellow Pages of your phone directory.

In addition, newspaper and magazines occasionally carry advice on this specialized topic. Begin clipping and keeping a file of these columns. The basic reference books by Emily Post and Leticia Baldridge each have small sections on gift-giving in international business. Also, ask your business associates what types of gifts have proven successful in their experience.

SPECIFIC TABOOS

If someone gave you a lily at any time other than Easter, you might be surprised because in our culture a lily is regarded as a symbol of death. Husbands here might be piqued if some well-intentioned visitor gave their wives scanty and provocative undergarments. Those are just two examples of taboo gifts in America.

So it is with other cultures. We can't possibly recount all of the taboos here—indeed, they probably are not all listed anywhere. However, the following list covers some key taboos:

□ The Japanese customarily wrap their gifts in paper, but they don't use white paper (color of death); they don't use bright colored paper; and they don't use bows.

□ Don't give four of anything to a Japanese or Korean; it is the "bad luck" number, like the number 13 here.

□ Don't give a clock to a Chinese; the word for clock in Chinese has a morbid, funereal connotation to it.

□ For someone from Hong Kong, giving two of something, or a pair, carries better luck than a single item.

□ Among Latin Americans, the gift of a knife or knives suggests the "cutting" of a relationship; yet this notion can be blunted by including a coin with the knives.

□ In the Middle East, a handkerchief suggests tears or parting, and therefore is inappropriate as a gift.

☐ Flowers carry all kinds of symbolism: purple flowers are the flowers of death in Mexico and Brazil; the same with white flowers in Japan; and white chrysanthemums are the flower of death in many European countries. Also, it is considered bad luck in many European countries to present an *even* number of flowers. Therefore, always present an odd number (except for 13, of course.)

☐ When you present flowers to a person from West Germany, always unwrap the bouquet first.

☐ Giving red roses in West Germany signals that you have strong romantic interests. In fact, throughout history, the rose has signified "secrecy." Consider the Latin word *sub rosa*, meaning secret, and note that many confessional booths in Catholic churches have carvings of roses above the doors.

☐ Giving a French person a gift of perfume is carrying the proverbial coals to Newcastle.

☐ In the Middle East, any pictures of partially unclothed females (even of famous statues) or of pet animals, like dogs who are considered dirty and lowly, are inappropriate gifts.

☐ In Japan, a gift depicting a fox would signify "fertility," while a badger signifies "cunning."

☐ In rank-conscious societies like Japan, be careful to present gifts in accordance with position and prestige. If several people are involved and you are uncertain about the hierarchy, give the group a joint gift (e.g., a silver tray, a carving, porcelain statue, fine molded glass).

☐ Tone down corporate logotype markings on your gifts. Either make them very subtle or simply insert your business card with the gift.

☐ Certain colors carry special connotations (see Chapter 11).

If you have any questions about a specific gift for a specific occasion, telephone the Cultural Attaché Officer at the embassy of the nation involved. Ask if your intended gift will have any unpleasant or unexpected connotations.

SUMMARY

You may be surprised at how certain gifts, presented with fore-thought and good taste, can ring the winner's bell for you. This example of a success story involved visitors from the Middle East. They were reverent Muslims and when their American host ex-pressed polite but sincere curiosity about their religion the visitors proudly presented him with a copy of their holy book, The Koran, printed in both English and Arabic. To endeavor to reciprocate, the American purchased a sterling silver compass—yes, a compass—and had a special carrying case constructed. Reason? Muslims cus-tomarily pray several times each day and must face toward Mecca, the Holy City. In a strange country and city, the compass served the basic and useful purpose of orienting the visitors and helping point to the proper direction.

=10

DOING BUSINESS WITH THREE SPECIAL GROUPS

**Canadians: Our closest neighbors,
British: Our longest-term visitors,
Japanese: Our most enigmatic visitors.**

—A seminar participant

Take these three—Canadians, British, and Japanese—add Mexicans and West Germans, and you cover the great majority of international visitors, certainly business visitors, to the United States each year.

This chapter focuses our ambassadorial magnifying glass on the top three groups for a close look at each, plus some tips for hosting and doing business with them.

We will begin with the Canadians. In this case, these guidelines should be helpful to *both* sides—U.S. citizens and Canadians. The overall objective is to create better understanding on both sides of what is the longest, least guarded border in the Western Hemisphere.

CANADIANS

Let's start with one incisive observation about that North American dynamic duo, Americans and Canadians, that just may characterize the whole relationship:

Americans are benevolently ignorant about Canada, and Canadians are malevolently well-informed about the United States.

Are Americans ignorant about Canadians? If any U.S. citizen considers that statement unfair or untrue, then answer this test: Name five famous historic Canadian figures.

When I ask that at seminars in the United States, the result is usually embarrassed silence. However, at one session someone did shout out "Anne Murray and Michael J. Fox."

On the other hand, most Canadians can name a long list of famous Americans from our history books.

Try a second question: "What's the *one* characteristic you would use to describe Canadians?"

American audiences tend to quickly answer, "Oh, that's easy. Canadians are just like us." And that is precisely why Americans are accused of harboring "benevolent ignorance" about Canadians. The truth is that our friendly neighbors to the North are fiercely proud of their own, individual heritage and are chagrined when airily classified by Americans as ". . . just like us."

Still, it is fair to say there are more similarities than differences between our cultures. But when Americans host Canadians, and vice versa, it is essential to know a few, basic, introductory facts.

The first fundamental fact is that The Free Trade Agreement between Canada and the United States, signed into law by President Reagan in January, 1989, and ratified by the Canadian Parliament, will, over the next 10 years, create a near common market between the two nations. Under terms of that agreement, by 1999 tariffs will be gradually reduced to zero resulting in an unfettered flow of goods and services back and forth over what is already considered the friendliest border in the world.

To demonstrate the business importance of that historic agreement, here are a few facts:

□ Canada is already the U.S.'s largest single trading partner representing about $200 billion in two-way trade. (Interestingly, in a 1989 survey, 83 percent of the Canadians polled knew this fact but only 12 percent of the Americans were aware of it.) Japan is the second largest trading partner with the United States, but the United States sells more to the single province of Ontario than it does all of Japan.

□ The United States has almost as much trade with the 26 million people of Canada as with the 320 million people in the 12 countries of the European Common Market.

◻ In 1987, there were 180 million border crossings between the two countries; some 45 million Canadians visited the United States, many of those obviously being multiple visits; and in that year it is estimated Canadians spent $3.9 billion in the United States.

◻ More than 75 percent of Canadians live within 100 miles of the 3,987-mile east-west border with the United States.

In Canada in 1988, the issue of whether to sign this agreement or not took the form of a national election. When Canadians voted Prime Minister Brian Mulroney's party back into office, his election also represented a referendum approving the agreement.

Hosting Canadians: Things We Should Know

With our economic ties inevitably growing stronger over the next 10 years, the following tips and information should be useful when we fellow North Americans host one another:

◻ Canada is the second largest country in the world, after the Soviet Union.

◻ "Eskimo" is now considered a rude Indian word no longer in use. The preferred term is "Inuit," which has not yet found its way into many of our dictionaries.

◻ Both countries were settled largely by emigration from Central European countries, and therefore both have a mixed ethnic "mosaic" heritage as a result. Principal ethnic groups in Canada are French, British, Irish, German, and Scandinavian, with some Oriental, Dutch, Ukranian, Italian, Polish, and many others. And don't forget Inuit and native American Indians.

◻ People in the United States tend to forget that when Colombus made his well-remembered voyage to the Caribbean, Canada had been known to the Northern European explorers for more than 500 years.

◻ The 1988 Winter Olympic Games, held in Calgary in the province of Alberta, did much to increase the world's poorly stocked store of information about Canada. World's Fairs in Montreal and Vancouver have also helped.

□ It is a misuse, but common and accepted, to speak of "French-Canadians" as a totally separate group. They are more correctly referred to as French-speaking Canadians.

□ Canada is, by law, a bilingual country, with about 25 percent who consider French their first language. In Quebec, that figure rises to about 80 percent, but visitors will find French spoken in pockets all the way to and including Vancouver. Such bilingualism should be watched carefully by citizens of the United States for it is rapidly germinating here as well, with Hispanic rapidly becoming an unofficial second language.

□ Most, if not all government employees in Canada are bilingual.

□ For those who regard Canada as a vast Northern wilderness consisting only of Inuit, Mounted Police, and polar bears, that perception is as inaccurate as it is out-of-date. Geographically, it is also helpful to know that Moose Jaw, Saskatchewan is almost on the same latitude as London, England.

□ Principal religions in Canada include Roman Catholic, Anglican, Baptist, and other Protestant churches.

□ Favorite sports are: hockey, speed and figure skating, football, baseball, soccer, rugby, curling, skiing, tennis, swimming, golf, lacross, field hockey, track and field, and gymnastics.

□ Some of the many Canadians who enjoy celebrity status in the United States are: John Candy, Rich Little, Wayne Gretzky, Robin MacNeil, Mary Pickford, Lorne Green, Paul Anka, William Shatner, Peter Jennings, Saul Bellow, John Kenneth Galbraith, former Senator Sam Hayakawa, and Alan Thicke.

□ Canada has a parliamentary government structure within a federal government. In the provinces, governments have authority over issues of education, property laws, and medical facilities. The House of Commons in Canada is elected by the populace whereas the Senate is appointed. The prime minister is the leader of the dominant political party in the House.

□ Like trivia? *The Canuck Book* by Ian Walker and Keith Bellows (General Publishing, Don Mills, Ontario, 1978) claims to contain "Canada's biggest, best, longest, least, oddest, oldest, and most ridiculous." One entry in the book records that "The world's most audacious streaker is Montreal's Michel Leduc. He trotted out among 500 dancing Catholic schoolgirls during the closing ceremonies of the 1979 Olympics (in Canada) and was seen by a television audience of some two billion people."

We'll conclude this segment on Canada with a scholarly description of Canada and its people from Claude T. Bissell, formerly president of the University of Toronto: "Canadians move slowly, but when they are aroused they move with remarkable speed. Someone suggested recently that our way of life is 'puritanism touched by orgy.' Our history is a record of stolidity broken by bold imaginativeness."

THE BRITISH

For many Americans, our closest international cousins seem to be the British. In school, we are taught about the courageous voyage of the Mayflower from Plymouth, England, in 1620, of the Colonies and how they were settled largely by the British, and of the epic struggle of the Revolutionary War.

Our kinship was dramatically heightened in this century when British "Tommies" and American "G.I.'s" fought side-by-side in two World Wars. There seems to exist today a warmth and kinship between our two societies that is unparalleled in the global community.

One of the nicest compliments I ever received was in the mid-1960s when, as a very junior executive, I worked for four years in London for my company's subsidiary firm there. The Managing Director of the British firm was Mr. L. Jack King, who with his crisp mustache, wonderful athletic ability, and keen business acumen was universally admired within our company. It was he who supervised my tour of duty. And, when it was finished, he sent this summary report about me back to our headquarters: "He came to us as a nice American lad, and we return him to you as a proper English gentleman."

Hosting the British: Things You Should Know

Our so-called "common language" is loaded with tricks and traps. Be wary. A delightful book titled *English/English* by Norman W.

Schur (Verbatim, Essex, CN 1980) lists thousands of word differences between American-English and English-English. As just one example, take the automobile. There are no less than 60 different terms used by Americans and the British to describe various parts of an automobile. This kind of ambiguity leads to a general tip: whenever controversy arises in business or social discussions with the British, check back over vocabulary—the root may easily lie in the definition of a single word or term. Sir Winston Churchill documented this very experience when he recorded that ". . . long and acrimonious debate resulted from a misunderstanding over one word, the verb 'to table' when used 'to table' a matter for discussion." To an American, that means "to set it aside" for later discussion, but to an English person it means just the opposite: "to lay the subject on the table for immediate discussion." With that type of potential confusion, it's no wonder we went to war with each other.

Let's discuss a few of the terms that deserve attention:

□ The designation "Great Britain" refers to the island containing England, Scotland, and Wales. When Northern Ireland is included, the correct designation becomes "The United Kingdom." The term British usually refers to anyone who is a citizen of England, Scotland, Wales, and Northern Ireland.

□ It is an Americanism to refer to "Britishers," which is considered a slightly pejorative term to U.K. ears. The same is true of the term "the Brits." It is better to refer to "the British" or "Britons."

□ While most traveling Britons have become accustomed to Americanisms, in their own society, they prefer certain rules of conduct. For instance, they tend to be more formal and more conservative than most Americans. The British even poke fun at themselves saying, "We tend to be so conservative that when the world comes to an end, it will come to England 20 years later."

□ They also tend to book business appointments well in advance and prefer face-to-face meetings rather than trying to conduct business over the telephone.

□ At social gatherings, the customary American conversational gambit is to ask "What do you do?" meaning what is your profession or work. This is considered a bit forward and rather personal among the British, who greatly value personal privacy. Also, *who* you are as an individual is more important than *what* you do.

□ The British are avid animal lovers. That offers an American host a wonderful ground of common interest for either conversation or general entertainment (e.g., admiring household pets, attending a horse or dog show.)

□ Similarly, most British are accomplished gardeners and will enjoy studying and learning about American flora and fauna.

□ Professional soccer, known as football in Britain, is the most popular spectator sport. Cricket and squash also rank high for recreation, as do tennis, golf, lawn bowling, and horse racing. Rugby is another very popular sport and is played both professionally and in amateur ranks. Another difference between our two countries is that generally in Britain how one plays the game is most important, whereas in the United States we tend to place more emphasis on the result.

□ While the Church of England is Anglican, or Episcopalian, and is the dominant religion in the United Kingdom, about 7 percent of the population is Roman Catholic.

□ Striped neckties can have considerable symbolism. Military regiments, universities and colleges, varsity teams, and prep schools in Britain have each adopted a specific patterned striped tie that are often worn proudly by alumni of that group and by alumni only. One unprepared American businessman reported visiting England, having a Briton spot his tie, and then ask him "Royal Engineers?", to which the American innocently replied, "No, Saks Fifth Avenue."

□ Education through high school is free in Great Britain and there is practically no illiteracy. Prestigious private schools— called "public schools" in Britain—require high fees and therefore only about one-sixteenth of the British youth are educated in them. Success in the British business world can be influenced by which of these schools a man or woman attended.

□ Pride is taken in self-control and seldom will the British resort to quarrelsomeness or violence.

□ Birth and position are still respected in Britain, and honorary or inherited titles still bear meaning and significance.

□ Plain, solid food without sauces is the most popular dining fare. A substantial breakfast is also usually served, with soft boiled eggs perhaps the most popular single choice. Among professional classes, lunch is taken at 1 P.M.. "High tea" is a blue-collar supper, and "afternoon tea" is what some stubborn Americans mistakenly call "high tea." At all meals, tea is more popular than coffee. As in many other countries, the main meal is often taken at midday, with the evening meal customarily served at 7:00 P.M.

□ As for social drinking, Scotch whisky is the most popular spirit, called just "whisky." One or perhaps two mixed drinks (usually Scotch whisky and either soda or water with little or no ice) precede dinner which then may be accompanied by wine. Gin and tonic is also very popular, and American beer is referred to as "lager," drunk chilled, which distinguishes it from the several unique British beers (dark, bitter, or stout) which are drunk at what Americans would regard as a cool room temperature. Cider is another popular British beverage; it is not apple juice but, instead, a fairly alcoholic brew.

□ Several different accents can be heard by British speakers, each accent identifying the region where the speaker lives, as is also the case in the United States. The cultured or so-called "proper" accent is spoken by British Broadcasting Company radio and television announcers. This is also termed the "received Southern English" or "Standard English," sometimes called the Oxford accent. However, in recent times, more announcers are being heard with distinct regional accents.

□ The United States and United Kingdom have frequently exchanged popular television programs. For example, "Dynasty" has been extremely popular in the United Kingdom. Likewise, the classic TV series "All in the Family," so popular in the United States, was actually based on an original British series called "'Til Death Do Us Part."

□ In frequent polls over many years, a strong majority of British citizens clearly favor and support the role of the Queen and the monarchy.

□ Some peculiarities that separate us are as follows: the way we handle eating utensils, with the British constantly keeping the fork in the left hand; driving and the fact that the British drive on the left-hand side of the road; our law enforcement officers are usually armed with heavy pistols in holsters, while the English counterpart, the "Bobby," carries only an 18-inch nightstick and a pair of handcuffs—no guns, bullets, or Mace. (*Note:* a limited number of London police are now armed against terrorists but never carry arms when off duty.)

□ Here is a result of a survey among Americans taken by the Anglo-American advertising agency, Ogilvy & Mather, reporting on how Americans describe the average Englishman: "Reserved, polite, intellectual, conservative, cultured, courteous, conventional, self-controlled, sensible, and tradition-loving." (Most Britons, hearing such fulsome praise, would self-deprecatingly dismiss such a sugary description and quickly change the subject.)

□ "Americans are often considered by the British as optimistic, overtly patriotic, and earnest," says William E. Phillips, Chairman of the Ogilvy Group. " (Americans) like to have fun but we take the world and our country seriously. We celebrate our national institutions, and though we may mock individual Presidents, we would never run commercials that mock the Presidency, as an office. In British advertising, by contrast, little is sacrosanct. [This] comes as a surprise to Americans, considering how stodgy we Americans imagine the British to be."

□ Americans are usually captivated by the sophisticated-sounding British accent and eloquence of their wit. Consider Commander Whitehead who became the much advertised spokesman for Schweppes tonic. Remember how he charmed American audiences with both accent and wit? Accordingly, one American executive cautions "You've got to watch those Brits—get them to *write* to you because when they speak it always sounds so irresistible."

□ I actually heard one unschooled American ask a British business executive when and how they celebrated Thanksgiving in England. The Briton paused and slyly responded, "Actually I suppose you could say we celebrate Thanksgiving each Fourth of July."

JAPANESE

Travel writers frequently describe faraway places as "lands of contrast," but as Japan-watcher John C. Condon says, the country of Japan can rightly be described as the "land of contradictions."

Visit Japan and you will see the ancient abacus sitting next to the electronic calculator, traditional kimonos side-by-side with mini-skirts, chopsticks next to knives and forks, and calligraphic brushes and ink next to ballpens and word processors.

When the Japanese come to this country, the contrasts continue. A culture born to graceful bowing, they often come here employing the acquired, firm Occidental handshake. Japanese women accompanying their husbands to the United States discard centuries of subservience and begin to dress, shop, and play golf like any American woman. Children of those expatriates quickly learn fluent and flawless English, only to return to Japan lagging behind their contemporaries in the rigid and demanding educational system there.

But if the contrasts within the Japanese society are glaring, then the contrasts between our societies is astounding. Americans tend to view the Japanese as enigmatic, inscrutable, mysterious, and every other synonym in the thesaurus that means "difficult to read and understand." Famed anthropologist Edward T. Hall uses perhaps the best word: "baffling."

The Japanese are trying mightily to understand our culture, perhaps moreso than we theirs. They realize that to continue their amazing success in the world economy, they must abandon their behavioral insularity and learn the ways of the world. Evidence of this is that when my first book, *Do's and Taboos Around the World,* was translated into Japanese, they did so verbatim, even though it was written in American-ese. When asked why, they replied, in effect "So our readers will not only learn the do's and taboos for other countries but so they can read it through American eyes—in that way they'll learn twice as much."

The ironic result is that, in the process of learning and using one another's nuances of behavior, they can clash into one another in midstream. Here is an example:

Two behavioral characteristics among the Japanese deal with eye contact and periods of silence. The Japanese tend to avoid direct eye contact, considering it impolite and intimidating. And as for silence, business discussions with the Japanese will often be punctuated by periods of silence which are expected and perfectly acceptable. Americans, on the other hand, prefer direct eye contact and shun awkward periods of silence.

A lawyer from North Carolina, experienced in negotiations with the Japanese, reports that at least one of his Japanese counterparts has turned this knowledge of contrasting styles into a disarming negotiating tactic. After an American client presented his proposal, the Japanese negotiator actually stared at the American but maintained complete silence. That totally untypical eye contact plus the long silence so unnerved the American, that he began revealing his second and even third negotiating positions without the Japanese businessman saying one word.

Speaking of negotiations, we Americans might have ordinary dialogue with a Japanese and be caught up by our own language. An example occurred when an American businessman said to his Japanese counterpart, "Right, then. Our thinking is in parallel." The Japanese man nodded and said "O.K." Weeks passed with no word from the Japanese. The American finally contacted him and asked, "What happened? I thought our thinking was in parallel?" The Japanese replied, "I looked up that word 'parallel' in the dictionary. It means 'two lines that never touch.'" The Japanese obviously thought the American was saying they were "apart in our thinking."

Hosting the Japanese: Things You Should Know

Here are some pointers:

□ The bow is the traditional Japanese greeting, but as we have learned, they have quickly adapted to handshaking. Some may even go so far as to emulate the Western firm grip and direct eye contact, but don't be surprised if the grip is limp and the eyes are averted.

□ It would be courteous and respectful to make a slight bow when meeting any Japanese person. It signals that, while he has adopted your customs, you also respect and are aware of his. Americans will probably never learn the full art of Japanese bowing, but the general rule is the lower you bow, the more respect you are demonstrating. And respect and humility are key tenets in the Japanese society.

□ Business cards are almost always exchanged. The sequence may consist of variations of the following: (1) the card is held respectfully between thumbs and forefingers and presented with both hands, accompanied by a slight bow; (2) a moment is taken by both parties to read and study the card; (3) then, at this point, handshaking will likely take place. It is considered impolite to receive a card and not offer one in return. Other do's and don'ts: don't shove the business card unceremoniously into your pocket; don't write on it, at least in the presence of the giver; do have your title clearly explained because your status is very important; and do place the card in front of you on table or desk for reference and as an additional sign of respect. This whole process of exchanging business cards is called *meishi* in Japanese.

□ Avoid jumping to first names until invited. Also, some Americans have learned that it is proper to attach the word *san* to a Japanese man's last name, which is a custom in Japan, but it should not be done prematurely. It is best to approach this gingerly, perhaps carefully asking your acquaintance about this custom, how it works, and when it is appropriate.

□ Style ranks alongside substance. This means the *way* something is done is almost as important as *how* it is done. This characteristic appears frequently: gifts are carefully wrapped, tea is served via a graceful and elaborate ceremony, the appearance of food is just as important as the taste, and in business dealings respect and modesty should be equal partners with honesty and integrity.

□ Conformity is another important characteristic among the Japanese. A popular saying is "The nail that sticks up gets hit with the hammer." This is evidenced in the conservative and uniform-like clothing of the Japanese business person.

□ While we see films of Japanese crammed sardine-style in trains and subways, in all other situations *touching* is unacceptable. So, don't clap your Japanese guest on the back or grab him around the shoulders like your best college buddy.

□ Other important gestures: the open mouth is considered rude in Japan so avoid yawning in public, or issuing a wide-open laugh; pointing and beckoning are done with the whole hand, palm downward; chewing gum in public is impolite.

□ Western sports popular in Japan are baseball, soccer, volleyball, tennis, skiing, and jogging; traditional Japanese sports are wrestling, judo, kendo (fencing with bamboo poles), and karate.

□ Japan still has a male-oriented society, but women are making great headway. One manifestation of this was the record number of women elected to the Japanese parliament, called the Diet, in the summer of 1989.

□ When entertained in the United States, many Japanese enjoy the opportunity to play golf, visit American homes, visit gambling casinos, tour famous U.S. sites, and purchase gifts to take home for families and associates.

□ Your Japanese visitors will very likely arrive bearing gifts, which you must never refuse. Gift-giving is almost ingrained in their culture. (Be certain to review Chapter 9.)

□ The "water business" is a euphemism in Japan for the so-called entertainment trade there: bars, cabarets, nightclubs, spas, and inns. Boye De Mente, in his excellent book *Japanese Etiquette & Ethics*, Passport Books, Lincolnwood, IL, 1987, advises that social drinking and entertainment are an important part of the Japanese businessperson's life. Ritualistic drinking, he writes, goes back to religious life in ancient times. A second reason is the strict hierarchy that exists in Japanese business, and so social drinking is the only outlet for informality and frankness. De Mente writes that ". . . they drink to loosen up and enjoy themselves, to be hospitable and to get to know their drinking partners, (and) they are suspicious of anyone who drinks and remains formal and sober. They call this 'killing the *sake*,' with the added connotation that it also kills the pleasure."

□ "Yes" does not necessarily mean "Yes, I agree." It usually means "Yes, I hear you." It does not automatically convey assent. In fact, much has been written about the unique ways the Japanese have to avoid saying "no." The reason for this is that any negativism is, for them, a sign of disrupting harmony, and harmony is sought above all.

□ The Japanese tend to smoke cigarettes more than Westerners, and sometimes even during meals. Also, they may not offer you a cigarette because it is considered a personal thing, and so they may not ask your permission to smoke.

□ Loud nose-blowing is considered rude. Furthermore, handkerchiefs are used for drying the fingers or forehead, but paper tissues are used for nose-blowing. One guidebook counsels that the Japanese "will sniff, snort, and spit with relish, but nose-blowing will certainly cause offense."

□ Speaking of offenses, the worst possible one would be to embarrass a Japanese visitor. This comes under the famous Oriental heading of "face." The origins of this come from the Japanese emphasis on groups as opposed to the more important role of an individual. Thus, when one is embarrassed, in Japan it is a direct reflection on one's group. Suicide in Japan is the ultimate means of taking responsibility for having brought shame to one's group. For more information on business relationships with the Japanese, a useful booklet to obtain is titled "Doing Business in Japan," published by JETRO (Japanese External Trade Organization), Suite 660, 401 N. Michigan Ave., Chicago, IL 60611. One purpose of JETRO is to assist U.S. businesses in exporting to Japan.

And speaking of "face," John Condon in his book *With Respect to the Japanese*, (Intercultural Press, Yarmouth, Maine, 1984) points out how Americans and Japanese see things in anatomical opposites—where they save face, we cover our ass.

The Japanese society is, indeed, complex. As guests, Americans tend to find the Japanese almost always enjoyable, happy, polite, respectful, generous, and gracious.

Hosting the Japanese particularly well is deserving of additional time and reading. I recommend any of the books cited in the Appendix.

SUMMARY

Wrapping up this advice on hosting these three dissimilar groups is not an easy job. From one vantage, the Canadians often consider us *uninformed*, the British often consider us *informal*, and the Japanese often consider us *insincere*. Yet in spite of this, each nationality has become, and is, a close ally, a valued trading partner, and each is anxious to build solid friendships with Americans. We must be doing something right. But it's worth doing more, especially with these three important groups of visitors. If I could recommend one word it would be "homework" . . . which is precisely what you have begun by reading these last dozen pages. Next, grow the invisible antenna that we talk about in this book, to receive all the new, incoming signals. These two—your homework and your invisible antenna—can be a powerful combination to win the continued amity of this valued trio: our closest, our longest-term, and our most enigmatic visitors.

=11

More Tips for Good Hosting

"Eureka!"

—*Archimedes*

When Archimedes discovered, while bathing, that he could measure the volume of an irregular solid by the object's displacement of water, he supposedly exclaimed "Eureka!" meaning "I have found it." In today's laboratories, research scientists speak of the search for the "Aha! factor."

When researching and outlining this book, I wanted a similar, albeit less dramatic, exclamation than either of those. I wanted the reader to frequently think, or even say aloud, "Ah, I didn't know that!"

In this chapter, a few more discoveries about sometimes overlooked areas of hosting will be added.

HOTELS

In some West German hotels, nude bathing is allowed in the swimming pools, but only on certain days and at certain times. Imagine the reaction of an unknowing and unsuspecting American visitor to Germany who decides to take a refreshing splash at one of those designated times.

Like that American hotel guest in Germany, when international visitors check in to a U.S. hotel, they may be registering for some shocks and surprises as well. Just walking through the doors of an American hotel may generate questions such as these:

□ Is there someone on the hotel staff who speaks my language?

□ When I check in, they ask at the desk how I intend paying. I reply "By credit card." Then they say "Can I make an *imprint*?" What does that mean?

□ How much do I tip the bellboy? Are other gratuities automatically included in my hotel bill (as is often the case in other countries)?

□ Am I required to leave my passport at the desk (as is required in some foreign countries)?

□ Why is there no 13th floor in an American hotel? The lights in the elevator jump from the 12th floor to the 14th floor. Of course, there is a 13th floor! Why isn't it designated? (The superstition about the number 13 is unknown in many other countries.)

□ Are menus available in my language?

□ How do various services work: the telephone, the thermostat, room service, laundry service, security, and so on.

□ Am I expected to tip the room maid?

□ Will the electrical currents and outlets work for my personal appliances?

□ Is a house doctor available?

□ If I place my shoes outside the door at night, will they be shined (as is often the custom in many other countries)?

□ Finally, as we have already learned, the question may arise, "What are the hours for nude bathing?"

These are just a sampling of questions a visitor might ask when checking into a U.S. hotel. More and more American hotels are reacting and responding to these questions. It is not only good hosting, it is good business. At the New York Hilton Hotel, 30 percent of its guests are from outside the United States. The Sheraton Washington Hotel in Washington, DC hosts over 75,000 international guests each year. The Days Inn motel chain reported that international guests accounted for over 100,000 room nights last year.

In leadership hotels like these, international guests might be pampered in many special ways: employees wear flags in their lapels representing the languages they speak; Japanese language newspapers are supplied to Japanese guests; luggage stickers come in five languages; jogging maps are supplied; English tea is served to guests from the United Kingdom; South American guests sip Brazilian coffee; room literature is printed in five languages; electrical adaptors are provided when requested or are already installed in rooms.

The American Hotel & Motel Association and American Express Co. have cosponsored two manuals to help hotel staffs. They are titled *The Care & Feeding of Guests from Abroad* and *The World Is Your Market*. Tips in those booklets include: Don't refer to guests from abroad as foreign; don't call guests from abroad by their first names; advise international guests immediately which language services are available; post internationally adopted signs and symbols for everything from safe deposit boxes to emergency exits.

But for business hosts, the message here is: Don't assume your local hotel has adopted all these worldly amenities. Check them out in advance. When depositing your guests at any hotel, make certain they are fully acquainted with all the customs and services.

Here is a brief checklist that identifies you as a considerate host:

1. Determine in advance what type of accommodation your guests prefer: single, double, smoking or nonsmoking, suite, lower floor, and price. Also, is it clear who is paying—the host or the guest?

2. Can you pre-register the guest? This small, often forgotten gesture, signals that you planned ahead. The same applies to obtaining a corporate rate for the room.

3. Does the visitor warrant gifts of flowers, candy, a fruit basket, liquor, or soft drinks placed in the room in advance?

4. Does the guest fully understand prevailing customs and practices for the following: tipping, room service, minibars, self-serve ice makers and vending machines, security, dress codes, exercise facilities, telephone service, thermostat controls, safety precautions, house doctors, wake up calls, sightseeing

services, business services, currency exchange, express check-out services, and methods of payment.

5. Provide a list of telephone numbers for you and your associates; a tin of homemade cookies for that personal homelike touch; a copy of the business agenda for the duration of the visit; a list of names, titles, and addresses of the people your guest will be meeting; historical information on your company and your city; newspapers from your guest's country; arrangements for golf or tennis; a special social program for the guest's spouse.

Another example of endearing yourself in the eyes of your guest, especially if he or she comes from Germany, France, Scandinavia, and such European countries, is to ask the hotel if it can provide a "duvet." This is what we Americans would call a down comforter, but in Europe they provide them routinely and they are fitted with covers, like a giant pillowcase. Thus, a duvet replaces our top sheet and blankets.* Your guest may sleep more comfortably with this touch of home and also give you high marks for thoughtfulness. (In 1988, we had a 20-year-old Danish man live in our home for six months. So important was his duvet that he bundled it up and carried it along with him all the way from Copenhagen.)

The conscientious host will discover many unsuspecting ways to make the guest more comfortable. For example, Ken Kirkpatrick, Nashville international business executive, reports that his French visitors invariably commented about American *washcloths*. In France, he learned, two washcloths are sewed together to form a mitt, or glove, so that one can scrub more efficiently while bathing. "Your washcloths come in a single piece," the French complained. "How do you make them work? They either slip out of my hand or it takes two hands."

While Kirkpatrick now solves the problem by providing each guest with personalized French-type wash-mits in advance, he adds "I'm not too distressed over their complaint. I keep thinking of how many Americans when visiting France have accidentally squirted themselves in the eye when examining a French bidet."

---

* If you wish to purchase a duvet for a visitor, one mail order source is The Company Store, LaCrosse, WI, a firm specializing in down-filled products.

TOASTING

The President of the United States does it frequently. Best men at weddings are required to do it, too. People from other countries do it more often than Americans. We're talking about presenting a toast.

Toasting is a skill most Americans never hone, but at a dinner or banquet, in less than a minute, a well-composed toast can convey more elan and diplomacy than a month of slick talk. But in the United States, more often than not, if the international guest rises at the dinner table to offer a warm and eloquent toast, most ill-prepared Americans will reciprocate by responding with a barely adequate "Cheers."

My first encounter with the art of toasting was in Hong Kong in 1968. During a twelve-course Chinese meal, my colleague in the next chair gently punched me with his elbow and said, "Now." I said "Now, what?" He whispered "Now is the time to give the toast."

What had happened is that after about a half-dozen courses, the shark's fin soup was served. At Oriental meals, that is the apex of the meal—and therefore the moment for toasts to be given. My first lesson in toasting had hit me literally in the middle of my shark's fin soup.

The moral here is this. Whenever hosting international guests, be prepared with a small repertoire of toasts for all occasions: a gracious thank you to your guest for his/her visit; a comment about the friendship between your countries; a remark about the great history of your guest's country; an appropriate quotation, sentiment, or anecdote.

When and how do you toast? Here are some tips:

□ On your home ground, you can decide when to make the gesture. Protocol around the world says the host usually toasts first.

□ You should stand, or, if in a small group, just gather everyone's attention, and address the toast to the senior guest.

□ Make good eye contact with all guests.

□ Keep it short (three minutes maximum and one minute is ideal).

- □ Keep it simple. But try to make it sincere, appropriate and memorable. Don't read it unless it's absolutely necessary.

- □ By all means avoid the temptation to recite a joke. A humorous, flattering anecdote, yes, but avoid the "did-you-hear-the-one-about" type story.

Toasting in other cultures can be as simple as saying "Prost" or as complicated as conjugating a Swedish verb. Among Scandinavians, for example, the ritual is to toast one person at a time by making eye contact, lifting the glass, sipping, making eye contact again, another lift of the glass, and then down to the table. Among older traditions in Sweden, the glass should be lifted from the seventh button down on the waistcoat, and one should never toast the hostess if she has less than seven guests. (Reason: For seven guests or less, she probably won't have kitchen help so one shouldn't overdue the toasting lest she imbibe too much.)

In much of the Orient, the standard toast is "Kam-pie" (with variations on that pronunciation). It literally means "bottoms up" and in Taiwan, for example, you are expected to physically turn your glass upside down to show that you have, indeed, drunk the whole contents.

A list of standard, one- or two-word toasts for more than two dozen languages can be found in the Appendix.

If you'd like to have a good, all-purpose toast, here's one suggestion. Begin by explaining this will be a toast "to friendship" and "how to enjoy life," two always safe subjects. Incidentally, I've heard this particular toast ascribed as "an old German toast" but on another occasion in Hong Kong it was attributed to Confucius, so it obviously has strong credentials and is well-traveled. The modern version goes like this:

> How to enjoy life:
>   To enjoy life for one hour, get drunk.
>   To enjoy life for one day, go play golf.
>   To enjoy life for one month, get married.
>   To enjoy life for one year, inherit a million dollars.
>   But, to enjoy life for a *lifetime*, have good friends.
> Here is to good friends.

A shorter all-purpose toast comes from Swedish philosopher Piet Hein:

Live while you have life to live.
Love while you have love to give.

Allen Fredericks, Associate Editor of Travel Magazine, journeyed to China where one host's toast was much less philosophical and certainly more pointed. Toward the end of the evening, the host rose, thanked his guests, raised his glass in a toast, drank, and then said: "Now go home."

Translations of toasts from one language to another can pose unexpected problems, but the result can also be memorable. Consider this true incident:

———— □ ————

A Latin American government official once visited my company and, after a delightful day of business and socializing, he turned to me at dinner and said in Spanish: "I wish to make a toast to our group which I will translate into English from my language. Is that O.K.?" Assuring him that it was, he rose and said with a mischievous twinkle in his eye "This is the most fun I have ever had . . . dressed."

———— □ ————

If toasting while hosting has special interest for you, I recommend a paperback book with the simple title *Toasts,* by Paul Dickson, Dell, 1981. Another handy book is *Irish Toasts,* illustrated by Karen Bailey, Chronicle Books, 1987.

Finally, we should remember that our international guests can also experience slips of the lip when they attempt to use American language and customs. One example involved a young American woman who teaches English in Houston to Latins and Middle Easterners who come there to learn the oil business. At the completion of one of these courses, a Middle Eastern gentleman-student asked if he might take her to dinner to celebrate the end of the course and also to practice his English. She agreed. On the appointed evening, her host arrived in a stretch limousine, took her to the finest restaurant in Houston, and ordered the meal in perfect French. He then ordered a bottle of fine wine, gallantly poured two glasses, lifted his glass up to the candlelight, looked her in the eye and said with much dignity, "Well . . . up yours!"

Of course what he intended to say was "Bottoms up." When I asked the young lady how she reacted, she said "Well, to be perfectly honest, my immediate reaction was to flash a rude gesture at him . . . which I did, so I guess he learned that custom as well that evening."

YOUNG PEOPLE

One summer Sunday, I met 13-year-old Rikke Olsen at the international terminal of Chicago's O'Hare airport. She had just arrived from Copenhagen to spend six weeks as our guest. Her father and I were friends and business associates for three decades. Our daughter had spent six weeks in Denmark when she was a teenager and now it was Rikke's turn to visit the United States.

As we drove on the interstate highway, an Illinois state patrol car happened to glide alongside. Seeing the car, Rikke quickly exclaimed, "That's an Illinois state patrolman, isn't it." Somewhat surprised by her quick observation and knowledge, I said "Why, yes, that's right." She continued: "And they are not allowed to cross state lines to arrest people, are they." After I affirmed that was correct, I asked, "But, Rikke, how in the world did you know that?" With great confidence and casualness, she answered "Oh, I learned that from the movie 'Bonnie and Clyde.'"

Young people can be, at once, the most delightful, most challenging, and most disarming guests of all. Their observations and insights about our society can serve as object lessons for any American.

Here, for example, is advice from an Indian student to other visiting foreign students on how to behave if they are invited to an American home for Sunday dinner:

1. Ask your hostess if you may help set the table.

2. You may take off your coat and tie but not your shoes.

3. Your host expects you to sit first at the table, so don't wait for the hostess because she probably is in the kitchen getting things ready.

4. Look out for plates or bowls that may be coming from either left or right.

5. Pass on any plates coming to you . . . from any direction.

6. Don't put too much of each kind of food on your plate because you will have a heap of everything in front of you that will be impossible to finish. Your hosts may think that you have not eaten for at least a week.

7. Start eating when you hear the hostess say "Well, we are all set now."

8. Use paper napkins as you like. You cannot imagine how much the economy of this country depends on the waste of paper.

9. Talk while eating, but do not try to look others in the eye because everyone stops eating and then it will never finish.

10. To save yourself the trouble of talking most of the time, ask the hostess how she cooked the chicken, fish, or apple pie and this will keep everyone else quiet until the end of the dinner.

The observations and discoveries of young international visitors are as refreshing as they are unexpected. Young Rikke, for example had never seen a basement, could not understand why autos here had different license plates, had never been in a typical Midwestern summer thunderstorm, wanted to know why all our TV shows changed precisely on the hour or half hour, and had never seen lightning bugs on a summer's night. Also, when she left for home, her suitcase contained 10 bags of Oreo cookies, dozens of packets of bubble gum, and 25 pounds of crunchy peanut butter.

Another young visitor said "I understand why one American coin is called a quarter, but where do the words dime, nickel, and penny come from and why is a dollar called a buck?" If you know all the answers, you are among a few rare Americans. (Answers: Dime comes from Middle English meaning a tenth part; nickel comes from the fact that our five-cent coin is made of a nickel-copper alloy; and penny or cent, as in one cent or one-hundredth, comes from the Old English *penig*. The slang word buck for one dollar comes from the time of the American Indians when one buckskin was a unit of trade, and it became truncated to buck.)

Here is a potpourri of other impressions in the form of actual statements about America from young visitors:

□ *A girl from Turkey:* "People watch TV for so long. They just don't turn it off. When you go to a party, they automatically turn TV on."

□ *A girl from France:* "Why do some areas have curfews for young people? What can you do after 12 o'clock that you couldn't do before?"

□ *A girl from Uruguay:* "Here kids drink to get drunk. In my country, drinking is a social thing."

□ *A boy from Denmark:* "Junk food. That's my impression of America. Junk food."

□ *A boy from Brazil:* "The one thing that surprised me? Oh, that was an electric blanket. I'd never seen one before."

□ *A girl from Germany:* "At your supermarkets, you put your groceries in brown paper bags. In my country, everything is put in plastic sacks. Or, the shopper will bring a basket to carry groceries home."

□ *A Chinese boy:* "What do I find peculiar here? Drinking fountains, pumpkin pie, gum-chewing, the popularity of jogging, and your huge grocery stores."

□ *A French girl:* "The bread. It is sliced and loaded with preservatives that make it soft and mushy. At home, we make fresh bread every day."

□ *A Danish girl:* "I never know what to say when an American says to me 'Nice to meet you.' We don't say that in our language."

In 1989, a Gallup poll showed that the predominant single concern of the American population was drugs. This malady is reflected in the eyes of young foreign visitors as well. Teens from other countries are appalled over the drug use and alcohol abuse among American youth. In Europe, for example, young people come from homes where wine is taken as a normal part of family meals and moderate alcohol consumption has been part of the culture for centuries.

If you are contemplating being a host family to a foreign student or young international visitor, to prepare yourself you might enjoy reading *Host Family Survival Kit,* by Nancy King and Ken Huff (Intercultural Press, Inc., Yarmouth, Maine, 1985). This handy paperback walks you through the various stages and sequences of hosting a foreign student and provides helpful advice throughout.

The largest international cultural student exchange organization, American Foreign Service International, uses two benchmarks for choosing students to travel and live abroad. According to AFSI, if they have these two characteristics, they are most likely to succeed in living successfully with other cultures. What are those magic characteristics? A sense of humor and the ability to fail.

On reflection, those two qualities would benefit the lowliest cross-cultural traveler or the highest placed multinational business executive.

COLORS

Americans "see red" when they are angry; jealousy is green; blue signifies coolness, placidness; black is morbid . . . and so it goes in our culture.

In other cultures, however, the symbolism behind any particular color can vary as much as Japanese *sushi* differs from English sole.

Let's start with a seemingly safe one: **white.** In early history, white signified purity or virginity. Remember the Roman vestal virgins cloaked in white? Yet today for the Japanese and other Orientals, white is used at funerals as a symbolic representation of hope. Therefore, in Japan white chrysanthemums are the flower of death, much like our white lily. And when giving gifts in Japan, always wrap the gift but never use white paper; instead, use pastel colors, but never white or bold, bright-colored papers.

White is right for brides in the United States, but not in India. There they prefer red or yellow for wedding gowns. That's not so unusual, by the way. Brides have not always worn white. Many historians say Roman brides insisted on **yellow,** while others claim they wore white dresses with **orange** (for passion) veils. In the Middle Ages, the more colorful the wedding dress, the better. Medieval brides often wore **red** wedding dresses and in Victorian days brides wore their brightest finery, no matter the color.

Purple is never worn at Japanese weddings by either the guests or wedding party members. According to Japanese superstition, purple fades faster than any other color, and might signify the fading of marital happiness.

Here is a spectrum of color tips for American hosts:

□ The French, Dutch, and Swedes associate **green** with cosmetics and toiletries, yet it is considered the national color of Egypt and should not be used for packaging there.

□ In Malaysia, consumers complained about a **green** product because it was associated with the jungle and disease.

□ In the Orient, **green** symbolizes exuberance and youth. But in China, men should not casually wear a green hat—in some regions there, a man wearing a green hat advertises that his wife or sister is a prostitute.

□ **Green,** as in shamrock green, is the national color of Ireland but in Northern Ireland, **orange** is the national symbol.

□ In England, **red** is regarded as an "old" color but in Japan the combination of **red** and **white** is widely regarded as appropriate for happy and pleasant occasions. In the United States and many other countries, a "red light" district, red hearts, and a red nose (as in Rudolph) all have special meaning.

□ In England and France, **red** is regarded as more masculine than **blue.** And in the Orient, at the time of Chinese New Year, the most popular gift tradition is to present bright and distinctive **red** envelopes containing money.

□ In England, **yellow** connotes youth and humor. But in the Orient, **yellow** is considered the imperial color because it suggests grandeur and mystery.

□ In Brazil and Mexico, **purple** is the color of death. **Brown,** as seen in withered leaves, is the funereal color in Persia, and **blue** (for heaven) is used in Syria.

□ **Gold** and its various hues have symbolism, too. Just about everywhere it signifies wealth even though platinum and iridium are both rarer and more useful. In the Middle East and parts of the Far East, they much prefer gold products with "dark" or "orange" shades, whereas in the United States a more "champagne" or "light" gold color is preferred. The darker gold is thought to be "heavier" or having more gold metal content. (Gold can come in many colors: white, rose, dark, light, and so on, depending on what other metals are mixed with it.) Incidentally, the Japanese generally dislike gold jewelry and personal accessories, regarding it as "flashy." They seem to prefer products with **white** precious metals, such as sterling silver or white gold. Yet the reverse is true in Hong Kong, the Middle East, and most of Latin America.

□ In England, **black** cats are considered lucky.

□ **Blue** suggests high achievement (as in "blue ribbon") in most countries. This may have originated with England's King Edward III who, in the year 1348, chose a broad dark-blue ribbon as the badge of his newly formed Order of the Garter.

Finally, here are some commonly accepted color symbols around the world: the **white** flag of truce, which goes back to the eleventh century; **red**-letter days, which come from hand-lettered medieval calendars when feast days were featured in red; the **red-yellow-green** combination used on traffic lights around the world is standard, except in many countries the **yellow** light for "caution" flashes between every change and not just after the green, as is the custom in the United States.

LANGUAGE

"If English was good enough for Jesus Christ, it's good enough for me." That's how satirist H. L. Mencken summarized the ethnocentric attitude of many Americans toward foreign languages.

English is the native tongue of barely a dozen countries, but it is either widely spoken or studied in more than 90 others. (To determine the likelihood of your international visitors speaking English, refer to the Appendix for a listing showing where English is spoken around the globe.)

For business hosts, the good news is that international visitors will very likely speak English. The bad news is that they may not understand *your* English. That is because American/English is replete with slang, colloquialisms, idioms, jargon, buzz words, lingo, officialese, acronyms, and metaphors. It is not difficult to find examples.

——————— ▢ ———————

An American magazine editor was hosting a group of Chinese when one of them said, "Please, if you will, explain what is a turkey." The editor launched into a lengthy explanation of the ungainly American bird that has become the centerpiece at American Thanksgiving tables. And then, of course, he had to explain about the American holiday, Thanksgiving. The Chinese waited patiently and then replied, "Well, I still do not understand what is meant when you Americans say 'Come on, you turkey, let's get moving.'"

——————— ▢ ———————

Even when we threaten someone with "I'll clean your clock!" or "I'll fix your wagon!", as one foreign observer said, "Those aren't threats. Those are household chores."

Each and every word is often comprehended by our international listeners, but it's often the peculiar way we arrange them that causes confusion. An American government official being interviewed on television commented that "We don't have deep pockets. This may be the straw that broke the camel's back. If so, this project goes down the tubes." For any foreigner with limited knowledge of English, those metaphors sound like they got thrown into a cement mixer and came out a big, tangled block of nothing.

And then there is American sport terminology. "What this outfit needs is fewer tight ends and more wide receivers," is what one chief executive told his multinational staff. So prolific is our sports vocabulary that there is even a new dictionary on the market devoted entirely to baseball terms.

Military and cowboy metaphors also raid our daily language. A former military man might say "We want that report ASAP," (meaning, of course, "as soon as possible"). And a cowboy's prescription for a company's problem might come out as "A Smith & Wesson beats four aces," meaning that strong, threatening behavior might be preferred over more rational means.

In addition, with each new edition of world dictionaries of

English, thousands of new words are added. Recent examples are: acid rain, barf, bleeper, detox, dingbat, duty-free, foxy, greenmail, lap-top, nose job, passive smoking, and plastic money.

With this uncontrolled proliferation it should not be surprising that among certain sub-cultures we encounter specialized vocabularies. In the case of Wall Street, for example, it might be called "stockspeak." There terms like boiler room, cash cows, delisting, dutch auction, odd lot, poison pills, LBOs, scorched-earth policies, wallflowers, and white knights make a foreign visitor's head whirl like a runaway ticker tape.

Another pocket of communication confusion comes from words called "cognates." That means words that look or sound alike between two languages. Some cognates are twins in meaning. But others have important differences in meaning. Language expert and world traveler Barb Odland provides these few examples of convoluted cognates: a limousine to a Frenchman from Normandy is not a fancy auto but instead a type of cow; the Spanish word *embarrasada* does not necessarily mean "embarrassed—in fact in Mexico it means "pregnant"; a woman shopping for a "mattress" in Mexico might reach out for the word "matrix," which sounds similar, but actually means "uterus" in Spanish; when a French person uses the word *demand* he or she means "ask" because the French word *demander* means "to ask" in French and not "to demand"; and the Spanish verb *molester* does not mean "to molest" but, instead, a much softer "to bother" as in "Would it bother you if I smoked?"

Americans also tend to have short-term love affairs with catchy *au courant* phrases. The 1988 presidential campaign gave birth to "spin doctor," "read my lips," and "a kinder and gentler nation," all of which soon became standards among fad-conscious writers and stand-up comedians and then evolved into worn clichés. But America is not alone. One writer proposed a ban on Australian words that first caught our fancy, and then withered from overuse. Aussie phrases like "mate," "g'day," "spark up the barbie," and "too right" are just a few examples.

If you consider these just trendy fun with lexicography, think again. They can have dire international consequences. During the 1988 Olympic Games in South Korea, a T-shirt design by a group of NBC-TV workers created a furor. The design contained the popular (at that time) and reverse twist phrase "We're Bad" and pictured two U.S. boxer superimposed over a Korean flag. The symbol was intended to spur on the American boxers by using jive talk. But the words combined with the flag were interpreted as slights against the Korean people and a formal apology was demanded.

Gymnastics with American lingo can turn an innocent business discussion into a heated wrestling match. The message here is fairly obvious: keep it as simple as the ABCs—avoid acronyms. Banish buzz words. Conserve colloquialisms. Don't sling slang. And so on. In other words, what may sound like crystal clear, catchy conversation to Americans may sound, instead, like harsh and fuzzy dissonance to your international business guest.

Some U.S. firms are taking this matter very seriously, and, as we have learned here, with good reason. Sharon Richards, Cross Cultural Coordinator for Intel Corporation, has compiled a special glossary of American business slang just for Intel's foreign speaking employees. Employees there are also urged to interrupt any conversation or lecture where an unfamiliar word or phrase interferes with comprehension. Americans at Intel are trained to speak in simple terms, to rephrase and paraphrase, and to employ "echoing," meaning to stop for feedback on what the listener is hearing.

And finally, if you still have trouble accepting the premise that our language is extremely difficult for any non-English speaking person, the following ditty from an unknown source might win you over:

> I take it you already know
> Of tough and bough and cough and dough?
> Others may stumble, but not you
> On hiccough, thorough, slough and through.
> Well don't! And now you wish, perhaps,
> To learn of less familiar traps.
> Beware of heard, a dreadful word
> That looks like beard but sounds like bird.
> And dead: it's said like bed, not bead,
> For goodness sake don't call it deed!
> Watch out for meat and great and threat
> (They rhyme with suite and straight and debt).
> A moth is not a moth as in mother
> Nor both in bother, nor broth in brother,
> And here is not a match for there,
> Nor dear and fear, for bear and pear.

And then there's dose and rose and lose—
Just look them up—and goose and choose
And cork and work and card and ward
And font and front and word and sword
And do and go, then thwart and cart,
Come, come! I've hardly made a start.
A dreadful language? Why man alive!
I'd learned to talk it when I was five.
And yet to write it, the more I tried,
I hadn't learned it at fifty-five.

=12=

TIP LIST

A list of brief but helpful tips follows, nationality by nationality, on the following important aspects of hosting:

- □ Greetings
- □ Punctuality
- □ Gift-giving
- □ Protocol
- □ Conversational do's and don'ts

The discussion is organized, first, by general region—Europe, Africa, Middle East, Far East, Central and South America, and the Caribbean, in that order—and then by specific nationality within those regions, in alphabetical order. Although the format is generally consistent, the enormous diversity in cultures and customs makes a rigid style of giving this information impossible.

These are intended to be quick tips, but like all generalizations about people and cultures, when you host international guests you may and will encounter exceptions. Nonetheless, being generally aware of these accepted, albeit broad-brushed traits might save you some embarrassment in your hosting responsibilities.

One cautionary note: A gentle but sometimes confusing clashing of cultures may occur if your international guests have studied and learned American customs and protocol and want to demonstrate that knowledge. Therefore, in the following listings, where it may say "limp handshakes are the custom" or "arriving 30 minutes late for appointments is the norm," you should remember that those are the *indigenous* practices. Certain guests from those locales may surprise you with a bone-crushing handshake and split-second promptness simply because they have done their homework on American protocol, learned firm handshakes and punctuality prevail here, and decided to display that knowledge.

To begin this listing, it's only fair that we first hold a mirror up to the American image. After all, what's good for the guest is good for the host, too. This particular list of American traits is culled from a series of seminars where I asked both foreign and American audiences to describe the stereotypical American business person. Here is how Americans might be described in some foreign language text when the question is asked: "What quick tips, what traits should I know when hosting Americans?"

AMERICANS FROM THE UNITED STATES

Firm handshaking is the rule, along with direct eye contact. Avoid body contact when greeting men, for example, hugs, kissing. Generally, punctuality is practiced and is important. In business, little time is spent on small talk. The attitude is "Time is money, so let's get down to business." Americans quickly jump to the use of first names. They prefer light lunches, with the main meal in the evening. They may even schedule breakfast meetings. They rarely speak other languages, but use much American "lingo." If business gifts are exchanged, they usually are token gifts. Americans often enjoy entertaining business guests at home. Good topics: sports, family, and business; bad topics: dominance of American power.

EUROPE

Before examining individual countries in Europe, here are a couple of bits of protocol common throughout Europe:

□ When giving flowers, you should know that chrysanthemums are linked with death, so avoid giving them. Red roses signify a strong romantic interest and attachment, so it's best to avoid them, too. When presenting flowers, always unwrap the paper in advance. Never give an *even* number of flowers—that's bad luck, but it is also unlucky to give 13 flowers. Finally, Europeans always seem to carry flowers in an upright position, while Americans tend to carry them in a downward position.

□ Another idiosyncrasy among almost all Europeans is that the second floor (in U.S. terms) is the "first" floor. This is because they call the "first floor" of any building the "ground floor."

Austrians

- □ Never call an Austrian a German.
- □ Are punctual.
- □ May bring flowers or chocolates if invited to your home.
- □ May call the toilet the "W.C." (for "water closet").
- □ Use a firm handshake (both men and women).
- □ Keeping hands in the lap when dining considered impolite.
- □ Are uncomfortable with first names, until friendship established.
- □ Good topics: history, art, music, sports, wines.
- □ Bad topics: money, religion, politics.

Belgians

- □ Value privacy.
- □ Use frequent handshaking at both greetings and farewells.
- □ Use first names only with old friends.
- □ Embrace among Belgians and other close friends.
- □ Cheek-kissing with other Belgians and close friends—three times, alternating cheeks.
- □ Like punctuality.
- □ Will joke about the Dutch and vice-versa.
- □ Great gourmets; they revere good cooking.
- □ Dislike being confused as being "French."
- □ Half the country speaks a dialect similar to Dutch.
- □ Snapping fingers or putting hands in pockets when conversing impolite.
- □ Good topics: soccer, biking, history.
- □ Bad topics: French-Flemish rivalries.

Bulgarians

- □ Frequent handshaking.
- □ Not many speak English; German and Russian are often spoken.

- □ Make appointments well in advance; very punctual.
- □ When dining, may use bread to mop up gravy and sauces.
- □ May bring flowers, candy, or wine to your home.
- □ A nod means "no"; shaking the head side-to-side means "yes."
- □ Good topics: family, home life, professions.
- □ Bad topics: politics and social conditions in Bulgaria.

Czechoslovakians

- □ Very punctual.
- □ Two republics: Czech and Slovak.
- □ Two separate languages but understood well by both.
- □ Handshaking very common: arriving, leaving, business, social.
- □ Make appointments well in advance.
- □ May bring flowers, wine, or cognac as gifts to your home.
- □ Toasting common at special occasions.
- □ Putting elbows on the table impolite.
- □ Good topics: sports and don't mind personal questions.
- □ Bad topics: politics, socialism, and U.S.S.R.

Danish

- □ Punctuality very important.
- □ Firm handshaking common among men, women, and even children.
- □ Toasting with the word "skoal" very common.
- □ Guests of honor sit to left of hostess.
- □ Guests of honor expected to make a toast.
- □ Like long, slow dinners with much conversation.
- □ Not accustomed to tipping taxi drivers or waitresses.
- □ Very impolite to "cut in" while dancing.
- □ Complimenting clothing is personal and considered odd.
- □ Don't like to be confused with Norwegians or Swedes.
- □ State church is Lutheran but few attend.
- □ Normally don't show emotions.
- □ Not a back-slapping, touching society.
- □ Substance more important than style.
- □ Good topics: food, Danish culture, current events.
- □ Bad topics: personal subjects like religion, income.

Dutch

- □ Officially, the Kingdom of the Netherlands.
- □ Called "Holland" but that is actually a province.
- □ Punctuality expected.
- □ Handshaking with everyone present, even children, common.
- □ Always introduce yourself or they may consider you rude.
- □ Don't exaggerate or present fluff in business proposals.
- □ Avoid haggling.
- □ Business gifts customarily wrapped.
- □ Not prone to touch and not physically demonstrative.
- □ Take pride in: land reclamation, art, history, furniture.
- □ Good topics: politics, travel, sports.
- □ Respected worldwide as sound, honest business traders.
- □ Usually fluent in English, plus other European languages.

East Germans

- □ Handshaking customary on greeting and leaving.
- □ Upset by confusion with West Germans.
- □ Respect punctuality.
- □ Standing with hands in pockets considered rude.
- □ Officially, the "German Democratic Republic."
- □ It is also "Berlin" and never "East" or "West Berlin."
- □ Good topics: sports, families, professions.
- □ Bad topics: politics, ties with U.S.S.R.

English, Scots, Welsh

- □ Each national group likes individual recognition.
- □ English more formal than others.
- □ Conservative in dress and social, business practices.
- □ Tend to use understatement in business matters.
- □ Titles and honors highly important.
- □ Usually have great fondness for household pets.
- □ Appointments, well in advance, are the rule.
- □ Punctuality important.
- □ Respect personal privacy—avoiding personal questions.
- □ Adopting American customs of first names, light lunches.
- □ When eating, declining "seconds" is considered polite.

- ☐ Accustomed to cooler room temperatures than Americans.
- ☐ Striped neckties denote military or school affiliations.
- ☐ Handshaking common among both men and women.
- ☐ English normally do not say "you're welcome"; Scots do.
- ☐ May appear stand-offish until formally introduced.
- ☐ Call a Scot a Scotsman, not a Scotchman or Scottish.
- ☐ If you smoke, offer cigarettes to everyone.
- ☐ Good topics: history, architecture, gardening.
- ☐ Bad topics: religion, Northern Ireland, money, and prices.

Finnish

- ☐ Considered "Nordic," meaning geographically grouped with Scandinavians.
- ☐ Linguistically and racially different from Scandinavians.
- ☐ Reflect Scandinavia in other customs and lifestyle.
- ☐ Firm handshakes the custom.
- ☐ Hugs and kisses not the custom.
- ☐ Tend to be quiet and unemotional.
- ☐ Punctuality preferred; same with advance appointments.
- ☐ Not formal, but may offer a toast at beginning of a meal.
- ☐ Good topics: hobbies, sports, travel, politics.
- ☐ Bad topics: personal questions about job, religion, politics.

French

- ☐ Tend to be formal and conservative in business protocol.
- ☐ First names rarely used, even among colleagues.
- ☐ Take great pride in French history, language, and arts.
- ☐ Frequent handshaking, but shorter and less firm than most.
- ☐ Highly value good cuisine and fine wines.
- ☐ Main meal of the day is usually at midday.
- ☐ Mineral water is often sipped in addition to wine.
- ☐ Avoid personal questions, politics, and money in conversation.
- ☐ Take great pride in French educational system.
- ☐ Chauvinistic about country and language.
- ☐ Decisions made usually after much deliberation.
- ☐ Dinnertime conversations are important and often long.
- ☐ Good topics: food, sports, culture.
- ☐ Bad topics: money, prices, very personal questions.

Greeks

- Respect the elderly.
- Shake hands, embrace, even kiss when meeting.
- Punctuality *not* a must.
- Prior appointments not necessary, but appreciated.
- Extremely hospitable, warm, and demonstrative.
- If you admire an article, he/she may give it to you.
- Main meal of day served at noon.
- Smiles when happy, but also when very angry.
- Signals "no" with uptilted chin and raised eyebrows.
- Good topics: sports, music, politics, Greek culture.
- Bad topics: Cyprus, Turkey, American political intrusions.

Hungarians

- Customary greeting the handshake.
- Socialist country, socialist beliefs.
- Self-deprecating when complimented.
- "To your health" a common toast before sipping wine.
- "Good appetite" the customary phrase before eating.
- Good topics: food, wine, history.
- Bad topics: political party membership or religion.

Icelanders

- Use first names among their own countrymen.
- Expect foreigners to use last names.
- Language: Icelandic (oldest living language in Europe).
- Punctuality not required.
- Customarily bring a small gift to a hostess.
- Service charges included on bills, so they don't tip.
- Political ties to Denmark.
- Fishing industry predominates.
- Good topics: absence of crime, history, and culture.
- Bad topics: weather and social problems.

Irish

- Not overly conscious about time and punctuality.
- Giving business gifts is not a common practice.
- English spoken liberally; Gaelic infrequently.
- Avoid discussion of religion or politics.

- □ Divided country.
- □ Strong emotional ties to the United States.
- □ Irish tell British jokes and vice versa.
- □ Jolly, warm temperament.
- □ Refusing a drink or failing to buy your round is bad.
- □ Other ways to offend the Irish: unkindness, be pro-British.
- □ Good topics: beauty of the country, culture, sports, weather.

Israelis

- □ More formal than the United States, but less than Europe.
- □ Shake hands when meeting and leaving.
- □ Usual spoken greeting is *shalom,* for departures, too.
- □ Titles are less important than in America.
- □ Saturday is the Sabbath to Orthodox Jews.
- □ Sabbath actually begins on Friday at sunset.
- □ Punctuality appreciated.
- □ Flowers and books are appreciated as gifts.
- □ Strong attachments to the United States.
- □ Sensitive conversation subjects: U.S. aid, West Bank situation, depressed economy.
- □ Good topics: culture, history, religion.

Italians

- □ Demonstrative and emotional by American standards.
- □ Use strong and frequent hand and body gestures.
- □ May shake hands accompanied by grasping the elbow.
- □ Men who are good friends will also embrace and pat backs.
- □ Titles are common among university graduates.
- □ Don't use first names until well acquainted.
- □ Punctuality not a virtue, at least for social events.
- □ Normally the big meal of the day at midday.
- □ Don't use bread plates; they break rolls next to the plate.
- □ Exchanging business gifts common among business people.
- □ Don't talk business at a social event.
- □ Good topics: world events, soccer, family.
- □ Bad topics: Mafia, politics, religion, taxes.

Luxembourgers

- □ Appreciate being recognized for own achievements.
- □ "Benelux" refers to: Belgium, Netherlands, Luxembourg.

- Handshaking the customary greeting.
- Good friends kiss cheeks, one on each side.
- Punctuality important.
- Speak both French and German.
- National language Luxembourgeois.
- Good topics: history, national independence.
- Bad topics: anti-Catholic issues, internal politics.

Norwegians

- Strong on punctuality and precision.
- More restrictive in using first names than Americans.
- May refer to you by your last name only.
- "Designated driver" originated in Norway due to harsh driving-while-intoxicated laws.
- Proud of history and culture.
- May consider Americans and both glib and too casual.
- Dislike being lumped with Swedes and Danes, but accept it.
- Normally bring gifts to a hostess.
- "Skoal" the customary toast.
- Good topics: winter sports, hobbies, Viking heritage.
- Bad topics: employment, salary, social status.

Polish

- First names used by close friends only.
- Men may kiss a woman's hand when greeting and departing.
- Usually bring flowers to a hostess.
- Chewing gum while conversing impolite.
- Don't use first names until invited to do so.
- Toasting often done at both formal and informal dinners.
- Cognac a popular drink.
- Proud of their history and culture.
- May know much about the United States from relatives here.
- Catholic religion practiced extensively.
- Good topics: national history, culture, solidarity movement.
- Bad topics: past linkages with U.S.S.R. and Germany.

Portuguese

- Men customarily embrace and slap backs.
- For women, a kiss on both cheeks is customary.
- Do not use extensive gestures like Spanish neighbors.
- Promptness appreciated.
- Discussing business at lunch O.K., but not at dinner.
- Instead of business gift-giving, dinner invitations prevail.
- Good topics: family, history, personal interests.
- Bad topics: politics and government.

Romanians

- Handshaking the customary greeting, done often.
- A very punctual society.
- First names used only among very close friends.
- Curious about Americans; may ask how much you earn.
- Enjoy entertaining by invitations to dinner.
- Good gifts: quality pens, lighters, perfume, coffee.
- Good topics: sports, travel, music, fashion, books.
- Bad topics: attitudes toward Soviet Union, communism, economy.

Russians

- The proper name is the Union of Soviet Socialist Republics or Soviet Union; Russia is just one state.
- *Glasnost* (new openness) on every Russian's mind.
- Same with *perestroika*, the restructuring of the economy.
- They want to know what Americans *really* think.
- When greeting, Russians shake hands and announce their name.
- Among friends, the "bear hug" and cheek kissing are common.
- Good gifts: jeans, quality pens, music albums, books.
- Many speak at least some English.
- Chief topic of conversation: peace.

Spanish

- Main meal between 1:30 and 4:30.
- Known for dining very late at night: 10:00 or later.
- Close male friends exchange an *abrazo*, or hug.

- □ Women friends greet and part with slight embrace.
- □ Punctuality only important when attending a bullfight.
- □ Prefer much small talk before getting down to business.
- □ Dahlias (and chrysanthemums) associated with death.
- □ Mr. Lopez-Cardenas addressed as Mr. Lopez.
- □ May interrupt you, but that's eagerness not rudeness.
- □ Good topics: sports, travel, history, politics.
- □ Bad topics: dislike of bullfighting, religion, family, job.

Swedes

- □ Handshaking common; touching and back-slapping uncommon.
- □ Appreciate awareness of differences with Danes, Norwegians.
- □ Punctuality a must but the business pace unrushed.
- □ May seem stiff and overly serious at first.
- □ Compliments often denied—don't blow your own horn.
- □ Toasting common at meals—look in eyes and say Skoal.
- □ Proud of social advancements, their history and culture.
- □ Take great joy in nature.
- □ Pride taken in Viking heritage.
- □ Good topics: Sweden's high standard of living, sports.
- □ Bad topics: high taxation, neutrality during World War II.

Swiss

- □ Trilingual: Swiss/German, French, Italian.
- □ English spoken freely, especially by businesspeople.
- □ Tricultural: distinct German, French, and Italian influences.
- □ Provinces known as "cantons."
- □ Proud of independence, high standard of living, history.
- □ Punctuality and overall courtesy highly valued.
- □ Conservative and dislike displays of wealth.
- □ Virtually every male serves in the military defense force.
- □ Impersonal gifts like flowers and candy popular.
- □ Common toast is simply "To your health."
- □ Good topics: sports, Swiss heritage, travel, politics.
- □ Bad topics: questions about age, job, family, diets.

Turkish

- □ Conservative in dress.
- □ Make appointments well in advance and be punctual.

- □ Most businesspeople speak English, French, or German.
- □ Business meetings begin with extensive small talk.
- □ Turkish hospitality generous, sincere, sometimes almost overwhelming.
- □ Consider a casual "We must have lunch" as sincere and real.
- □ To say "no," raises chin, shuts eyes, and tilts head backward.
- □ Most common form of entertainment: restaurant dining.
- □ Good topics: families, professions, hobbies.
- □ Bad topics: politics, communism, the Cyprus-Greece conflict

West Germans

- □ Firm handshakes (often one pump) the rule.
- □ Never use first names until invited.
- □ Rank important in business dealings.
- □ Punctuality extremely important.
- □ Full name: the Federal Republic of Germany.
- □ Most appreciative of American military support.
- □ Proud of economic renaissance.
- □ Northern Germans more quiet and reserved.
- □ Southern Germans more gregarious.
- □ Hands in pockets when conversing impolite.
- □ Answer the phone by stating their names.
- □ Discuss business after a meal; breakfast meetings are out.
- □ When eating, don't place your hands in your lap.
- □ Good topics: autos, soccer, good food.
- □ Bad topics: references to World War II, American sports.

Yugoslavians

- □ Greetings will be the customary handshake, also extended when leaving.
- □ Generally punctual.
- □ Offer business guests coffee, tea, maybe a drink and snack.
- □ More open in discussing political views.
- □ May ask personal questions: Married? What work do you do?
- □ More knowledgable than their neighbors about Western world.

- ☐ Good topics: lifestyles in United States, sports, family, fashion.
- ☐ Bad topics: religion and particularly sensitive politics.

AFRICA

It is first important to recognize there are three subdivisions of this continent: South Africa, the black African countries, and the northern nations that are generally grouped around the Mediterranean Sea. As for protocol and etiquette, the northern African nations follow Arabic or Muslim customs, while the middle nations are oriented to black multicultures, and South Africa has Dutch, English, and tribal black African influences.

In the Muslim portion, where the Muslim religion is practiced, there are several extremely important customs that apply throughout that region. To learn what they are, jump ahead to the section on The Middle East, (p. 183).

Algerians

- ☐ Handshaking common, on both meeting and leaving.
- ☐ Cheek kissing (both cheeks) done among close friends.
- ☐ First names not used in business discussions.
- ☐ Professional titles widely used.
- ☐ Punctuality somewhat relaxed.
- ☐ Business discussions begin with small talk.
- ☐ Small gifts may be exchanged during second business visits.
- ☐ Good topics: industrialization and agrarian reforms.
- ☐ Bad topics: politics and economic problems.

Egyptians

- ☐ Normal work week Saturday through Thursday.
- ☐ In the Muslim world, Friday is the day of rest.
- ☐ Friendship and trust come before any business relationship.
- ☐ Social engagements usually held late in the day.
- ☐ Good topics: history, national advancements, antiquity.
- ☐ Bad topics: Mid-East politics.

Ghanians

- □ Notable for having diverse ethnic groups within the country.
- □ Difficult to pinpoint specific, common customs.
- □ Shaking hands the common form of greeting.
- □ Probably observe Western rules for punctuality, but at home, punctuality very relaxed.
- □ Avoid gestures with the left hand.

Ivory Coast

- □ Official name *Cote d'Ivoire.*
- □ A former French colony, with that influence.
- □ Traditional handshaking the custom.
- □ Official language French, but English very common.
- □ Make appointments well in advance; be punctual but don't be surprised if your guest is not punctual.
- □ Good topics: achievements, history, culture.
- □ Bad topics: politics, inefficiency of industries.

Kenyans

- □ Call them "KEN-yans," not "KEEN-yans."
- □ Swahili the most common language, but English well known.
- □ As a former English colony, many English traits common.
- □ Shake hands at greetings and departures.
- □ Flowers usually express condolences.
- □ Good topics: Kenyan track stars, history, culture, wildlife.
- □ Bad topics: British occupation period, Mau-Mau period.

Libyans

- □ Economy almost entirely state-controlled.
- □ Political relationship with West very tense, even warlike.
- □ Strong militaristic and religious attitudes.
- □ In all other respects, Libyans are like other Mid-Easterners.

Moroccans

- □ Shaking hands customary.
- □ Good friends—male and female—kiss cheeks.
- □ Punctuality relaxed.

- □ Admire an object and you may receive it as a gift.
- □ Good topics: history, culture.
- □ Bad topics: Mid-East tension, religious zeal.

Mozambiquens

- □ First names rarely used.
- □ Professional titles should be used.
- □ Good topics: history, culture.
- □ Bad topics: politics, regional disputes.

Nigerians

- □ Important to recognize variety of customs and cultures.
- □ Diverse life-styles.
- □ Avoid discussing religion.
- □ O.K. to discuss African politics.

Senegalese

- □ Shake hands when introduced.
- □ Relaxed attitude toward punctuality.
- □ Muslim practices common.
- □ Good topics: national achievements, and culture.
- □ Bad topics: politics, religion, government leaders.

South Africans

- □ White culture (17 percent of the population) derived from Dutch/English settlers.
- □ Proud of accomplishments.
- □ Whites sensitive and defensive about apartheid.
- □ Punctuality expected.
- □ Proud of role as a world source for essential minerals.
- □ Almost all speak English, but Afrikaans official language.
- □ Majority population black, with many tribal languages.
- □ Good topics: all sports, natural beauties and resources of South Africa.
- □ Bad topics: racial unrest, boycotts.

Tanzanians

- □ Shaking hands the prevailing custom for greeting.
- □ Small gifts often exchanged in business situations.

- □ Good topics: Tanzanian parks, African culture.
- □ Bad topics: politics.

Ugandans

- □ Punctuality important.
- □ Handshaking common.
- □ Guests will probably bring small gifts for a hostess.
- □ Most topics can be discussed freely.
- □ Most common topics: world affairs and arts.

Zambians

- □ Shaking hands with the left supporting the right common.
- □ Use courtesy or professional titles.
- □ When dining, Zambians may ask for food; it is impolite not to.
- □ Improper to refuse food.
- □ Gifts should not be given to government officials.
- □ For others, small gifts of modest value acceptable.
- □ Avoid discussing Zambian politics or economic problems but O.K. to discuss international politics.

THE MIDDLE EAST

There are certain, extremely important customs you should learn regarding this intriguing part of the world. They include:

- □ Devout Muslims never drink alcohol and dietary rules are important (see Chapter 3, Dining).
- □ Eat only with the right hand because the left hand is used for bodily hygiene and considered "unclean." (When handing out business cards or giving business gifts it is best to use only the right hand.)
- □ Women usually have second-class status. Muslim men are embarrassed when women cross their legs or show off their bodies in any way.
- □ Middle Easterners are more of a touching culture, meaning they will stand closer than Americans are accustomed, touch arms, and even hold hands for short periods.
- □ They are generous and may bring you expensive gifts.

◻ Take care about admiring possessions like, say, a briefcase because your guest may immediately insist that you accept it as a gift.

◻ Middle Easterners may also toy with small sets of beads, which are *not* like a Catholic rosary, but instead are "worry beads." In other words, they are a form of relaxation and therapy, nothing more.

◻ In many Middle Eastern countries, the business work week ends on a Thursday, with Friday being the day of rest. Business affairs then resume on Saturday.

◻ A devout Muslim is required to pray five times daily: sunrise, three times during the day, and at sunset. They must face Mecca while praying. Often they are given dispensations when traveling abroad, but you might discretely inquire if they would like times set aside for personal prayers. If they say yes, then arrange for a quiet, private room and politely indicate which direction is East.

◻ Many Middle-Easterners will frequently say, "God willing" or as it is said in Arabic, *Inshallah.* In our parlance, this is comparable to saying "Well, I hope so." and therefore it is used often.

◻ It is impolite to sit in any position where you might show the sole of your shoe to your guest.

Gulf Residents

◻ Unofficial designation; refers to five separate states: Bahrain, Kuwait, Oman, Qatar, and United Arab Emirates.

◻ Important to know political and cultural differences of each.

◻ Customary greeting is *salaam alaykum.*

◻ Shaking hands and saying *kaif halak* comes next.

◻ A touching society, so be prepared.

◻ Punctuality important.

◻ Live on the "Arabian Gulf" not the "Persian Gulf."

◻ Good topics: horses, falcons, families.

◻ Bad topics: politics, religion, male-oriented society.

Iran

◻ Handshaking and slight bow is the customary greeting.

◻ Divided into "anti-West" and "pro-West."

- ☐ Most who visit United States in "pro-West" category.
- ☐ Farsi is the official language.
- ☐ Most are devout and far right Muslims.
- ☐ West-oriented businesspeople good negotiators.
- ☐ Good topics: ancient history and culture.
- ☐ Bad topics: current unrest and antipathy to United States.

Iraq

- ☐ Greetings are similar to other Mid-East nations.
- ☐ Punctuality flexible.
- ☐ When entertained, alcohol more common.
- ☐ Good topics: ancient history and culture of Iraq.
- ☐ Bad topics: Iran-Iraq war, other politics.

Jordan

- ☐ Greetings a mixture of Western and Middle-Eastern.
- ☐ Usually bring warm feelings for America.
- ☐ May refuse invitations twice before accepting.
- ☐ Dislike high-pressure business techniques.
- ☐ Punctuality relaxed.
- ☐ Good topics: history, culture, families, the King.
- ☐ Bad topics: relationships with Israel, other politics.

Lebanese

- ☐ Punctuality not especially important.
- ☐ About half are Christian, and half Muslim.
- ☐ Descended from early world traders: the Phoenicians.
- ☐ Will probably want to talk business only after a meal.
- ☐ Hospitality an unspoken rule among Lebanese.
- ☐ English, French, and Arabic the common languages.
- ☐ Before the civil wars, they were the Swiss of the Mid-East.
- ☐ Good topics: business, children, education.
- ☐ Bad topics: politics, religion, sex, Israeli relations.

Saudi Arabians

- ☐ Greetings can be elaborate.
- ☐ Handshaking may be accompanied by touching arm or shoulder.
- ☐ After several visits, men may even embrace in greeting.

□ Enjoy giving luxury gifts.

□ Are usually the strictest about religion and dietary rules.

□ Men bring wives to the United States but they're unseen in Saudi.

□ Like to develop long, close business friendships.

□ Dislike U.S. business custom of changing sales/marketing representatives.

□ Dislike dogs as household pets.

□ Good topics: history, culture, respect for Islamic faith.

□ Bad topics: any blasphemy, Israel, role of women, blue jokes.

Syria

□ Handshaking and embracing common greetings.

□ Women friends kiss cheeks.

□ Relaxed about punctuality.

□ Appreciate respect for their history and culture.

□ Avoid conversations on Mid-East politics and alignments.

United Arab Emirates

□ A country comprised of seven sheikdoms: Abua Dhabi, Dubai, Sharjah, Ras al-Khaimah, Alman, Umm al-Qaiwain, and Fujairah.

□ Important to recognize separate leaders in each.

□ Customs and protocol similar to other Mid-East countries.

THE PACIFIC AND ASIA

This is one of the most diverse regions of the world, however there are still some generalizations that withstand the test of diversity. Here are a few of them:

□ Style is often equal to, or more important than substance. This is especially true in Japan, but also among all the others there is an exquisite sense of politeness and patience. The role of personal friendships cannot be overemphasized. Losing face, which in American terms simply means to be embarrassed, is another taboo. Do nothing that might possibly embarrass your Oriental guest.

☐ English is either spoken or being studied in every country in the Asian crescent. They are diligently learning American customs and protocol, so be prepared to run into a sometimes surprising overlapping of behavior. For example, the Japanese normally give what we would consider a mild, even weak handshake because to grip firmly is considered aggressive in their culture. However, the Japanese have become eager learners and are adopting Western ways. Consequently, you might find some Japanese who'll give you a handshake so vigorous you'll think you're on some American used-car lot.

Australians

☐ Called by some "Chicagoans with an accent."
☐ Warm, friendly, and informal.
☐ Firm handshakes prevail.
☐ Speak frankly and directly; they dislike pretensions.
☐ Dislike class structure and distinctions. Example: If alone, may sit in front with the taxi driver.
☐ Value close personal friendships.
☐ Use the word "Mate" often.
☐ Know much about the United States but feel we know little of them.
☐ Will not shy away from disagreement.
☐ Appreciate punctuality.
☐ Have good sense of humor, even in tense situations.

Bangladesh

☐ Men shake hands, but women merely nod.
☐ Hindus, in the minority, greet with palms held in prayer.
☐ Most businesspeople speak English.
☐ Punctuality highly regarded.
☐ Originally part of Pakistan.
☐ Heavily Muslim.
☐ Use the right hand for eating.
☐ The "thumbs up" gesture is considered rude.
☐ In conversation, avoid criticizing the country or government.
☐ Business travelers enjoy talking about travel and professions

Chinese (People's Republic of China)

- □ In China when meeting, a nod or bow may be sufficient, however, here they may offer their hand for handshaking.
- □ Seniority and rank both very important when hosting.
- □ Dual-language business cards recommended.
- □ Usually have three names; first one is the family name.
- □ May ask very personal questions: income, value of your home.
- □ Have difficulty saying no.
- □ Any type of touching uncommon—hugging, back-patting.
- □ Toasting common, as is applauding even simplest acts.
- □ Among businesspeople, personal relationships important.
- □ Gifts should be kept modest, or give one gift to a group.
- □ Avoid talking about Taiwan.
- □ Good topics: history, culture, family, progress in China.
- □ Bad topics: cultural revolution, sex, wealth, politics.

Chinese (Hong Kong)

- □ Largest free market in the world, it reverts to China in 1997.
- □ Strong British influence because of 100-year-rule.
- □ English spoken by all businesspeople.
- □ Handshaking is the customary greeting.
- □ Chinese may have three names; first one the family name.
- □ Some Chinese have adopted Western first names.
- □ Politeness, humility, and grace appreciated and respected.
- □ Do nothing to cause embarrassment.
- □ Not a touching society, so avoid hugs or holding arms.
- □ Winking or beckoning with the index finger considered rude.
- □ Good topics: food, families, hobbies, travel.
- □ Bad topics: politics on mainland China and the 1997 take-over, although these are difficult to avoid.

Chinese (Taiwanese or Republic of China)

- □ Taiwan a province of the mainland before 1949 revolution.
- □ Inhabited by Nationalist Chinese.
- □ Refer to the "other" China as "Mainland China."
- □ Very friendly to Westerners and most speak English.

- □ Dual-language business cards are frequently exchanged.
- □ Most businesspeople have adopted English surnames.
- □ Patience, humility, and respect are highly valued traits.
- □ Close personal friendships valued in business.
- □ Toasting common and "Kam-pie" means "bottoms up."
- □ Gift-giving common, and they may present expensive gifts.
- □ Good topics: Chinese antiquities stored in Taiwan, food, and art.
- □ Bad topics: politics, trade friction, smuggling.

Fijians

- □ Greet one another with a smile and raised eyebrows.
- □ But handshaking common with all others.
- □ "Respectful friendliness" goes a long way, say Fijians.
- □ Punctuality respected but life's pace slower there.
- □ Good topics: personal experiences, culture, history.
- □ Bad topics: displays of intellect frowned upon.

Filipino (The Philippines)

- □ Handshaking common with maybe even a pat on the back.
- □ English the language of business, government, education.
- □ American practices prevail in business and when hosting.
- □ May send a small gift to a hostess following a dinner.
- □ Easy to entertain, they smile, are warm and friendly.
- □ May have anti-American feelings.
- □ Good topics: family, culture, history, business.
- □ Bad topics: politics, religion, corruption, foreign aid.

Indians

- □ Men shake hands with one another.
- □ When greeting a woman, put palms together and bow slightly.
- □ Hindus do not eat beef and the cow is a sacred animal.
- □ Great respect shown elders.
- □ Muslims usually follow their strict dietary rules.
- □ Orthodox Sikhs wear a turban, don't smoke, or eat beef.
- □ Use your right hand for passing food.
- □ Many British colonial customs still prevail.

- Good topics: culture, tradition, other people, and travel.
- Bad topics: personal matters, poverty, foreign aid.

Indonesians

- Handshaking and a nod of the head customary greetings.
- Punctuality important.
- Respect for the individual a trait of their society.
- Business dealings may be long and slow by U.S. standards.
- Impolite to refuse a gift.
- Good topics: history, culture, tradition.
- Bad topics: local politics, socialism, and foreign aid.

Japanese

- Adopting Western customs quickly.
- Pleasing to them when a host exhibits their protocol.
- Business cards exchanged before bowing or handshaking.
- A bow the traditional greeting; the lower the better.
- Handshaking common, but it may seem like a weak grip.
- Impolite to have long or frequent eye-to-eye contact.
- First names rarely used.
- The personal side of business extremely important.
- Style just as important as substance.
- Patience, politeness, and humility great virtues.
- Gift-giving ingrained in the culture; be prepared.
- Phrase questions so they can be answered with "yes."
- Harmony important, so the word "no" is shunned.
- Good topics: history, culture, art.
- Bad topics: avoid discussing World War II; anything that will embarrass.

Malaysians

- Either "Malaysians" or "Malays" correct.
- Predominant ethnic group Malay, then Chinese and Indian.
- Handshaking common when they visit the West.
- Among themselves, they hold palms outward and touch fingers.
- English commonly spoken but second to Malaysian.
- Touching uncommon, especially the top of one's head.

- □ Never beckon someone with the curled index finger.
- □ Use the right hand to eat, touch people, or things.
- □ Don't clear your throat or blow your nose while dining.
- □ In business, decision-making slow.
- □ Good topic: your guest's business or social achievements.
- □ Bad topic: comparing standards of living with the West.

New Zealanders

- □ Handshaking the customary greeting.
- □ Formality may rule at first, but then ease off.
- □ Make good guests because they are frank yet friendly.
- □ Dislike being identified as being Australians.
- □ Loud speech considered rude and irritating.
- □ Napkins called *serviettes*; a napkin is a diaper.
- □ Rank in business minimized; they prefer equality.
- □ Good topics: rugby, cricket—anything about New Zealand.
- □ Bad topics: personal questions, religion, nuclear energy.

Pakistanis

- □ The common greeting a handshake, though close friends may hug.
- □ Men usually do not shake hands with or touch women.
- □ Refrain from using first names, until invited.
- □ Islamic code of conduct prevails.
- □ English common but Urdu the major language.
- □ Names complicated, so study carefully or simply ask.
- □ Staring fairly common in this culture.
- □ Showing the soles of your shoes is a rude gesture.
- □ Good topics: culture, history and Pakistani crafts.
- □ Bad topics: criticizing Islam, discussing India or Israel.

Samoans

- □ Before business meetings, formal greetings exchanged.
- □ Samoans can be very eloquent.
- □ Exchanging gifts common.
- □ Avoid pointing your legs toward the center of the room.
- □ Good topics: culture and history.
- □ Bad topics: American aid and political dominance.

Singaporeans

- □ Western-style handshaking the custom.
- □ Business cards presented respectfully with two hands.
- □ Take special care with name pronunciations.
- □ Punctuality prized.
- □ All speak English even though the heritage Chinese.
- □ Pride taken in being practical, straight and to the point.
- □ Unlike the Japanese, gift-giving uncommon in business.
- □ Business lunches can be long and informal.
- □ Unlike other Asian countries, power breakfasts common.
- □ Blunt questions may be asked, such as "How much do you earn?"
- □ Virtually a nonsmoking society.
- □ American negotiating methods considered pushy.
- □ Women treated as equals in business.
- □ Good topics: clean, economically healthy country.
- □ Bad topics: being disrespectful over the country's size.

South Koreans

- □ Men bow slightly and shake hands, sometimes with two hands.
- □ Women refrain from shaking hands.
- □ Family names come first, then the surname.
- □ The open mouth considered rude; cover it when laughing.
- □ Impolite to blow your nose in public.
- □ Women play secondary roles in their society.
- □ Patience, humility, and respect for age are important traits.
- □ Business entertainment important and extensive.
- □ Solo or group singing a tradition after dinner.
- □ Called "The Irishmen of the Oriental world."
- □ Good topics: culture, history, the successful Olympic Games.
- □ Bad topics: political unrest, secondary role of women.

Sri Lankans

- □ Handshaking the common form of greeting.
- □ Punctuality respected.
- □ Tea the national drink.

- □ Country originally called Ceylon; now pronounced "SHREE-lanka."
- □ Different castes have different religious restrictions.
- □ Predominant ethnic group the Sinhalese (Buddhists).
- □ Minority group the Tamils (Hindus).
- □ Smoking during introductions considered impolite.
- □ English commonly spoken.
- □ The left hand considered unclean.
- □ Nodding your head means "no"; shaking it means "yes."
- □ Good topics: hobbies, families, schools, history, culture.
- □ Bad topics: ethnic frictions, caste system, religion, sex.

Thais (Thailand)

- □ Putting palms in a prayer position is the Thai greeting.
- □ In the West, Thais will adopt the handshake.
- □ First names used frequently.
- □ You may be addressed as "Mr. Bob" or "Mr. Tom."
- □ Displays of both temper and affection in public are bad.
- □ Western humor and sarcasm often misunderstood.
- □ Be patient. Businesspeople take a long time to decide.
- □ Never point to anything using your foot, or show your sole.
- □ Don't pat a Thai on the head.
- □ Good topics: culture, history, Thai food.
- □ Bad topics: criticizing politics, the Royal Family, or religion.

CENTRAL AND SOUTH AMERICA

The first rule when entertaining Latins is to recognize that there are some 40 different countries south of the Rio Grande River. This means there are important and distinct differences within this major region of the world. But there are also some common habits and similarities, so let's begin with them:

□ All of them speak Spanish, except in Brazil where the national language is Portuguese.

□ In all Latin countries, the attitude toward time is less rigid than among North Americans and a 30 minute delay should not be a surprise. In fact, among close associates, it is recommended that, when setting times for appointments or pick-ups, ask *"la hora inglesa, o la hora espanol?"* This means "the English hour" (meaning

"Promptly at the time specified?") or "the Latin hour" (meaning "If I say 7 o'clock, don't be surprised if I don't show up until 7:30 or even later").

□ Latins will usually stand closer together during conversations, so be prepared for that plus casual touching and, of course, the *abrazo*, or embrace, among good friends. You may even be startled to have a Latin businessman hold your elbow while conversing, or walk down the street arm-in-arm.

□ Latins are warm and friendly people and enjoy social conversation before getting down to business. This is a calculated process aimed at getting to know you personally. Latins tend to be more interested in you, the person, than you as a representative of some faceless corporation.

□ The main meal of the day is usually taken at midday throughout all Latin American countries. However, this should not deter you from also hosting your business guests over dinner in the evening. Most Latin businesspeople know about American dining customs and, indeed, in their own country will entertain in the evening at a restaurant for special occasions. When toasting, the host customarily is expected to make the first toast with the guest then probably responding.

Argentines

□ Handshaking common when meeting for the first time.
□ Titles important.
□ Italian and German the second and third languages.
□ Strong Italian, German, British, and Spanish heritage.
□ Tender beef and red wine virtual national symbols.
□ American beef and red wine compare poorly to theirs.
□ Long meals and conversation the norm.
□ Crossing the knife and fork signal "I am finished."
□ Never pour wine back-handed; it's considered impolite.
□ Good topics: soccer, history, culture, home and children.
□ Bad topics: the Peron years, religion, Falkland Islands conflict.

Belizeans

□ Formerly British Honduras, now Belize.
□ Handshaking customary.

- An exception: Punctuality practiced in business.
- English the official language but Spanish common.
- Titles important.
- Refusing food considered impolite.
- Pushing the plate forward indicates "I am finished."
- Good topics: Mayan culture, coral reefs and jungle in Belize.
- Bad topics: religion, politics and race.

Bolivians

- Shaking hands the customary greeting.
- Direct eye-contact important during conversations.
- Titles important.
- Midday the time for the main meal.
- Tea and cakes common around 4:00 and repeated at 9:00.
- When a full evening meal is taken, it may be around 9:00.
- Bolivia has the highest everything: airport, lake, capital.
- Good topics: auto racing, soccer, families and food.
- Bad topics: poverty, Chile, and other political subjects.

Brazilians

- Handshaking, often for a long time, is common.
- Shake hands for hello and good-bye; use good eye contact.
- Touching arms and elbows and backs very common.
- First names used often, but titles important.
- Music and long, animated conversation favorite habits.
- When conversing, interruptions viewed as enthusiasm.
- Enjoy joking, informality, and friendships.
- The "O.K." hand signal a rude gesture in Brazil.
- Midday the normal time for the main meal.
- A light meal common at night, unless entertaining formally.
- American coffee is a mere shadow of Brazilian coffee.
- In Brazil, restaurant entertainment prevails versus at home.
- Good topics: politics, soccer, family, and children.
- Bad topics: Argentina, politics, poverty, religion.

Chileans

- With first introductions, a handshake is the custom.
- Close friends hug and rub cheeks.

- ☐ In business, punctuality respected.
- ☐ Light conversation customary before business discussions.
- ☐ Men customarily wear suits and ties for social events.
- ☐ Don't serve wine with your left hand.
- ☐ Wines, especially white wines, a national pride.
- ☐ Women have advanced in the professions in Chile.
- ☐ Good topics: families, children, Easter Island, history.
- ☐ Bad topics: politics, human rights, 1988 grape export scare.

Colombians

- ☐ Handshaking the customary greeting in business.
- ☐ Among friends, expect the *abrazo*.
- ☐ Punctuality relaxed.
- ☐ Businesspeople prefer relaxed conversation before business.
- ☐ Titles are respected.
- ☐ People with university degrees can be called "Doctor."
- ☐ Impolite to yawn in public.
- ☐ Bullfighting popular; don't make negative comments.
- ☐ Good topics: history, culture, soccer, coffee, gold museum.
- ☐ Bad topics: drug traffic, politics, religion.

Costa Ricans

- ☐ Handshaking the common greeting.
- ☐ *Abrazos* not as common as in other Latin countries.
- ☐ Titles important and respected.
- ☐ Call themselves *Ticos* (TEE-kos).
- ☐ Gifts frequently exchanged on special occasions.
- ☐ Politics freely discussed because of stability there.
- ☐ Businesspeople are more formal and serious than other Latins.
- ☐ Women active in business.
- ☐ Good topics: children, history, art.
- ☐ Bad topics: any personal criticism, religion.

Ecuadorians

- ☐ Handshaking common when arriving and when leaving.
- ☐ Men friends embrace and women friends kiss.

- □ Relations with neighbor Peru have always been strained.
- □ A girl's fifteenth birthday extremely important.
- □ Midday the customary time for the main meal.
- □ A famous part of Ecuador are the Galapagos Islands.
- □ Good topics: family, culture, history.
- □ Bad topics: politics, U.S. political influence.

El Salvadorians

- □ Handshaking the usual form of greeting.
- □ Some people merely nod when meeting.
- □ Titles, especially among the elderly, very important.
- □ Touching more common here than in the United States.
- □ Some will insist they are "Americans" as well.
- □ Small gifts often exchanged.
- □ Good topics: history, geography, culture, families.
- □ Bad topics: local politics, religion.

Guatemalans

- □ Shaking hands and saying "mucho gusto" very proper.
- □ Handshake may seem limp, which is customary.
- □ Close friends embrace and pat each other's back.
- □ Titles very important.
- □ The Indian culture exists here more than elsewhere.
- □ Speaking softly considered the polite thing to do.
- □ Male guests sit to the right of the host; women to the left.
- □ Businesspeople usually punctual.
- □ Social conversation before business the custom.
- □ Business discussed at lunch and even breakfast.
- □ Good topics: Guatemalan geography, history, culture.
- □ Bad topics: politics or "the violence" since 1978.

Hondurans

- □ Handshaking the custom.
- □ Close acquaintances often greet with a hearty hug.
- □ *Machismo*—the idea that men are superior—prevails.
- □ Titles and family names used rather than first names.
- □ Hondurans are known for their gracious hospitality.
- □ Gifts not necessary, but token ones for women are nice.

- □ Good topics: Honduran history, culture, families.
- □ Bad topics: Current unrest and internal politics.

Mexicans

- □ Handshaking the custom.
- □ Longtime friends may embrace; women kiss the cheek.
- □ Punctuality not rigid.
- □ The midday meal the main one, taken about 1:00 to 4:00.
- □ Purple the color of death.
- □ Mexicans tire of hearing jokes about "Montezuma's revenge."
- □ Refrain from using first names until invited to do so.
- □ Titles important.
- □ Hands on hips suggest aggressiveness.
- □ Hands in pockets impolite.
- □ Mexicans refer to people from the United States as North Americans.
- □ While there is pride in Indian ancestry, don't dwell on it.
- □ Good topics: Mexican culture, history, art, museums.
- □ Bad topics: illegal aliens, earthquakes, poverty.

Nicaraguans

- □ When greeting, smile, shake hands, and use a Spanish phrase.
- □ The concept of *machismo* prevails.
- □ Dinner guests may bring small gifts, like flowers or candy.
- □ Approach politics warily; the country is split.
- □ There is a long, long history of unrest and disruption.
- □ Many respect and love the United States; others see us as an enemy.
- □ Good topics: family, history, culture.
- □ Bad topics: poverty, politics, religion.

Panamanians

- □ Handshaking the custom. Old friends embrace.
- □ Titles important.
- □ Spanish the official language but English very common.
- □ In business, conversations begin with much small talk.

- ☐ Panamanian women taking more and more managerial jobs.
- ☐ Gifts normally not exchanged when entertaining.
- ☐ The host sits at the head of the table opposite the guest.
- ☐ Good topics: family, hobbies, basketball, baseball.
- ☐ Bad topics: former Canal Zone, race problems, politics.

Paraguayans

- ☐ Handshakes and "mucho gusto" the custom.
- ☐ Good friends embrace; women kiss cheeks.
- ☐ Close friends may walk arm-in-arm.
- ☐ People stand close together when having conversations.
- ☐ Titles important to remember and use.
- ☐ Don't eat many vegetables.
- ☐ In business, decision-making may be a slow process.
- ☐ Good topics: family, sports, current events.
- ☐ Bad topics: local politics.

Peruvians

- ☐ Handshaking at greeting and parting customary.
- ☐ Embracing (*abrazo*) common among good friends.
- ☐ Titles important.
- ☐ The main meal of the day usually at midday.
- ☐ Tend to be more formal and conservative.
- ☐ Great pride in the Incan and Spanish heritage.
- ☐ The ruins at Machu Picchu are a national treasure.
- ☐ A gift of flowers appropriate for any occasion.
- ☐ Only a bullfight requires absolute punctuality.
- ☐ Dinner often taken after 9:00 P.M.
- ☐ It is polite, in Peru, to arrive 30 minutes late for dinner.
- ☐ Politeness requires eating everything on the plate.
- ☐ Good topics: families, culture, geography—a wide variety.
- ☐ Bad topics: politics, religion, racial prejudices.

Uruguayans

- ☐ Handshaking the usual way of greeting.
- ☐ First names used only among close friends.
- ☐ Titles important.
- ☐ Meetings tend to be formal but rarely start on time.

- □ Guests often send flowers or candy to a hostess.
- □ A European culture has been inherited here.
- □ Spanish the official language.
- □ Beef common fare for all meals in Uruguay.
- □ Good topics: history, culture, all sports—especially soccer.
- □ Bad topics: politics and Communism.

Venezuelans

- □ Handshaking by both sexes common and customary.
- □ Good friends hug and women kiss cheeks.
- □ People tend to stand very close together when conversing.
- □ Businesspeople punctual and small talk minimal.
- □ Titles important.
- □ Guests may bring or send flowers or candy to a hostess.
- □ The orchid is the national flower.
- □ In their country, guests rarely sit at the head of a table.
- □ Good topics: business, art, literature, history.
- □ Bad topics: local unrest, inflation, politics.

THE CARIBBEAN

The Caribbean is a polyglot of races, languages and cultures. It consists of independent countries as well as territories. Political associations range from Great Britain, to Holland, to France to the United States. It is therefore difficult to offer substantive tips about each and every country. James Michener's book, *Caribbean*, is an excellent resource in this area.

Following are some general comments on greetings, protocol and conversation, followed by specifics on Haitians and Puerto Ricans:

General Comments about Residents of the Caribbean

- □ The handshake is the common and customary form of greeting.
- □ English prevails but Spanish, French and Dutch are found.
- □ Table manners are informal.

- □ A more relaxed pace is practiced compared to the United States.
- □ Punctuality is not closely adhered to in this region.
- □ Business often begins with extended social conversation.
- □ Exchanging of gifts is not required or customary.
- □ Business cards are always important and used extensively.
- □ The main meal of the day is generally taken at midday.
- □ Good topics: weather, tourist business, economy.
- □ Bad topics: local politics, religion, racial conflicts.

Haitians

- □ Handshaking the customary greeting.
- □ French and the Creole dialect commonly spoken.
- □ Casualness and informality prevail.
- □ Per capita, the poorest nation in the Hemisphere.
- □ Good topics: food, local art, weather, culture.
- □ Bad topics: local politics, refugees in America.

Puerto Ricans

- □ Handshaking prevails as the customary greeting.
- □ Good friends embrace.
- □ Standing close customary; backing away impolite.
- □ Gifts often exchanged and opened on the spot.
- □ Polite to decline a gift at first.
- □ English spoken freely and fluently.
- □ Speaking some Spanish phrases appreciated.
- □ Object to open criticism, pushiness, and greed.
- □ Good topics: cultural heritage, rapid economic growth.
- □ Bad topics: statehood can be a hotly debated subject.

APPENDIX

RELIGIONS OF THE WORLD

A short, general description of each of the major religions of the world is given, followed by a country-by-country listing showing the predominant religions for each.

As a host, this information will be useful in your conversation and general hosting of any international guest.

Islam and Muslims

The Arabic word Islam means peace, submission, and obedience. The religion of Islam is the complete acceptance of the teachings and guidance of God as revealed to His Prophet Muhammad. A Muslim (or Moslem) is one who believes in God and strives for total reorganization of his life according to His revealed guidance and the sayings of the Prophet. "Muhammadanism" is a misnomer for Islam and offends its very spirit. The word "Allah" is the proper name of God in Arabic. It is a unique term because it has no plural or feminine gender. The Koran (or Quran) is the holy book of Islam and contains doctrines and teachings of Islam. There are five basic teachings of the Islamic faith, called "the five pillars": (1) Declaration of faith, (2) Prayers five times daily, (3) Fasting from sunrise to sunset during the month of Ramadhan (which varies from month to month by the Western calendar), (4) almsgiving or tithing, and (5) the pilgrimage to Mecca once during a lifetime, if it can be afforded financially and physically. There are two different sects composing the Islamic world: the Sunni Muslims and the Shi'ite Muslims. The majority group, the Sunni's, are generally found in the Arab states, Africa, India and Indonesia. The Shi'ites mainly inhabit Lebanon, Iraq, and the Arabian Gulf.

Hindu

Found predominantly in India, Hindu belief rests on the qualities of acceptance, tranquility, reincarnation, and transmigration. The entire religion relates to problems that are especially serious in the Indian environment, and so the actual practice of Hinduism varies from village to village. One especially distinguishing characteristic is the religion's interest in techniques of self-examination and control allowing believers to be in harmony with the world. The Hindu believes in the flow of life through many existences.

Buddhism

Buddhism is the thought and practice associated with Shakyamuni, the Buddha who lived in India in the 6th and 5th centuries B.C. Buddhist thinking does not center around a person, but rather focuses on the idea of teaching. The core of the Buddhist philosophy, or the Four Noble Truths, is the knowledge of suffering, the origin of suffering, the destruction of suffering, and how to extinguish suffering. There is a distinct emphasis on suffering and pain that is strongly linked to healing.

Shintoism

Common to the Japanese islands, the Shinto religion is a national religion based fundamentally on each individual shrine. Shinto practice is an individual matter, involving voluntary practice and observance. The principle of the life of the Japanese people, the religion is made up of the spirits, festivals, ascetic disciplines, social service, and other elements.

Taoism

A predominantly Asian religion, the aim of Taoism is to achieve harmony with all that is, by pursuing inaction and effortlessness. There is a quest for freedom as the Taoist turns away from society to the contemplation of nature, seeking fulfillment in the spontaneous and "trans-ethical." The ultimate goal of the Taoist is to become an immortal.

Animism

The belief that a spirit is active in aspects of the environment. Animism is most common in African countries.

Judaism

Judaism is based on the revelation of God to Moses on Mt. Sinai and on God's giving of the law. The Jews believe there is only one God, who is the creator and ruler of the whole world, basing their belief on the Old Testament of the Bible. The Jewish still await the coming of the Messiah.

Christianity

Descended from Judaism and the Old Testament, Christianity centers around similar beliefs with few changes. The significance of Jesus as the

Messiah causes Christian beliefs to be based on both the Old and New Testaments of the Bible. Jesus' birth, death and resurrection are the foundation for the religion. The Christianity movement has been subject to new thinking and interpretations, thus creating branches or off-shoots of the basic belief. The three major branches of the early church are the Eastern Orthodox (Greek, Russian, Syrian, Armenian, Coptic), the Roman Catholic, and the Protestant (Lutheran, Reformed/Presbyterian, Pentecostal, Anglican/Episcopal, Baptist, Methodist, and Free Churches.)

Table A1
Predominant Religions—Country-by-Country

AFGHANISTAN
Islam
Sunni 74%
Shi'ite 25%

ALBANIA
Nonreligious 55%
Islam 21%
Atheist 19%
Christian 5%

ALGERIA
Islam (Sunni)

ANDORRA
Roman Catholic

ANGOLA
Roman Catholic 69%
Protestant 20%
Traditional 10%

ANTIGUA & BARBUDA
Anglican and
Roman Catholic

ARGENTINA
Roman Catholic

AUSTRALIA
Roman Catholic 28%
Anglican 28%
Uniting Church 14%

AUSTRIA
Roman Catholic 89%

BAHAMAS
Baptist 29%
Anglican 23%
Roman Catholic 23%
Methodist 7%

BAHRAIN
Islam

BANGLADESH
Islam (official) 83%
Hindu 16%

BARBADOS
Anglican 70%
Methodist 9%
Roman Catholic 4%

BELGIUM
Roman Catholic 95%

BELIZE
Roman Catholic 62%
Anglican 12%
Methodist 6%
Baha'i 2.5%

BENIN
Transition 70%
Christian 15%
Islam 15%

BHUTAN
Buddhist 70%
Hindu 25%
Islam 5%

BOLIVIA
Roman Catholic 94%
Baha'i 3%

BOTSWANA
Christian 48%
Traditional 49%

BRAZIL
Roman Catholic 88%
Protestant 6%

Table A1 *(Continued)*

BRUNEI
Islam 60%
Christian 8%
Buddhist & Local 23%

BULGARIA
Atheist 65%
Eastern Orth. 27%
Islam 8%

BURKINA FASO
Animist 65%
Islam 25%
Roman Catholic 10%

BURMA
Buddhist 89%
Christian 5%
Islam 3%

BURUNDI
Roman Catholic 78%
Traditional 14%

KAMPUCHEA
Theravada Buddhist

CAMEROON
Roman Catholic 35%
Animist 12%
Islam 35%
Protestant 18%

CANADA
Roman Catholic 47%
Protestant 41%
No Religion 7%
Eastern Orth. 2%

CAPE VERDE
Protestant 41%

CENTRAL AFRICAN REPUBLIC
Protestant 33%
Roman Catholic 50%
Animist 5%
Islam 3%

CHAD
Islam 44%
Christian 33%
Traditional 23%

CHILE
Roman Catholic 90%

CHINA (PEOPLES REPUBLIC)
Non-Religious 59%
Folk Religions 20%
Atheist 12%

COLOMBIA
Roman Catholic

COMOROS
Islam

CONGO
Traditional 48%
Christian 47%
Islam 2%

COSTA RICA
Roman Catholic

CUBA
Roman Catholic 49%
Non-Religious 49%
Atheist 6%

CYPRUS
Greek Orth. 76%
Islam 19%

CZECHOSLOVAKIA
Roman Catholic 67%
Atheist 29%
Czechoslovak Church 4%

DENMARK
Lutheran

DJIBOUTI
Islam (Sunni) 94%
Christian 6%

DOMINICA
Roman Catholic
Anglican
Methodist

DOMINICAN REPUBLIC
Roman Catholic

ECUADOR
Roman Catholic 92%

EGPYT
Islam 93%
Christian 7%

EL SALVADOR
Roman Catholic

Table A1 (Continued)

EQUITORIAL GUINEA
  Roman Catholic
  Protestant
  Traditional

ETHIOPIA
  Ethiopian Orth. 49%
  Islam 31%
  Traditional 11%

FIJI
  Christian 50%
  Hindu 41%
  Islam 8%

FINLAND
  Lutheran 90%
  Greek Orth. 1%

FRANCE
  Roman Catholic 90%

GABON
  Roman Catholic 65%
  Protestant 19%

GAMBIA
  Islam 85%
  Christian 2%
  Traditional 11%

GDR (EAST GERMANY)
  Protestant 53%
  Roman Catholic 8%

FRG (WEST GERMANY)
  Protestant 49%
  Roman Catholic 45%

GHANA
  Christianity 63%
  Animist 21%
  Islam 16%

GREECE
  Greek Orthodox

GRENADA
  Roman Catholic 64%
  Anglican 21%

GUATEMALA
  Roman Catholic

GUINEA
  Islam 69%
  Traditional 30%

GUINEA-BISSAU
  Traditional 65%
  Islam 30%
  Christian 5%

GUYANA
  Hindu 34%
  Protestant 18%
  Islam 9%
  Roman Catholic 18%
  Anglican 16%

HAITI
  Roman Catholic 80%
  Baptist 10%

HONDURAS
  Roman Catholic

HUNGARY
  Roman Catholic 54%
  Portestant 22%
  Orthodox 7%

ICELAND
  Evangelical Lutheran

INDIA
  Hindu 83%
  Islam 11%
  Sikh 2%

INDONESIA
  Islam 87%
  Christian 10%
  Hindu/Buddhism 3%

IRAN
  Islam (Shi'ite) 93%
  Islam (Sunni) 5%

IRAQ
  Islam 96%
  Christian 4%

IRELAND (REPUBLIC OF)
  Roman Catholic 94%
  Protestant 5%

ISRAEL
  Jewish 82%
  Islam 14%
  Christian 2.3%

ITALY
  Roman Catholic 83%

Table A1 *(Continued)*

IVORY COAST
Folk Beliefs 44%
Christian 32%
Islam 24%

JAMAICA
Protestant 71%
Roman Catholic 10%
Rastafarian 7%

JAPAN
Shintoist
Buddhist

JORDAN
Islam (Sunni) 93%
Christian 5%

KENYA
Protestant 27%
Roman Catholic 26%
Traditional 19%
Islam 6%

KOREA (NORTH)
Atheist 68%
Traditional 16%

KOREA (SOUTH)
Buddhist 19%
Protestant 16%
Roman Catholic 5%

KUWAIT
Islam 92%
Christian 6%

LAOS
Buddhist 58%
Tribal 43%

LEBANON
Christian
Islam

LESOTHO
Roman Catholic 44%
Lesotho Evan. Church
Anglican

LIBERIA
Traditional 75%
Christian 10%
Islam 15%

LIBYA
Islam

LIECHTENSTEIN
Roman Catholic 86%
Protestant 9%

LUXEMBOURG
Roman Catholic

MADAGASCAR
Traditional 47%
Roman Catholic 26%
Protestant 23%

MALAWI
Christian 57%
Traditional 19%
Islam 2%

MALAYSIA
Islam 53%
Buddhism 17%
Chinese Folk Relig. 12%
Hindu 7%
Christian 6%

MALDIVES
Islam

MALI
Islam 90%
Traditional 9%
Christian 1%

MALTA
Roman Catholic

MAURITANIA
Islam

MAURITIUS
Hindu 52%
Roman Catholic 26%
Islam 13%

MEXICO
Roman Catholic 93%

MONACO
Roman Catholic

MONGOLIA
Lamaistic Buddhism

MOROCCO
Islam

Table A1 *(Continued)*

MOZAMBIQUE
   Traditional 48%
   Christian 39%
   Islam 13%

NEPAL
   Hindu 90%
   Buddhism 5%
   Islam 3%

THE NETHERLANDS
   Roman Catholic 36%
   Dutch Reformed 33%
   Unaffiliated 27%

NEW ZEALAND
   Church of England 26%
   Presbyterian 17%
   Roman Catholic 14%

NICARAGUA
   Roman Catholic 91%

NIGER
   Islam 90%
   Christian 10%

NIGERIA
   Islam 47%
   Christian 34%
   Animist 18%

NORWAY
   Evangelical Lutheran

OMAN
   Islam 86%

PAKISTAN
   Islam 97%
   Hindu
   Christian
   Buddhism

PANAMA
   Roman Catholic 89%
   Islam 5%
   Protestant 5%

PAPUA NEW GUINEA
   Protestant 64%
   Roman Catholic 33%

PARAGUAY
   Roman Catholic

PERU
   Roman Catholic

THE PHILIPPINES
   Roman Catholic 73%
   Islam 4%
   Protestant 3%

POLAND
   Roman Catholic 85%

PORTUGAL
   Roman Catholic

QATAR
   Islam 92%
   Christian 6%

ROMANIA
   Romanian Orthodox 80%
   Greek Orthodox 10%

RWANDA
   Roman Catholic 56%
   Protestant 12%
   Islam 9%
   Animist 23%

ST. LUCIA
   Roman Catholic 91%
   Anglican 3%

ST. VINCENT & THE GRENADINES
   Anglican 47%
   Methodist 28%
   Roman Catholic 13%

SAN MARINO
   Roman Catholic

SÃO TOME & PRINCIPE
   Roman Catholic
   Protestant

SAUDI ARABIA
   Islam

SENEGAL
   Islam 91%
   Christian 6%

SEYCHELLES
   Roman Catholic 90%
   Anglican 8%

Table A1 *(Continued)*

SIERRA LEONE
  Animist 52%
  Islam 40%
  Christian 9%

SINGAPORE
  Islam 15%
  Christian 10%
  Buddhism 40%
  Hindu 7%
  Taoist

SOLOMON ISLANDS
  Anglican 34%
  Roman Catholic 19%
  South Seas Evangelical 25%
  Protestant 15%

SOMLIA
  Islam (Sunni)

SOUTH AFRICA
  Dutch Reformed 40%
  Anglican 11%
  Roman Catholic 8%

NAMIBIA
  Christian
  Indigenous

SOVIET UNION
  Russian Orthodox
  Islam
  Judaism
  Lutheran
  Atheist

SPAIN
  Roman Catholic

SRI LANKA
  Buddhist 69%
  Hindu 15%
  Islam 8%
  Christian 8%

SUDAN
  Islam 73%
  Animist 18%
  Christian 9%

SURINAME
  Protestant
  Roman Catholic
  Hindu
  Islam

SWAZILAND
  Christian 77%
  Animist 27%

SWEDEN
  Swedish Lutheran 95%

SWITZERLAND
  Roman Catholic 48%
  Protestant 44%

SYRIA
  Islam 90%
  Christian 10%

TANZANIA
  Christian 40%
  Islam 30%
  Animist 30%

THAILAND
  Buddhism 95%
  Islam 4%

TOGO
  Animist 46%
  Christian 37%
  Islam 17%

TONGA
  Free Wesleyan 47%
  Roman Catholic 16%
  Hindu 25%
  Mormon 9%

TRINIDAD & TOBAGO
  Christian 64%
  Hindu 25%
  Islam 6%

TUNISIA
  Islam (Sunni) 99.4%

TURKEY
  Islam (Sunni) 99.2%

UGANDA
  Christian 63%
  Islam 6%

Table A1 *(Continued)*

UAE
  Islam
    Sunni 80%
    Shi'ite 20%

UNITED KINGDOM
  Church of England
  Church of Wales
  Church of Scotland
  Church of Ireland
  Roman Catholic
  Methodist
  Congregational
  Baptist
  Judaism

UNITED STATES
  Protestant
  Roman Catholic
  Judaism

URUGUAY
  Roman Catholic 60%

VANAUTU
  Presbyterian 47%
  Roman Catholic 15%
  Anglican 15%

VENEZUALA
  Roman Catholic

VIETNAM
  Buddhism
  Roman Catholic

Islam
Taoist
Confucian
Animist

YEMEN
  Islam (Sunni)

YEMEN ARAB REPUBLIC
  Islam
    Shi'ite 60%
    Sunni 40%

YOGOSLAVIA
  Greek Orthodox 41%
  Roman Catholic 32%
  Islam 12%

ZAIRE
  Roman Catholic 48%
  Protestant 29%
  Islam 10%

ZAMBIA
  Animist
  Roman Catholic
  Protestant

ZIMBABWE
  Christian 25%
  Animist 24%
  Syncretic 50%

TOASTS AND TOASTING AROUND THE WORLD

Nationality	Toast	Pronunciation
American	Cheers	Cheers
Austrian	Prosit	PROH-zit
Belgian (Flemish)	Op uw gezonheid	Op uv ga-ZON-hite
Bohemian	Naz Dar	Naz DAR
Brazilian	Saude or Viva	Sah-OO-Day, VEE-va
British	Cheers	Cheers
Chinese	Nien Nien Ju E	Nyen, Nyen, Zhu Ee
Czechoslovakian	Na Zdravie	Nah ZDROH-vee-yeh
Danish	Skal	Skohl
Dutch	Proost	Prohst
Egyptian	Fee Sihetak	Fee SAY-tak
Estonian	Tervist	TER-vist
Finnish	Kippis	KEE-pees
French	A Votre Sante	A Votre SAN-tay
German	Prosit	PROH-sit
Greek	Eis Igian	Ees IGEE-an
Hawaiian	Meli kalikama	Meh-lee kali-kama
Hebrew	L'chayim	Leh HAH-yim
Hungarian	Kedves Egeszegere	KED-vesh Eh-gay-say-gay-REH
Irish	Salinte	SLAHN-she
Indonesian	Selamat	Sell-a-mat
Italian	A la Salute (or) Cin cin	Ah lah Sa-LOO-tay Chin Chin
Japanese	Kampai	Kahm-PAH-ee
Korean	Kong gang ul wi ha yo	(As spelled)
Malayan	Slamat minum	Sla-mat min-um
Mexican	Salud	Sal-UUD
Norwegian	Skal	Skohl
Philippine	Mabuhay	Ma-BOO-hay
Polish	Na Zdrowie	Nahz DROH-fee-yeh
Portuguese	A sua saude	A sua SA-OO day
Russian	Na Zdorovia	Nah ZDROH-vee-ah
Scottish	Shlante	SHLAHN-tay
Spanish	Salud	Sa LUUD
Swedish	Skal	Skohl
Thai	Sawasdi	Sa-weh-do
Welsh	lechyd Da	YEH-hid Day
Yugoslavian	Na Zdravie	Nah ZDRAH-vee-yeh

WHERE ENGLISH IS SPOKEN

Is your international guest likely to speak English? Of the world's 4.8 billion people, nearly 750 million are familiar with English. English is the native tongue of barely a dozen countries, but it is widely spoken or studied in more than 90 others. A list follows of those countries where English is (1) the native language, (2) the official or semiofficial language, or (3) or, where it is studied widely.

The Native Language

English is the native language in 12 nations with 345 million people:

North America: Canada (except Quebec), United States.

South America: Guyana

Caribbean: Bahamas, Barbados, Grenada, Jamaica, Trinidad and Tobago.

Europe: Ireland, United Kingdom (England, Scotland, Wales).

Pacific: Australia, New Zealand.

Official or Semiofficial Language

In 33 other countries and Puerto Rico, English is considered an official or semiofficial language. This means it is often used in the conduct of government business. Those nations are:

Africa: Botswana, Cameroon, Ethiopia, Gambia, Ghana, Kenya, Lesotho, Liberia, Malawi, Mauritius, Namibia, Nigeria, Sierra Leone, South Africa, Sudan, Swaziland, Tanzania, Uganda, Zambia, Zimbabwe.

Asia, Pacific: Bangladesh, Burma, Fiji, India, Malaysia, Pakistan, Philippines, Singapore, Sri Lanka, Tonga, Western Samoa.

Mideast, Mediterranean: Israel, Malta.

Where English Is Studied Widely

English is required in school or studied widely in at least 56 other nations:

North America: Mexico

Central America, Caribbean: Costa Rica, Cuba, Dominican Republic, Honduras.

South America: Brazil, Colombia, Venezuela.

Europe: Austria, Belgium, Denmark, East Germany, Finland, France, Greece, Iceland, Italy, Luxembourg, Netherlands, Norway, Portugal, Romania, Soviet Union, Sweden, Switzerland, West Germany.

Africa: Algeria, Angola, Burkina Faso, Burundi, Central African Republic, Chad, Gabon, Guinea, Ivory Coast, Libya, Madagascar, Morocco, Niger, Senegal, Togo, Zaire.

Mideast: Egypt, Jordan, North Yemen, Saudi Arabia, Syria, Turkey.

Asia: Afghanistan, China, Hong Kong, Indonesia, Japan, Nepal, South Korea, Thailand.

SOURCES FOR HELP

The National Council for International Visitors (NCIV)

This Council is a network of 148 local and national nongovernmental organizations and institutions in 103 towns and cities in 41 states. Over 800,000 volunteers annually host and provide professional programs for approximately 5,000 visitors.

These visitors are customarily international leaders in government, industry, finance, labor, media, education, and the professions plus 3,000 international scholars and graduate trainees. The leaders are sponsored by the United States Information Agency (USIA) and the trainees by the United States Agency for International Development (USAID).

Most of NCIV's 103 local Councils for International Visitors (CIVs) are funded locally and operate as not-for-profit organizations with independent boards which include a cross section of community leadership.

While much of the thrust of the NCIV and the local councils is aimed at foreign governmental leaders, they also support the international work of state and local chambers of commerce and also help educate the public through extensive networks of volunteers and professionals in all walks of life.

Many of the local councils also provide limited service to nonsponsored international visitors and students. Those services may include:

- □ Information, maps, and guidance
- □ Escorted sightseeing
- □ Language aid
- □ Arrangements for professional meetings
- □ Hospitality with American host families.

This assistance is offered through the generosity of NCIV local volunteers, so not all requests can be accommodated.

The NCIV Directory of Members can be contacted by calling 1-800-523-8101.

U.S. Travel and Tourism Administration (USTTA)

This office is part of the U.S. Department of Commerce and is headed by an Under Secretary within that Department. The USTTA offers a wide range of publications dealing mainly with tourism in the United States. It offers extensive information on numbers of visitors, where they come from and why. For a bibliography of publications offered by the USTTA contact:

Office of Research
U.S. Travel and Tourism Administration
U.S. Department of Commerce
Room 1516
Washington, DC 20230
Telephone: (202) 377-4028

David M. Kennedy Center for International Studies

This is probably the finest single repository for resource information on cross-cultural information and communication. The Center offers a diverse collection of booklets, leaflets and other general information. Most notable, perhaps, is CULTURGRAMS, a unique, four-page cultural orientation for about 100 countries. These leaflets cover customs, manners, lifestyles, and other specialized information; they also include socioeconomic statistics, maps and addresses of embassies and national tourist offices.

For a complete list of offerings, contact:

David M. Kennedy Center for International Studies
Publication Services, 280 HRCB
Brigham Young University
Provo, UT 84602
Telephone: (801) 378-6528

Intercultural Press Inc.

This is a publishing organization that specializes in intercultural subjects. It offers an excellent variety of books and even videotapes on all subjects, including detailed studies of specific countries and cultural groups. For a listing of its offerings, contact:

Intercultural Press, Inc.
P.O. Box 768
10 U.S. Route 1
Yarmouth, Maine 04096
Telephone: (207) 846-5168

International Society for Intercultural Education, Training and Research (SIETAR International)

This is an association of professionals in the field of intercultural education, training and research. It is affiliated with Georgetown University. The membership in SIETAR is devoted to intercultural understanding through nonpolitical avenues for contact between people, for contacts among educators, trainers and researchers in this field, for professional development and for the exchange and dissemination of information and knowledge.

For more information on membership, meetings and publications of SIETAR, contact:

SIETAR International
1505 22nd St., N.W.
Washington, DC 20037
Telephone: (202) 296-4710

The Travel Reference Center

This center claims to have the largest collection of travel, tourism and recreation research studies available in any one place in the United States. It can, for a fee, conduct literature searches, information requests on specific reference questions, research assistance, and copies of articles, papers and other information. It is part of the College of Business and Administration at the University of Colorado.

For information, contact:

Director—Travel Reference Center
College of Business and Administration and
Graduate School of Business Administration
Campus Box 420
Boulder, CO 80309-0420
Telephone: (303) 492-5056

Going International Inc.

This was one of the first private consulting firms in the United States on the subject of cross-cultural training and information. Founded and operated by Lennie Copeland and Lewis Griggs, they began with the book *Going International, How to Make Friends and Deal Effectively in the Global Marketplace* (Random House, 1985). The book was followed by seven videotape training programs. More recently, Copeland and Griggs have expanded into the area they call "valuing diversity." This is a three-part film/video series showing specific situations that cause conflict and poor performance in the workplace. The programs address issues such as: stereotypes and assumptions, cultural differences, unwritten rules and double standards, the "white male club," communications styles and accents, and the stresses of being bicultural.

For more information contact:

Copeland-Griggs Productions Inc.
302 23rd Avenue
San Franciso, CA 94121
Telephone: (415) 668-4200

The Japanese External Trade Organization (JETRO)

This organization has been established in the United States by the Japanese government to foster trade and investment between the U.S. and Japan. JETRO offices offer more than two dozen booklets in English in the following areas: Marketing, Business Information, Japanese Industry and Trade, Import Promotion Activities, Guidebooks for Penetrating the Japanese Market, and Case Studies of Successful Foreign Firms in Japan.

JETRO offices are located in the following cities: 1221 Avenue of the Americas, New York, N.Y.; 401 North Michigan Ave., Chicago, IL; 725 South Figueroa St., Los Angeles, CA; 360 Post St., San Francisco, CA; 1221 McKinney, Houston, TX; 229 Peachtree St N.E., Suite 2011, Atlanta, GA; and 1200 17th St, Suite 1410, Denver, CO.

Recommended Books

A Handbook for Visitors to the U.S.A.
Beulah F. Rohrlich, former president of SIETAR, 1505 22nd St. N.W., Washington, DC 20037.

American Cultural Patterns
Edward C. Stewart, Intercultural Press, 1972, P.O. Box 768, Yarmouth, ME 04096. (A new edition is due soon.)

A Walk Across America and *The Walk West*
Peter Jenkins distributed by G. K. Hall and Morrow. An unusual and private perspective of America presented in a two-book series.

The Travelers' Guide to Asian Customs & Manners
Kevin Chambers, Meadowbrook, Distributed by Simon & Schuster, New York, 1988. How to converse, dine, tip, drive, bargain, dress, make friends and do business while in Asia, Australia and New Zealand.

The Travelers' Guide to European Customs & Manners
Nancy L. Braganti and Elizabeth Devine, Meadowbrook, distributed by Simon and Schuster, New York, 1984. How to converse, dine, tip, drive, bargain, dress, make friends and conduct business while in Europe.

The Travelers' Guide to Latin American Customs & Manners
Elizabeth Devine and Nancy L. Braganti, St. Martin's Press, New York, 1988. This includes information for Argentina, Belize, Bolivia, Brazil, Chile, Colombia, Costa Rica, Ecuador, Guatemala, Mexico, Panama, Paraguay, Peru, Uruguay, and Venezuela.

The Economist Business Traveller's Guides
Prentice Hall Press, New York, 1987. There are four separate guides— one each for: Japan, Britain, Arabian Peninsula, and United States.
   Each volume contains business practices and etiquette, plus information on: finances, politics, economics, industry, professions, hotels, restaurants, airports, taxis, trains, sightseeing, shopping, sports, local business services and resources, communications, planning and reference, maps, and charts.

Do's and Taboos Around the World
A Guide to International Behavior, compiled and edited by Roger E. Axtell, Wiley, New York, 1986. This offers information on the following topics: protocol, customs and etiquette; hand gestures and body language; American jargon and baffling idioms; gift giving and receiving.

American Ways

A Guide for Foreigners in the United States, Gary Althen, Intercultural Press, Inc., Yarmouth, Maine, 1988. This book contains information aimed at the non-American who comes to the U.S. to study or live. The author offers suggestions to these foreigners on how to respond most effectively to the Americans they meet.

Living In The U.S.A.

Alison R. Lanier, Intercultural Press, Inc., Yarmouth, Maine, 1988. This book is aimed at the foreign visitor or business manager especially those who come to live or work here. It tells of American customs and courtesies and gives practical advice for living here.

The International Businesswoman: A Guide to Success in the Global Marketplace

Marlene L. Rossman, Praeger Publishers, New York, 1986. This guidebook is written for the American businesswoman who enters the international marketplace, giving advice on preparation, careers, negotiating, barriers, marketing, traveling and family.

RECOMMENDED BOOKS ON JAPAN

Japanese Language and Culture for Business and Travel
Kyoko Hijrida and Muneo Yoshikawa, University of Hawaii Press, Honolulu, 1987. This is an extremely helpful introduction to the language of modern Japan. It focuses on business and travel language with excellent cultural insights along the way. A companion book, issued by the same publisher, is *Japanese Culture and Behavior* by Takie Sugiyama Lebra and William P. Lebra (Eds.), 1986. A collection of selected readings, this book is helpful to beginners in the study of Japanese culture and society.

With Respect to the Japanese, a Guide for Americans
John C. Condon, Intercultural Press, Yarmouth, Maine, 1984, is a short (92 pages) and readable book covering the basic principles of understanding the Japanese.

Japanese Etiquette & Ethics in Business
Boye De Mente, Passport Books, Lincolnwood, IL, 1987, has had over 100,000 copies sold in previous editions. This would be an extremely useful book for any businessperson to read before, during and again after a visit by Japanese guests or when traveling to Japan. De Mente carries the reader right through the fundamental principles of the Japanese culture as they apply to business, and finishes with a valuable glossary of key Japanese business terms and their meanings.

Hidden Differences, Doing Business with the Japanese
Edward T. Hall and Mildred Reed Hall, Anchor Press/Doubleday, Garden City, NY, 1987. This renowned social anthropologist has collaborated with his wife in producing an excellent, rounded guide dealing with everything from space and time concepts in Japan to how to start a small business there. It is short (172 pages) but each page is a golden nugget of helpful information worth examining over and over again.

How To Do Business With The Japanese, A Strategy for Success
Mark Zimmerman, Random House, New York, 1985. This covers much of the same ground as the previous books, but adds sections on how to compete with the Japanese in the U.S., in foreign markets or in Japan itself. Zimmerman, who died in 1983, served at one time as president of the American Chamber of Commerce in Japan.

Getting Your Yen's Worth
How to Negotiate with Japan, Inc., Robert T. Moran, Gulf Publishing Co., Houston, 1985. This compact reference book describes the appearance, behavior and negotiating tactics for American executives to use

and it also explains how Japanese executives perceive such efforts. It orients the reader with some historical and cultural background but primarily focuses on negotiating styles and techniques that should and should not be used, including an executive's negotiating posture, proper social interactions, and key words and concepts critical to understanding the Japanese negotiating style.

SPORTS

One sure way to make conversation is to talk about a guest's interest in sports. Following is a listing of the most popular sports for each country. The countries are listed alphabetically.* (Note: The American term "soccer" is used here, but in most of the countries where it is played it is called "football." The term "American football" is used by most non-Americans to describe football in the United States.)

Table A2
Major Sports—Country-By-Country

Albania
soccer
gymnastics
volleyball

Antigua & Barbuda
cricket

Argentina
soccer
tennis
rugby

Australia
sailing
tennis
cricket
Australian football

Austria
skiing
mountaineering

Bahamas
All water sports

Barbados
cricket
surfing
sailing

Belgium
cycling
soccer

Bolivia
soccer

Brazil
soccer
water sports
basketball

Bulgaria
soccer

Canada
skiing
swimming
fishing
Canadian football
ice hockey

Chile
soccer
skiing
horse racing

*China, People's
  Republic of*
gymnastics
weight lifting
shooting

*China, Republic of
  (Taiwan)*
baseball
soccer
basketball

Colombia
soccer
basketball
baseball
bull fighting

Costa Rica
soccer

Cuba
baseball
basketball
swimming
boxing

Czechoslovakia
soccer
ice hockey
skiing

Denmark
soccer
cycling
rowing
sailing

Dominican Republic
baseball
basketball
boxing

Egypt
soccer
swimming
tennis

El Salvador
soccer

Ethiopia
distance running

Finland
skiing
running
rowing

Worldmark Encyclopedia of the Nations, 7th Edition, 1988, Vol. 2-5, **Worldmark Press, Ltd, Publisher.**

Table A2 *(Continued)*

France
soccer
skiing
tennis

German Democratic Republic
swimming
skiing
soccer

Federal Republic of Germany
soccer
tennis

Greece
swimming
sailing
water skiing

Guyana
cricket

Haiti
soccer

Hong Kong
horse racing
cricket
soccer

Hungary
handball
soccer
tennis

Iceland
swimming
fishing
pony trekking

India
cricket
field hockey
polo

Iran
skiing
weight lifting

Ireland
golfing
fishing
sailing

Israel
soccer
basketball

Italy
soccer
lawn bowling
tennis

Jamaica
cricket
golf
water sports

Japan
baseball
wrestling

Jordan
swimming
tennis
squash

Kenya
distance running

Korea (North)
wrestling
tug-of-war
chess

Korea (South)
soccer
baseball

Liechtenstein
swimming
tennis
hiking

Luxembourg
swimming
hiking
cycling

Malaysia
horse racing
soccer
rugby

Mali
soccer

Malta
soccer

Mexico
baseball
soccer
jai-alai
bull fighting

Mongolia
wrestling
archery
horse racing

Morocco
soccer
swimming
boxing

Netherlands
soccer
tennis
swimming

New Zealand
horse racing
soccer
cricket

Nicaragua
basketball
cock fighting
bull fighting

Niger
fishing
swimming

Nigeria
swimming
sailing
tennis

Norway
skiing
ice skating
fishing

Oman
water sports
spear fishing

Pakistan
mountain climbing

Panama
water sports
tennis
golf

Table A2 (Continued)

Papua New Guinea
golf
tennis
rock climbing

Paraguay
soccer
tennis
horse racing

Peru
soccer
baseball
basketball

Philippines
basketball
baseball
soccer

Poland
camping
hiking
soccer

Portugal
soccer
bull fighting

Romania
soccer
skiing
hiking

Saudi Arabia
soccer
falconry
camel and horse racing

Singapore
badminton
basketball
boxing

Solomon Islands
rugby
football
soccer

South Africa
golf
tennis
rugby

Soviet Union
track and field
volleyball
skiing

Spain
soccer
bull fighting
pelota

Sri Lanka
water sports
golf
tennis

Sweden
soccer
skiing
ice skating

Thailand
soccer
baseball

Tonga
fishing
swimming
sailing

Trinidad & Tobago
cricket
soccer

Turkey
water sports
mountaineering
soccer

United Kingdom
soccer
golf
horseback riding
rugby

Uruguay
soccer
basketball
cycling

Venezuela
baseball
football
bull fighting

Yugoslavia
soccer
swimming
gymnastics

A Case Study:
How to Gather Hosting Information

□ How does one cultivate more knowledge about hosting international visitors?

□ Where does information about cultural idiosyncrasies come from?

□ To answer those questions, following is a case study. It is a typical example of how information can be accumulated to make you a nonpareil host of international visitors.

It began when my wife and I received what appeared to be, on the surface, an ordinary invitation to a small dinner party.

The hostess, Virginia Matheson, is a world-traveled and vivacious woman with not just a circle of acquaintances but a global group of good friends. She tends to make friends easily, which is probably just a reflection of her own warm and kind personality.

On this occasion, the party happened to be in honor of a couple from New Zealand, a surgeon and his wife who, as it happened, had also lived for eight years in the United States back in the 1970s.

I decided this might be a good setting to acquire more insight about New Zealanders, their customs and protocol, and particularly about their views of America. More specifically, I wanted to learn what they considered peculiar about Americans and the United States.

Admittedly I was aided by the fact that New Zealanders are outgoing and easy to talk with, coupled with disarming frankness and humor. I told them outright I was interested in their observations of America—not deep philosophical or political opinions, but rather the common, everyday things that make up the veneer of a culture. "Well, then" the surgeon responded, "let's begin by talking about American *plumbing.*"

As the evening progressed, here are the notes I scribbled:

On Plumbing . . .

We call them "faucets." They call them "taps."

Our faucets are inconsistent: the cold water is on the right, but not always; some turn outward, others turn inward; some are knobs, others are handles; and on some there is just a single control.

The same applies to bath outlets. "Your plumbing, like your license plates, is not standard and seems to vary from state to state," they said. "Why is that?"

Eating . . . and American Restaurants

What we call the "entree" is called the "appetizer" in New Zealand (and most European countries). This can lead to considerable confusion. They could end up with a bowl of soup and no main course.

A "napkin" here is actually the word for a "diaper" in New Zealand (and England and Canada)—another misunderstanding that could cause red faces.

We call the waiter for the "check," but they call for the "bill."

Our sandwiches come with a weird variety of strange names: Reuben, Triple-Deckers, and Whoppers.

Toast in New Zealand is white (occasionally "grown," meaning whole wheat); here the waitress invariably asks "White, whole wheat, or rye?"

When ordering soup in New Zealand, there is no distinction between a "bowl" of soup and a "cup" of soup as there is here.

And finally on the subject of eating and restaurants, "Don't order tea in America," they warn. "It's horrible." New Zealanders and others in the old Commonwealth (meaning England, Australia, South Africa, Canada and others) all treasure tea and tea-making. We can't seem to duplicate it in America. "Why is that?" they ask. (The frank answer is: I don't know.)

Table Manners . . .

This, incidentally, is a dandy way to get a conversation started about different cultural idiosyncrasies. There are so many different teachings and views. Here are some conversation-starters our dinner group developed:

- Ask your visitors about the etiquette of putting elbows, or wrists, on the table. What were they taught? Germans, for example, are taught to keep both hands on the table at all times and that placing the hands in the lap is rude.

- Ask about eating with the fork constantly in the left hand. How did that originate?

- Ask about a desert spoon and fork placed atop the plate. Is that common in their country?

- How does one signal they are finished eating—by placing the knife and fork across the plate?

- Finally, why do Americans keep the same knife for several dishes?

Miscellaneous Observations

- Americans call the first floor of a building just that, the "first floor," but to New Zealanders it is the "ground floor." So, our second floor becomes their first floor. On that basis, an American and a New Zealander could agree to meet in a certain building and miss each other by a whole floor.

□ Our light switches flick the wrong way. Also, in New Zealand, lights are often turned on by pressing buttons.

□ Water in our basins swirls clockwise. In New Zealand, it swirls counter-clockwise (as does the water all through the Southern Hemisphere; it's called the Coriolis Force.)

□ "Your TV color is poor quality compared to ours," they advised. "And why do you have so many channels? And the numbers also vary from community to community. Why do all programs start precisely on the hour or half hour? Is that necessary?" they ask. "On the other hand, you have a wonderful assortment of TV programming and it is offered throughout the day. In our country, TV broadcasting doesn't start until nearly midday."

□ Why are there so many different license plates on American autos? Not only between states, but *within* states. And some states require plates front and back; others on the back only. Also, personalized license plates are strange to see. In other countries, license plates give helpful information about city or region of domicile. For example, in New Zealand, the letters on the plate signify the *age* of the car.

□ Certain American words are considered "blue" words in New Zealand. One of those words is "stuffed." Let us just say here that it is related to sexual intercourse. So you want to be certain at the dinner table to say "I'm full" instead of "I'm stuffed." And another word is "randy" which, in New Zealand parlance means "horny." This allowed me to tell the true story about an acquaintance of mine named Nino Amato who once visited a single's bar in New Zealand. When a pretty local girl approached him with the greeting "Are you randy?", he replied, "No, my name is Nino."

What was their *biggest* gripe against Americans? It was when we mistakenly call a New Zealander an Australian.

A good researcher/reporter always tries to verify information from a second source. Accordingly, several weeks later I had occasion to dine with Mr. Ross M. Jansen, and his wife. Mr. Jansen is the Mayor of Hamilton in New Zealand. I asked the Jansens about each of the observations I had collected at the dinner party. The Jansens not only confirmed each point, but added these:

1. What is the most common single question Americans usually ask of New Zealanders (or at least of the Jansens)? Answer: Where is New Zealand?

2. Americans should learn that the kiwi is not only a fruit indigenous to New Zealand but it happens to also be a bird, as well as the national symbol of their country.

3. Many words are different between us. For example, the word "certify" in America means to confirm, guarantee or acknowledge. But in New Zealand it means "to commit someone, usually to an institution." Important difference! Also, the letter "Z" in the alphabet is pronounced "zed" in their country, which becomes important when spelling aloud "New Zealand."

4. They acknowledge that they probably know more about America than vice versa. "We're so small we must know about the rest of the world. America is so big. I guess we can't expect you to know much about such a little place tucked away to the right of Australia."

5. What facts did some Americans seem to know about their country? Answers: that Kiri Ti Kanawa is a famous, lovely operatic star, and that the native Maoris in New Zealand rub noses as a traditional greeting.

6. Finally, in New Zealand they tell ethnic jokes, just as we do in America. But in New Zealand they tell ethnic jokes about the Irish.

There you have it. A typical case study on expanding your world of cross-cultural information. Try it yourself some evening.

INDEX